D1440924

From Decision to Heresy

Urbanomic/Sequence Press Titles:

The Concept of Non-Photography, François Laruelle

Fanged Noumena: Collected Writings 1987 – 2007, Nick Land

The Number and the Siren: A Decipherment of Mallarmé's Coup de Dés, Quentin Meillassoux

Synthetic Philosophy of Contemporary Mathematics, Fernando Zalamea

FRANÇOIS LARUELLE

From Decision
to Heresy

Experiments in Non-Standard Thought

Edited By

ROBIN MACKAY

URBANOMIC

sequence

Published in 2012 by

URBANOMIC
THE OLD LEMONADE FACTORY
WINDSOR QUARRY
FALMOUTH TR11 3EX
UNITED KINGDOM

SEQUENCE PRESS
36 ORCHARD STREET
NEW YORK
NY 10002
UNITED STATES

Liberté • Egalité • Fraternité
RÉPUBLIQUE FRANÇAISE

This book is supported by the Institut Français
as part of the Burgess programme (www.frenchbooknews.com).

Library of Congress Control Number: 2012951173

BRITISH LIBRARY CATALOGUING-IN-PUBLICATION DATA

A full catalogue record of this book is available
from the British Library
ISBN 978-0-9832169-0-2

Copy-editor: Michael Carr
Printed and bound in the UK by
the MPG Books Group, Bodmin and Kings Lynn

www.urbanomic.com
www.sequencepress.com

CONTENTS

List of Sources   vii

Bibliography   xi

Introduction: Laruelle Undivided   1

A Rigorous Science of Man   33

Toward a Science of Philosophical Decision   75

Revolution within the Limits of Science Alone   107

The Transcendental Method   135

The 'Non-Philosophical' Paradigm   173

What Is Non-Philosophy?   185

Philosophy and Non-Philosophy   245

Non-Philosophy as Heresy   257

A Summary of Non-Philosophy   285

From the First to the Second Non-Philosophy   305

The Degrowth of Philosophy:
     Toward a Generic Ecology   327

Appendix I

Experimental Texts, Fictions, Hyperspeculation   353

Variations on a Theme by Heidegger   355

Leibniz Variations   371

Letter to Deleuze   393

Universe Black in the Human Foundations
     of Colour   401

What the One Sees in the One   409

Appendix II

Transvaluation of the Transcendental Method   425

List of Sources

'A Rigorous Science of Man [Une science rigoureuse de l'homme]' originally appeared in F. Laruelle, *Biographie de l'homme ordinaire* (Paris: Aubier, 1985), 7-30. 'Toward a Science of Philosophical Decision [Pour une science de la décision philosophique]' in *Cahiers du Collège International de Philosophie*, 4 (1987), 25-40. 'Revolution within the Limits of Science Alone [De la révolution dans les simples limites de la science]' in *Cahiers du Collège International de Philosophie*, 7 (1989), 111-26. 'The Transcendental Method [La méthode transcendantale]' in A. Jacob (ed.), *L'univers philosophique* (Paris: PUF, 1989), 693-700, © PUF, 1989. 'The Non-Philosophical Paradigm [Le paradigme non-philosophique]' in F. Laruelle, *En tant qu'un* (Paris: Aubier, 1991), 69-76 respectively. 'What is Non-Philosophy?

[Qu'est-ce que la non-philosophie?]' in J. D. Blanco (ed.), *Initation à la pensée de F. Laruelle: la philosophie en commune* (Paris: L'Harmattan, 1997), © Editions l'Harmattan. 'Philosophy and Non-Philosophy [Philosophie et non-philosophie]' in F. Laruelle, *En tant qu'un* (Paris: Aubier, 1991), 61-8. 'Non-Philosophy as Heresy [De la non-philosophie comme hérésie]' in Non-philosophie, le Collectif, *Discipline hérétique. Esthetique, psychanalyse, religion* (Paris: Kimé, 1998). 'A Summary of Non-Philosophy [Abrégé de non-philosophie]' in F. Laruelle, *La Lutte et l'utopie à la fin des temps philosophiques* (Paris: Kimé, 2004), 29-42; the English translation first appeared in *Pli – The Warwick Journal of Philosophy*, 8 (1999). 'From the First to the Second Non-Philosophy [De la première à la seconde non-philosophie]' is the text of a lecture delivered at the University of Warwick, UK, in 2010. 'The Degrowth of Philosophy' is the text of a lecture delivered at Miguel Abreu Gallery in New York in 2012. 'Experimental Texts, Fictions, Hyperspeculations [Textes Expérimentaux; Fictions; Hyperspéculation]' originally appeared in F. Laruelle (ed.), *La décision philosophique* 7 (Paris: Osiris, 1989). 'Variations on a Theme from Heidegger [Variations sur un thème de Heidegger]' in F. Laruelle (ed.), *La décision philosophique* 1 (Paris: Osiris, 1987). 'Leibniz Variations [Variations Leibniz]', 'Letter to Deleuze [Lettre à Deleuze]' and 'Universe Black in the Human Foundations of Colour [Du noir univers dans les fondations humaines de la couleur]' in F. Laruelle (ed.), *La décision philosophique* 5 (Paris: Osiris, 1988); the latter first appeared in English translation in *Hyun Soo Choi: Seven Large Scale Paintings* (New York: Thread Waxing Space, 1991). 'What the One Sees in the One [Ce que l'Un voit dans l'Un]' originally appeared in F. Laruelle (ed.), *La décision philosophique* 7 (Paris: Osiris, 1989). 'Transvaluation of the Transcendental Method [La Transvaluation de la méthode transcendantale]' in *Bulletin de la Société française de Philosophie* 73 (1979), 77-119.

Bibliography

PHILOSOPHY I

1971

– *Phénomène et différence. Essai sur l'ontologie de Ravaisson* [*Phenomenon and Difference: Essay on Ravaisson's Ontology*] (Paris: Klincksieck).

1976

– *Machines textuelles. Déconstruction et libido d'écriture* [*Textual Machines: Deconstruction and the Libido of Writing*] (Paris: Seuil).

1977

– *Nietzsche contre Heidegger. Thèses pour une politique nietzschéenne* [*Nietzsche Contra Heidegger: Theses for a Nietzschean Politics*] (Paris: Payot).

– *Le déclin de l'écriture* [*The Decline of Writing*] (Paris: Aubier-Flammarion).

1978

– *Au-delà du principe de pouvoir* [*Beyond the Power Principle*] (Paris: Payot).

PHILOSOPHY II

1981

– *Le principe de minorité* [*The Minority Principle*] (Paris: Aubier Montaigne).

1983-5

– *Pourquoi pas la philosophie?* (I : Descartes, mission terminée, retour impossible ; II : Les crimes de l'histoire de la philosophie ; III: Théorie de la décision philosophique ; IV : Le philosophe sans qualités ; V : Le mystique, le pratique, l'ordinaire ; VI : Métaphysique du futur) [*Why Not Philosophy?* (*I: Descartes, Mission Terminated, No Return; II: The Crimes of the History of Philosophy; III: Theory of Philosophical Decision; IV: The Philosopher Without Qualities; V: Mysticism, Practice, the Ordinary; VI: Metaphysics of the Future*)] (Paris: A series of 'casebooks' published by the author).

1985

– *Une biographie de l'homme ordinaire. Des Autorités et des Minorités* [*Biography of the Ordinary Man: Authorities and Minorities*] (Paris: PUF).

1986

– *Les philosophies de la différence. Introduction critique* (Paris: PUF), trans. R. Gangle as *Philosophies of Difference: A Critical Introduction to Non-Philosophy* (London/New York: Continuum, 2010).

1989

– *Philosophie et non-philosophie* [*Philosophy and Non-Philosophy*] (Liège/Brussels: Mardaga).

1991

– *En tant qu'un. La «non-philosophie» expliquée aux philosophes* [*As One*: '*Non-Philosophy*' *Explained to Philosophers*] (Paris: Aubier).

1992

– *Théorie des identités. Fractalité généralisée et philosophie artificielle* [*Theory of Identities: Generalised Fractality and Artificial Philosophy*] (Paris: PUF).

2011

– *Le concept de non-photographie / The Concept of Non-Photography* (Falmouth/New York: Urbanomic/Sequence Press). Bilingual edition, trans. R. Mackay (texts dating from c.1992).

PHILOSOPHY III

1995

– *Théorie des Étrangers. Science des hommes, démocratie, non-psychanalyse* [*Theory of Strangers: The Science of Men, Democracy, and Non-Psychoanalysis*] (Paris: Kimé).

1996

– *Principes de la non-philosophie* (Paris: PUF), trans. A. P. Smith & N. Rubczak as *Principles of Non-Philosophy* (London/New York: Continuum, forthcoming 2013).

1997

– *Die nicht-borgessche Hypothese. Versuche einer Wissenschaft von Buch und Bibliothek.* [*The Non-Borgesian Hypothesis: Toward a Science of the Book and the Library*] (Stuttgart: Jutta Legueil).

1998

– (with collaborators) *Dictionnaire de la non-philosophie* [*Dictionary of Non-Philosophy*] (Paris: Kimé).

2000

– *Ethique de l'étranger* [*Ethics of the Stranger*] (Paris: Kimé).
– *Introduction au Non-Marxisme* [*Introduction to Non-Marxism*] (Paris: PUF).

PHILOSOPHY IV

2002

– *Le Christ futur, une leçon d'hérésie* (Paris: Exils), trans. A. P. Smith as *Future Christ: A Lesson in Heresy* (London/ New York: Continuum, 2011).

2003

– *L'ultime honneur des intellectuels* [*The Ultimate Honour of Intellectuals*] (Paris: Textuel).

2004

– *La Lutte et l'utopie à la fin des temps philosophiques* (Paris: Kimé), trans. D. S. Burk as *Struggle and Utopia at the End Times of Philosophy* (Minneapolis: Univocal, 2012).

2007

– *Mystique non-philosophique à l'usage des contemporains* [*Non-Philosophical Mysticism for Contemporary Usage*] (Paris: L'Harmattan).

PHILOSOPHY V

2008

– *Introduction aux sciences génériques* [*Introduction to Generic Sciences*] (Paris: Petra).

2010

– *Philosophie non-standard* [*Non-Standard Philosophy*] (Paris: Kimé).

– *L'Anti-Badiou: Sur l'introduction du maoïsme dans la philosophie* (Paris: Kimé), trans. R. Mackay as *Anti-Badiou: On the Introduction of Maoism into Philosophy* (London/New York: Continuum, forthcoming 2013).

2012

– *Théorie générale des victimes* [*General Theory of Victims*] (Paris: Mille et une Nuits).

– *Photo-fiction, une esthétique non-standard / Photo-fiction, A Non-Standard Aesthetics* (Minneapolis: Univocal). Bilingual edition, trans. D. S. Burk.

Introduction: Laruelle Undivided

Robin Mackay

> *One day, after I had completed my studies, I sat at my*
> *desk, and I cleared away all the books, everything that had*
> *already been written. I started again with a new blank*
> *sheet of paper, and I began to search myself.*
>
> FRANÇOIS LARUELLE[1]

It's an episode easily disavowed as a moment of weakness, an intellectual lapse on the part of the reader of philosophy: glancing up from the page, one undergoes a jarring shift of perspective. All-encompassing conceptual edifices abruptly concertina into the localised precincts of a life of which they now seem an inadequate and tendentious caricature. Who will admit to having indulged this momentary discomposure, as if it could have some pertinence to the practice called 'philosophy', and the endless repetitions and reexaminations to which that practice seems consigned? Perhaps only a naive reader, but perhaps also one perturbed by a creeping sense of circumscription, a sense

---

1   The italicized passages throughout the Introduction are drawn from a recorded conversation with Laruelle in Paris, February 2012.

of being compelled and interpellated by systems that serve some other authority. François Laruelle's work ultimately stands for the courage to take hold of this moment of 'naivety'; to bring this perturbation to bear upon the powers of philosophy, patiently and delicately drawing out the threads of thought from their philosophical warp according to the rectitude of its 'weak force'.

In the figure of the thinker who presumes to sweep away canonical texts to make room for a new mode of thought, we are liable to suspect a petulant dismissal of philosophy on the grounds that it fails to minister to the therapeutic or pragmatic demands of 'real life'; or another anti-philosophical polemic, in which philosophy would be debunked as a grandiloquent mask for some more mundane power. But although Laruelle's work begins with the conviction that there is something prior to and indifferent to philosophy, the real of which it speaks owes nothing to the spontaneous self-evidence of everyday realities. And far from summarily dismissing the tradition, the project of 'non-philosophy' or 'non-standard philosophy' is the outcome of a long and assiduous philosophical apprenticeship, albeit that of a thinker who has never really been of the establishment, and whose entry into the discipline had no air of predestination about it.

I am from a family that is difficult to define, because they were far from being cultured. But at the same time, in the family there was a very, very strong religious protestant culture. They were not cultivated people, in the sense of City people, not at all. But they were very strong believers. And I had a rather strict religious education – a Kantian education! – there was the sensible world and the intelligible world, invisible things … doubtless I retained something from that.

But I can't speak of any special experience that drove me into philosophy. I found myself in a class where I did a year of philosophy, before I chose to continue it – but I remember that I hesitated for some time over whether to study literature or philosophy. In the end I chose the latter, and it went very well. But I always used to write very 'literary' texts about philosophy. When it came to doing History of Philosophy, explaining already-written, readymade texts, I was not so good, although eventually I learned how to write like that too. And then, as I said, after I graduated I had this moment where I cleared everything away, and I started to write a text, very much influenced by Michel Henry, which was already on the One. Then I wrote a master's thesis, 'The Absence of Being', after having seen a film, Antonioni's La Notte. At first I was going to write something on the young Hegel. But I came back from vacation, having seen La Notte, and I told my supervisor, Paul Ricoeur, that I renounced Hegel! (Not that the young Hegel isn't interesting…) So yes, that film was also a turning point, curious things like that happen.

So, I would say that in entering into non-philosophy, I was a philosopher, like everyone is! I studied philosophy in the classical manner, I graduated, and so on. It was a very long *process, of course. I wrote five books that I consider were still entirely philosophical. But something had already started to move, something seismic inside of philosophy.*

These early writings developed a Nietzschean genea-logical method, identifying the libidinal 'machines' at work in various modern and contemporary philosophies, including that of Derrida. Laruelle's heterodox 'machinic deconstruction', operated against the 'ideology of the signifier', soon saw him excommunicated from decon-structionist circles. But equally, he came to understand that revolutionary theories of philosophy, overturnings or subversions of philosophy (including Nietzsche's and Derrida's) were ultimately revolutions *for* philosophy. They invariably reaffirmed and further fuelled an expan-sive, self-differentiating dynamic behind which Laruelle divined the immobile motor of 'Philosophical Decision'. Beyond the schizophreny of a still-philosophical material-ism of philosophy, then, a theoretical apparatus began to take shape fit to engage with the syntax of Decision – without thinking it, once again, philosophically. Laruelle claimed that there was a real alternative, in the form of the disinterested stance of science (so often accused by philosophy of irreflexive 'naivety', just as often co-opted as a gnoseological ideal). For science does not assume that 'doubled' relation of co-constitution with its object that sets philosophy spinning in its endless circles.

For me, it had to do with Nietzsche, ultimately. In Nietzsche, you have this idea that philosophy is always excessive – the will to power, to philosophise is to dominate. Thus it is motivated by excess, by overpowering. But at the same time there is in Nietzsche a constant critique of philosophies, as being still gregarious, frozen in relations of domination that are dogmatic or fixed – doctrines of metaphysics, ontology. So in Nietzsche there is already a kind of internal contradiction that I felt very strongly. I was very Nietzschean in the first four or five books. And then I realised that I had to work in a 'doubled' way: to use Nietzsche, but against philosophy itself, already. And therefore against Nietzsche too, since he was already working against himself.

And then was forged the idea to write a new book, which gave rise to The Minorities Principle, *and most importantly,* Biography of the Ordinary Man. *It is here that I started to invert the movement. That is to say, to find a more precise and stronger way of working with science in the interior of philosophy – inside philosophy, not as an object of philosophy, but on the inside of it. From this moment, little by little, I identified the Principle of Sufficient Philosophy, and above all its form, its expression, which is what I call double-transcendence, the doublet-form of philosophy. Foucault identified a transcendental-empirical doublet. But that's not all – there is a second, transcendental-real, doublet, which we can see at work in Kant, in Heidegger. There are two doublets, three or four terms. Once this analysis of philosophy as double-transcendence was made* (*and it came to me rather late, in its precise and massive form, as the Principle of Sufficient Philosophy*), *then everything fell into place: Philosophy's appearing as a necessary medium for thinking – absolutely necessary, but excessive. And above all the way in which, in its affirmation of itself, it becomes a mode that is, as Kant says (about Plato) – given to divagation, to extravagances. It tends toward the mad, the delirious.*

There are many ways of defining philosophy. We can talk about it as an Encompassing – a phrase of Jaspers's – the idea that there are necessarily two terms, but one of them ends up coming back over the duality that they form, enveloping it in some way, enveloping the first duality in a second moment. And what expresses the auto-encompassing character of philosophy is that one cannot speak of philosophy, one cannot understand a philosopher, unless one is oneself a philosopher. One cannot understand Dasein unless one is oneself Dasein. It is an 'auto-' system; philosophy is an activity of auto-definition (a very complex one, of course) and of auto-position. For instance, Being is the positing of beings, but the relation or difference Being/beings is itself re-posited from the point of view of Being, not from the point of view of beings. It's the same with Kant's distinction between empirical and transcendental, but one can generalise it beyond Kant's vocabulary.

Although Laruelle concerns himself very early with decoupling the 'transcendental method' from any of its specific philosophical instantiations, the Kantian transcendental deduction remains perhaps the most explicit model of Philosophical Decision. And Kant's thematisation of philosophy's tendency toward 'transcendental illusion' remains central to non-philosophy, as does his pioneering attempt to circumscribe philosophical pretensions (albeit, in Kant's case, so as to consolidate Reason).

Philosophy has always been characterised by its marginality: it continually haunts its own borders. Kant is an important figure, in so far as, up until Kant, philosophy had been marginal and had constantly tried to exit itself, but only 'theatrically', through a series of rejections of the foregoing philosophy, but always nevertheless advocating Philosophy as such. With Kant there is a genuine break, whose effects are felt to this day. For Kant distinguishes two ways of thinking: the analytic of truth (a science), and metaphysics ('transcendental dialectic').

Is non-philosophy a continuation of Kantian critique? I have often said (although maybe this is too easy) that non-philosophy is a continuation of every philosophy! But it's true – non-philosophy is Parmenidean, it is Zen, it is Spinozist, it is Malebranchist... non-philosophy is not a circle, but a straight line which, like a tangent, touches many philosophical circles, many philosophical systems. Maybe we can understand it in that geometrical way: given a straight line, one can touch upon a great many circles...

So, Kant is indeed a model, in the sense that one speaks, in science, of models and modelisation. A model that I use very often; however it's just one model for the doctrinal continuum that I examine under the name of 'Philosophy'. All philosophies are possible models for Philosophy. This is the problem of the generalisation of 'Philosophy-Capital-P'. When I say 'Philosophy', I mean to imply precisely that Philosophy is no longer seen from within its own self-encompassing, but from another perspective which is that of non-philosophy or non-standard thought. It is the latter that allows me to say 'there is Philosophy', to consider it as completed, if not closed.

This suspension of philosophy's sufficiency through its theoretical circumscription as Decision is not merely a matter for philosophers. As Laruelle insists, if the domain of possible action, the 'world', appears as always already *philosophisable*, this testifies to the co-constitution of philosophy and the world. To defend a non-philosophisable real is to defend the possibility of non-standard worlds; and, inversely, from within the 'standard' model of the world, the outlook is inevitably, if not philosophical, then philosophisable.

Of course it's not necessary to read philosophy to philosophise, just as it's not necessary to go to church to be a believer. More exactly, even if one does not professionally, dogmatically, 'do philosophy', all of the vocabulary of more or less general notions one uses is philosophisable. For me, everything that is philosophisable is ultimately philosophical – which is to say that,

*even if the philosophical is very limited, in reality, from the
moment when everything is philosophisable, from the moment
it could pass through the screen of the philosophy of the concept, then we must act as if it were philosophised. This is why I
postulate that the extent of philosophy is truly immense – it is
all-encompassing, auto-encompassing. Once again, this notion
of 'The Encompassing' upon which Jaspers's existential (not
existentialist) philosophy is founded: There are limit experiences – death, grief, affects like these, crises – where experience
is taken to its last limit in some way. These experiences are not
necessarily expressly philosophical or philosophized explicitly
in some book or other, but they are in principle philosophisable.
And that they are philosophisable is enough, for me, to class
them in principle inside philosophical sufficiency. My critique
is a critique of all possible philosophy.*

*And so, I wish to make something non-philosophisable,
something that would no longer be possible for philosophy.*

Although non-philosophy or non-standard thought may
appear to the non-initiated as a rather severe and abstract
mode of thought, Laruelle ceaselessly reminds readers
that the struggle against philosophical sufficiency can
only be prosecuted from a stance at once immediate,
concrete and human. Yet this 'ordinary' that orients the
work remains itself to be determined *by* it – no apodictic
deduction or any spontaneous knowledge of it is assumed.
It falls precisely to non-standard thought to discover

this genericity – to chart the effects of introducing into thought that moment in which an individual is nothing-more-than-individual, comprising neither difference nor distance – a moment that corresponds to no received image of self, or to any of the various subjects constructed by philosophy.

Indeed, rather than furnishing a philosophical 'proof' of the existence of this undivided 'One', so as to provide a ground for non-standard thought, Laurelle employs an axiomatic approach that also brings the messianic aspect of his project into view: It is through the axiomatic positing of a non-philosophisable experience that non-philosophy is able to *experimentally* realise the 'thought-force' of a generic humanity unbound from its admixture with the Logos. This experiment proceeds by way of the shift in perspective that Laruelle calls 'vision-in-One', a generic effectuation of the essentially irreflexive mode of 'seeing' characteristic of science, through whose optic philosophy is 'prepared' for a non-philosophical usage.

Non-standard thought is centred on the term of 'man', on man and on the knowledge that we can have of humans. And yet it is not really a centre, since 'man' is a somewhat marginal instance of a theoretical apparatus that is necessary to approach the problem of man. This non-standard thought is at once abstract – it involves a quite highly-developed theoretical apparatus, which refers to philosophy and to science – but also claims to be concrete, arising from an experience or experimentation. There are various terms for the latter, including 'vision-in-One'. This term is just a formula that sums up a set of phenomena or experiences.

So, this is a difficult thought for those who are not initiated in philosophy. Although for philosophers themselves it is also very difficult, because it goes counter to philosophy as traditionally practised, in the course of the great philosophical tradition.

But at the same time it is a thought that claimed from the start to be for the ordinary man, or what I now call generic man. So, the paradox of non-standard thought is that it struggles against philosophy, against philosophical authority, and it does so by making use of philosophy (and of science also – the combination of the two is very important); but at the same time, it is undertaken so as to avail oneself of a field of experience (itself rather paradoxical) that might be called the human phenomenon or phenomena.

All of this gives Laruelle's work a complex relation to his contemporaries' antihumanism:

If, within non-standard thought, the knowledge of human nature (to put it in traditional terms) remains entirely problematic, not at all becoming the object of some dogmatic knowledge, this only goes to show that there is no absolutely determined knowledge of the human, of man; and in particular it aids the struggle against every dogmatic definition of human nature – against racism, for

11

example: if one has no absolutely certain knowledge of human nature, it is far more difficult to develop a racist thought.

It's an antihumanism in the sense of a broadly speaking structuralist anti-metaphysics. It is above all the structuralists who brought about this term – theoretical, not practical, anti-humanism. And I am also a theoretical antihumanist. From the point of view of theory, one can speak of man, but not in terms of humanism. For traditionally, humanism is, despite everything, a form of thought very much marked by metaphysics (as Heidegger says), or else marked by idealism, by bourgeois ideology (as Althusser says). So, generic man is a man without humanism, I would say. This is not to say that practically speaking one abandons man. Quite the contrary, but one defends him against what? Precisely against the superior, dominant authority of philosophy, of the Principle of Sufficient Philosophy.

The disenthralling effects of a 'science of Man' that would no longer be anthropo-logical (a philosophical amalgam of man and logos) have fundamentally Marxian political stakes. Take Marx's rejection, in *The Jewish Question*, of Bauer's claim that true political emancipation requires religious affiliation to give way to a primary commitment to the secular state. This 'theological problem', Marx argues, only serves to obfuscate the more radical question of the state as such, and the ways in which the *political* emancipation it offers falls short of *universal human* emancipation. The state is in fact consummated

12

in its secular form, which allows the real forms of power that oppress man (including religion and capital) to fall outside its purview. Its empty universality and 'freedom' herald a form of power that accommodates its citizens to the inevitability of the world as it is.

We could say that Laruelle extends this critique to the entry requirements for becoming a citizen of one of the various (more-or-less united) states of Philosophy: In them, as in the secular nation-states Marx addresses, the human accedes only to a 'devious' emancipation, by way of an intermediary ('however necessary this intermediary may be') in whose bureaucratic profile it will henceforth recognise itself – as a subject defined by certain a priori universal attributes. In return, the citizen may be allowed the privilege of private attributes that do not fall under its legislation (the spurious particularities of sensation, the right to speculation within reason). But the political freedom brokered by and enjoyed through this intermediary falls short of universal human emancipation, since it disjoins the real human from the subject. By the lights of the polity of philosophical subjects, 'insofar as he appears both to himself and to others as a *real individual* he is an illusory phenomenon'; and as *homo philosophicus*, he appears to himself 'divested of his real, individual life, and infused with an unreal universality'. Just as, for Marx, political emancipation is thus merely 'the final form of human emancipation within the framework of the prevailing social order', for Laruelle the history of the philosophical subject, for all its radical renovations, radicalisations and revolutions, amounts only to a drawn-out subtilisation of the philosophical order. In presuming to represent it in and for thought, Philosophy adulterates the 'thought-force'[2] that constitutes its real productive basis. How, then, to challenge this state's auto-positing, self-legislating character, its claim to have always already encompassed the possibilities of thought *tout court* ('it appears like lightning, too terrible, too sudden...' [Nietzsche]); and how to defend the human against it?

Laruelle's defence of humanity as immanence unaffected by any transcendence whatsoever undoubtedly owes a great debt to Husserl, who radicalised transcendental thought, reinvigorating its attempt to expunge the categories of empirical experience from the transcendental ego. But his defensive strategy owes more to two borderline non-philosophical thinkers for whom the Husserlian transcendental ego itself continues to imprint upon radical subjectivity predicates drawn from objective transcendence.

For Michel Henry, Husserlian phenomenology reiterates the 'murder' that is the founding act of philosophy: Since 'immanent perception' still involves a phemomenological distancing between given and givennness,

---

2   Laruelle's 'force-(de)-pensée', echoing 'force de travail', Marx's 'labour power'.

Husserl, despite himself, participates in philosophy's elimination of the heterogeneity of subjective 'Life' by imbuing it with the predicates of transcendent perception. Meanwhile, Emmanuel Levinas claims that Husserl remains motivated by the philosophical drive to gnoseological immanence, which deprives his Ego of the founding moment of absolute transcendence heralded by the experience of the 'face of the Other'. Henry and Levinas both move to delimit philosophy, as a relatively narrow space of thought that must be supplemented by something extra-philosophical (quasi-religious, even) – 'Life', 'the Other' – in order for the real nature of the subject to be registered. They constitute two cardinal points – absolute immanence, absolute transcendence – whose 'impossible' superposition allowed Laruelle to sharpen his defence of the real against the philosophy-world's mixtures of transcendence and immanence.

The humanity of generic man is radically distinct from the world – which is not to say absolutely distinct. This is where we depart from Husserl. For Husserl, consciousness, the transcendental ego or transcendental consciousness is distinct in a certain way – Husserl uses a vocabulary of 'absoluteness', but I am content to say radically distinct. That is to say, for me, there is a distinction in principle between two regions that are ontologically totally distinct, different. But they are unilaterally different. That is to say, nothing of the world enters into the definition of human

15

FROM DECISION TO HERESY

nature, but nevertheless human nature is affected by, or has to do with, the solicitations or occasions coming from the world, from objects, attention, the psychological, the political, etc.

So, this is very close to Michel Henry, yet at the same time, there is not that type of break that we find in Henry. In particular, there is not the same kind of cut or separation between a transcendental ego, a moment of radical or absolute immanence, as Henry sometimes says, and the world as being, as horizon.

Both Henry and Levinas salvage radical subjectivity only by defining it against – and thus once more in relation to – the worldly (whether as transcendent objectivation or immanent adequation). Laruelle's logic of 'unilateral duality' refuses the mutual imbrication or 'othering' implied by such a relative definition. The One, radical immanence, is not thought *against* transcendence, but as *indifferent* to it. Consequently, if there is a difference or distance between this immanence and the transcendent objectification it undergoes, such a difference is operative *only on the side of the latter*. It is this *unilaterality* that philosophy, which habitually thinks in terms of dyads *and* their unity, fails to grasp. Indeed, unilaterality entails that the One is utterly foreclosed to thought except in so far as it allows itself to be 'cloned', modelled in thought as 'determination-in-the-last-instance'. It is through this procedure that non-philosophy 'unilateralises' its philosophical materials, consuming the philosophical only once it has been meticulously prepared, as one might dine on *fugu* once an expert chef has disemboweled it and removed its toxic organs of reproduction.

Thus non-philosophy's advocacy of real immanence goes hand-in-hand with its modesty in acknowledging that it sets out, not from a 'pure' immanence, but from the interference pattern between the philosophy-world that gives it occasion to think (occasional cause), and a real that unilaterally determines all worldly phenomena and thought (the One). This interference or double-causality is the very condition of non-philosophy. Unilateral duality (a 'relation of relation to non-relation') thus replaces unitary thought (in which dyads are always encompassed by unity). Accordingly, the human arrives in thought only as already 'harassed' by the philosophy-world; and yet, in so far as it is the locus of a radical ('prior-to-priority') experience, the human cannot be said to be either tragically predestined to its fate, or intimately affected or alienated by it.

Harassment, in my problematic, replaces alienation. And Philosophy is the mistress of harassment! It is not a matter of alienation; it is not the idea, as in Hegel or in the young Marx, of a becoming-other of consciousness through objectivation. I am far closer to the later Marx, who, reading Feuerbach, affirms that man is not alienated, in the Hegelian manner, qua object-consciousness; but that objectivation is what there is that

17

is positive in the relation to the world. Alienation was therefore an overhasty interpretation of objectivation. Objectivation is necessary: the human being (even the human being qua generic, so to speak) expresses himself objectively in the world and through his objectivation, and we must not say that he alienates himself in doing so. The alienation occurs subsequently, through a bad interpretation of this objectivation. In Marx we have this distinction between objectivation and alienation – so we shouldn't reduce Marx too quickly to the Hegel of the Phenomenology. *The world is not the other of man. I would rather say, if pushed, that man is the other of the world. But the human being as generic is not alienated in, does not confuse himself with, the world. He has to do with the world, or it has to do with him. Of course, the world is a perpetual occasion of stimulation for human thought. But in itself, the world is not, in the classic sense, an alterity in which one may be alienated. The world is the milieu in which man necessarily is involved – and here I come closest to Heidegger's being-in-the-world. But even for Heidegger, there is the idea that there is a sort of correspondence between Dasein and the world, through this being-in the-world, which is a kind of comportment in regard to the world. For me what replaces Dasein is generic man; and generic man does not comport himself with the world, that is to say he does not realise a synthesis with the world. He is solicited, motivated, by the occasions of the world, but remains foreclosed in a certain way to being constituted in any way by the facticity of things.*

It must be seen that all of this is governed by a certain type of relation which is a 'relation-without-relation': unilateral duality. This is fundamental, though perhaps abstract and difficult to understand, because it is very much opposed to the common representation of things, which tends to place instances or terms in a pre-existing space, so that the relation between A and B is always in reality a doubled relation – not just A to B but also B to A, reversibly or reciprocally. If, in this way, one places this 'A to B' in a space presumed to pre-exist it in reality, then one has already made the trajectory to B a first time, and one then merely goes on to do it again a second time. That is to say, there is a whole system of relations that is reflected in itself.

In unilateral duality one is dealing neither with external relations between atomic points, nor entirely internal relations. Because internal relations suppose that the world or the object is an accident of thinking substance. Now what replaces thinking substance for me is generic man, and generic man has nothing to do with substance, we cannot know it as substance. In which case the world is not an accident, either. There is a sort of dualism or duality between generic man and the world, but this duality is unilateral – that is to say, there is a sort of relation that takes place between generic man and the world, the world is not completely foreign to us, it is interiorised, passing into immanence, in the same way that Husserl says that the noema is immanence, the immanent side of things. Whereas the things always remain relatively independent or autonomous in relation to generic man.

Laruelle's analysis of philosophy's self-evident sufficiency positions him in an unusual relation to the critique of the 'spontaneous', one of the pillars of the French philosophical convergence between Marxist critique and epistemology. Althusser, undoubtedly a major influence on Laruelle's thinking, still upheld the distinction between spontaneous philosophy and philosophy 'proper', proclaiming the impossibility of taking up any position that would not be within the philosophical 'circle'. Indeed, in order to demonstrate the impossibility of escaping it, Althusser declares that he 'enters the necessary circle deliberately'. Laruelle's neat answer is that the non-philosopher renounces the dream of exiting the circle, once she realises that she (qua One) never entered it. Philosophy, as formalised in the axiomatic of Decision, is a circumscribed and suspended body of thought, and can no longer exert its all-encompassing mode of capture. Other modes of thought also lose their respective principles of sufficiency, becoming, like philosophy, mere *models* of the One, determined in the last instance *by* the One.

It's true that what I call 'Non-philosophy' is a way of delivering us – locally, but at the same time in a certain way globally, each time – from philosophical spontaneity, which I call the Principle of Sufficient Philosophy. For me it was absolutely capital when I arrived at this idea of philosophy sufficiency – and not only philosophical, because every discipline very soon arrives at its own sufficiency, in the sense that it tends to auto-finalise itself, raise itself to the level of a total, complete or all-powerful thought.

So, the problem is that of demarcation: Is one to constitute a device, an apparatus that one calls historical materalism, or dialectical materialism, to make this difference between ideology (spontaneous philosophy) and a more 'scientific' philosophy? This is what Althusser calls the line of demarcation – and, incidentally, Deleuze also speaks of lines of demarcation, he says that the first philosophical act is to trace a line of demarcation. Plato himself says this, if not in the same way: tracing a line between the shadows, the flux of sensations, objects, and the Ideas and the Good. In Kant, we also find this, between the judgement of experience and the judgement of perception – the latter is human sensation, whereas the judgement of experience is also governed by mathematicised physical laws.

Instead of tracing such a line, I propose a special device that I call generic, and which does not share the topography of historical materialism – structure, superstructure, etc. I proceed through a sort of reduction of the amplitude of philosophy. Philosophy is a type of thought that goes to extremes, that traces the diameter from one extreme to the other – from the most empirical, meaningless experience, up to God. Philosophy itself plays the role of mediation between science and theology (yes, theology as the crowning moment of philosophy – obviously this might not be such a popular idea!). But I reduce this range, this amplitude. First of all by observing one very particular feature of it – it takes the form of a hierarchy: Theology comments on philosophy globally, and then philosophy comments on science, and then there are other smaller local hierarchies within each level. What I do is to operate a reduction that I call generic. Generic reduction consists in bringing together science and philosophy very closely, through an operation that I borrow essentially from quantum mechanics, that of superposition. A superposition of science and philosophy – so that we are no longer in a hierarchy. There is no longer a hierarchy of science in relation to philosophy, no 'philosophy of science'. Philosophy of science has always reaffirmed the privilege of philosophy, or a theology of philosophy, a theology of science. So I reduce in a certain way the extremes, and I attribute to this reduced sphere the term generic. Why generic? Because it is a reduction to the genus of knowledge. Knowledges are animated, propelled, by a desire of philosophy, a transcendental or even speculative desire. Knowledges surpass themselves because of this desire. Experience surpasses itself toward science, and science toward philosophy. But in the generic, there is no longer this vertical surpassing (from experience toward God). There is a different kind of surpassing, a purely horizontal surpassing. I call generic the usages of knowledge in so far as they are destined for man – made for man, for humans. Knowledges are not free of themselves, they are always taken up again by philosophy, by its sense of excess toward a theological dimension. On the contrary, qua generic these knowledges form a new sphere of reality or of the real that is at once philosophical and scientific. There is no longer a philosophy of science, nor a science of philosophy, in the sense of one being object, the other subject. A generic knowledge is one that is turned toward or quasi-finalised by humanity. Not by God, not by pure, completely autonomous technology or pure scientificity. But it is oriented toward humanity. I think that Hegel is the great disorienter of thought, in the sense that he can go in almost any direction. And my problem is that of the re-orientation of thought, toward its usage to the profit of humans – the idea of a politics and an ethics of the defence of the human.

By 'colliding' bodies of knowledge reduced to this generic state, Laruelle's formidable masterwork *Non-Standard Philosophy* (2010) claims, with the aid of borrowings from quantum theory, to finally acquire the necessary means for the description of the 'structures of the ordinary man' anticipated at the dawn of *Philosophy II*.

This new project announces not so much a materialism as a *materielism*, noting the distinction between matter and *materiel*, a term appropriated from Max Scheler, who used it to describe something like Husserl's *Erlebnis* or lived experience.[3] Non-standard thought seems to envisage a theory of knowledges generically 'reduced' to this materiel register, which can then

---

3   Scheler sought to remove ethical values from the sole realm of pure reason, making of them material a prioris whose only existence lies in their being *felt*. With the English coinage *materiel* I seek to retain the neologistic character of Laruelle's French *material* – a word that does not exist in French, and which he introduces to mark the foreignness of Scheler's *materiale*.

23

be described without succumbing to their objective appearance (the latter, as the deliverances of models, are never to be confused with the real that they serve). Thus Laruelle arrives at a rigorous generic theory of the lived experience of knowledges qua materiel.

I distinguish the materiel from materiality. Max Scheler speaks of Materiel Value-Ethics [materiale Wertethik]. *It's a difficult word because it is usually translated, in most languages, as 'material'. But materiel is a content, something continuous that needs a form or a syntax, an articulation: it is for me, essentially lived experience that is materiel – the phenomenological* hyle, *you could say. This is not a materialism, because a materialism is a thought where there is a philosophical positing of matter as being, in the sense of being or human being.*

For me, generic man is that which replaces – although not with the same site, or function – the subject. One can speak of a subject, but one must speak of a non-individual, generic subject – one can only qualify it as individual under condition of the philosophical. The device of materiality, which is scientific or algebraic, must at the same time be something human. Generic man is not traced from psychological man, even psychoanalytic man. It is rather the reverse that is true. Everything we call human is understood ultimately, perhaps better, through physical nature, through a (quantum-) physical-type procedure or event. The idea of superposition permits the fabrication of a non-individual generic. It allows us to fuse contraries into a

*quasi-identity, not a logical identity but an algebraic identity:
A+A=A. This is what I call a strongly analytic but weakly
synthetic relation. We remain in idempotence. We exit from
the analytic (since a synthesis is made) but in approaching the
synthesis we remain ultimately within things that are analytic,
that have hardly exited from the analytic. It is a thinking of
tension that can be annotated algebraically, particularly through
this relation of idempotence. And for me this is the principle or
the basis of superposition.*

*So obviously, there is no subject in the psychological sense, no
consciousness in the reflexive sense anymore, one has evacuated
this with algebra, with the formula of idempotence. And the lived
experience, the 'materiel-ity' that goes with this idempotence,
is no longer psychological. It is a neutralised lived experience,
Husserl's* Erlebnis *– only in Husserl, lived experience is a
lived experience of consciousness, whereas in my work it is one
of idempotence. An algebraic lived experience – it is fused here
with algebra, not a form of objectivity –* A+A=A *is not objective,
but a certified algebraic knowledge. Generic man is a fusion of
idempotence and lived experience.*

With idempotence taking the place of identity, and non-
commutativity taking the place of unilaterality, the science
of man now takes the form of a minimal transcendental in
the form of an algebra that, like quantum physics itself,
does not claim to bear directly upon objective phenomena, but on operators (not on objects, but on theories

of objects, i.e. philosophies and other knowledges), and in which the amplitude or tension between the One and its occasional effectuation in thought can be registered. In Laruelle's own classification of his works, the non-standard experiment opens a new chapter:

There is a continuous flow of work, which might well give the impression of being repetitive. And it's true that there is a globally invariant structure, with local modifications, but this continuous flux is divided up into Philosophy 1, 2, 3, 4 ... like waves, like pulsions, each number corresponding to a new push. So, it's not like the classification of Heidegger's or Wittgenstein's work into 1 and 2, into a before and an after. It is a multiple pulsion, each time oriented in a certain sense toward the same thing. But at the same time there is a great difference between Non-Standard Philosophy and my first two books, which are entirely philosophical. There is the large zone in-between which is non-philosophy, and Non-Standard Philosophy is again different.

Laruelle is at pains to point out that what he intends with his usage of quantum thought is something quite different to the philosophical fetishisation of a constituted science that he often criticizes (most recently in the polemical *Anti-Badiou*, with regard to Badiou's use of set theory). The generic reduction of knowledges (philosophy and science) is to be carried out 'under science' and not 'under philosophy' – that is, their combination is not to be submitted once again to the reflexivity of philosophy. That materiel has idempotence as a property is not to say that, for instance, the biological object of the brain is governed by the physical principles of quantum mechanics; or that the concepts of the latter, as elaborated in the very well-determined context of physical experiments, are applicable in a positive way to philosophy conceived as a physical mass.

There is a body of philosophy, a philosophical materiality, a conceptual and lived materiel, and one can treat philosophy as a part of physical nature – physical in the contemporary sense, that is to say in using methods from quantum thought. But this is not a philosophical fetishisation of science, because it is a generic generalisation of a science. It is not a physicalism – physicalism would mean a reduction of lived experience, of the concept, to physical positivity. I don't use Quantum Mechanics in this positivist way, but according to a usage I call generic, a generic usage of the discipline or of a body of knowledge. A generic usage of science, just like a generic usage of philosophy, consists in depriving it of its dimension of sufficiency or auto-promotion, of auto-affirmation – since every discipline arrives very soon at its own sufficiency, in the sense that it auto-finalises itself, it raises itself to the level of a total, complete or all-powerful thought. It consists of treating it simply as a reduced range or property of thought – reduced from the extremes, the extremes are eliminated. Theology remains theology. The most banal experience remains what it is, science remains what it is, but all of this outside the PSP, which is for me the Great Satan!

At the same time, my non-standard philosophy has its own contingency, in a certain sense. The contingency of any production of non-standard thought comes from the philosophical model one chooses – in my case, from the utilisation of the quantum mechanical reference. In a sense, nothing especially authorises it, but nothing prohibits me from doing it either! If someone wanted to prohibit me, I would wonder why!
So I can speak of contingency, contingency in the rather banal sense that it is my decision, a decision that I took that seems interesting and productive, not innovative but surprising.

And there you have it, now I am ready to know that it will all disappear ...

Exploring Laruelle's oeuvre, it is difficult to avoid the impression of a continual anticipation of the moment when non-philosophy will begin to function, to produce its promised heresy. The texts collected in this volume lead us from the programmatic *Biography of the Ordinary Man* to the new matrix of *Non-Standard Philosophy*, where this experiment is put into action. But toward the end of the eighties, Laruelle produced a number of experimental texts (a selection of which are collected in the Appendix) which seemed to set non-philosophy in motion in a very different way, once more scrambling expectations by identifying the science of philosophy with a poetics.

I have always wanted to write experimental texts, I would love to write more of them. But I am held back by scruples, or by a self-critique – shame, even. Because I know they will be judged harshly by poets, by philosophers, by pretty much everyone! I feel that this in fact is what I want to do, but I dare not do, any longer. I am still obsessed by the idea that one day I may write such a book, with texts that are freer like this. However, in most of my longer books there are sections that are at the limit, that become 'experimental' texts. Above all in the 'christo-fiction', or in the book on mysticism, there are texts that are really at the limit of a type of poetry of thought, or an experimental writing. So it is not something I have entirely distanced myself from. But I have these scruples, I dare not free myself completely.

My problem is really that of how to treat philosophy as a material, and thus also as a materiality – without preoccupying oneself with the aims of philosophy, of its dignity, of its quasi-theological ends, of philosophical virtues, wisdom etc... None of that interests me. What interests me is philosophy as the material for an art, at the limit, an art. My idea, which has been growing for some years, and may last a little longer, is to make art with philosophy, to introduce or make a poetry of thought, not necessarily a poetry made of concepts, a poetry that would put forward some philosophical thesis – but to make something poetic with concepts. Thus, to create a practice that could destroy, in a certain way, the classical usage of philosophy. Obviously, in the books I have published, I still respect the dignity of philosophical work – at least, I hope so. I still make those books for philosophers. But my experimental texts, I don't know who those are written for. I don't know. Which is rather embarrassing for me! When people speak favourably about them, I say, yes, but even I myself don't know how to evaluate them, I have no judgement on them. They are a sort of non-sense, even for me!

Laruelle's term 'philo-fiction' may be understood as referring primarily to the 'fictionalist' school of philosophy of mathematics, where the warring ontological commitments of traditional debates are eliminated by taking up a stance of hypothetical 'acceptance' with regard to the implications of the various objects they propose. In a similarly modest spirit of acceptance, the non-standard approach is content to allow all knowledges equal validity as fictions or partial models of the real that determines them in the last instance. Every philosophy, once its intricate and dense meshwork of decision is combed through by the unilateralising force of generic thought, tells us something about how the Individual fares in its inevitable struggle with the Authorities of the world – a one-sided struggle that non-philosophy refuses to make into a confrontation, all the better to issue an 'ultimatum' from its position of eternal weakness – from the *uni-verse* that is the human's true habitat – to the philosophy-world, its doublets and its subjects.

However, considering that phenomenology, in its stringent attempts to describe the phenomena and their mode of givenness, always risked becoming a formalist counterpart of the modern novel, Laruelle's radical consummation of transcendental method, his phenomenology-without-logos, does present us with a 'fiction' in this other sense: Setting out from a science aiming to describe the 'structures of the ordinary man', non-standard thought today still speaks of an algebraic 'description of the human phenomenon'. This reduced description or performance of the experience of the philosophy-world, on the part of a colourless Stranger-subject lacking all recognizable characteristics, makes for a 'novel without qualities' – philosophy as the material for a (non-) art. In Laruelle's black universe, as in Antonioni's Milanese night, this Stranger scans the surfaces of the world, of language, of thought, without finding in them anything that reflects, expresses or relieves her inner forces – forces that remain a non-given. Character without action, struggle without confrontation, interior life reduced to the finest thread of a generic humanity – this remains the insistent promise of Laruelle's work, from the biography of the Ordinary Man to the quantum xenography of the Stranger.

If the reader is disappointed with my 'programmatic messianism', yes, messianity is what I do. There is nothing else to announce, it must be announced many times, repeated – as Bergson said, a philosopher has only one idea.

NOTES ON THE TRANSLATIONS, ACKNOWLEDGEMENTS

A sizable group of translators contributed toward this book. My thanks to them all for their hard work and patience as the project progressed. As editor, I took responsibility for ensuring a consistency not only of technical vocabulary but also of tone, in the hope of rendering Laruelle's prose as readable and idiomatic as possible while preserving its rigour and its inherent strangeness.

Useful in preparing this volume were John Mullarkey and Anthony Paul Smith's volume *Laruelle and Non-Philosophy* and Gabriel Alkon and Boris Gunjevic's collection *The Non-Philosophy Project*. I also found invaluable Hugues Choplin's pedagogical guides *La non-philosophie de François Laruelle* and *De la phénoménologie à la non-philosophie*, along with the indispensible writings of Ray Brassier, the thinker who first introduced myself and many others to Laruelle's work, and who has been most helpful at key points in the editorial process. My thanks to Miguel Abreu and Katherine Pickard at Sequence Press, to Anne-Françoise Schmid for many clarifications and valuable discussions, to Marjorie Gracieuse for her advice, and above all to Louise for her patience and support as this project slowly came to fruition alongside our own. And finally, thanks to François Laruelle – we hope that this volume will contribute to the growing awareness and discussion of his work.

A Rigorous Science of Man

(1985)

Translated by Robin Mackay

1. FROM THE HUMAN SCIENCES TO THE SCIENCE OF MAN

There is every reason to revolt against philosophers. But to what end? Is revolt its own reason, one more reason? Isn't it philosophers who, dispensing reason, and in particular the reasons for revolt, dispense revolt? Should we not finally cease to revolt, founding our existence on a firm yet tolerant indifference toward philosophy? 'Ordinary man', the finite individual we also refer to as the *Minorities*, maintains himself in this indifference, which he draws from himself rather than from philosophy. We shall defend five 'theses', or in truth five 'theorems' – human theorems:

1. Man really exists, and is really distinct from the World: a thesis that contradicts almost all of philosophy;

2. Man is a mystical living being condemned to action, a contemplative being bound to practice for reasons he knows nothing of;

3. As practical living being, man is condemned a second time, and for the same reasons, to philosophy;

4. This double condemnation organises his destiny, a destiny called 'The World', 'History', 'Language', 'Sexuality', 'Power', etc. – what we designate in general as *Authorities*;

5. A rigorous science of the ordinary man – that is to say, of man – is possible; a biography of the individual as Minorities and as Authorities; a theoretically-founded description of the life he leads between these two poles, which suffice to define him.

This description may be facilitated (but not replaced) by an introductory outline of the most general programme of a *rigorous science of man* designed to replace philosophy and its avatars, the 'human sciences'; a *transcendental Science*, of course, which is to say one that is not empirical – but not 'philosophical' either...

In their existing form, at the moment of their triumph, the Human Sciences are not sciences, and do not bear upon man: and these two for the same reason. What is at issue here is something other than their conflict with philosophy, or the fact that they lack exact empirical procedures – two debates into which we shall not enter.

What we condemn is the globally non-scientific character of these occasional sciences, which do not form *a* science; and the complementary fact that they relate to no real object. We shall not take up the old combat: defending philosophy against the human sciences. Does one defend a father against his sons, or let him die? Rather, we defend man against this authoritarian family in league against him and (this is not at all contradictory) we attempt to constitute him as the object of a rigorous science.

Man has never been the object of the human sciences. Man does not recognise himself in this authoritarian and predatory activity; and the human sciences think something other than man. They combine in a strange way the plural and the singular: we are supposed to understand, now, that there exists man in itself, inexhaustible, which multiple, impotent and irreal sciences try to circumvent; now, that man does not exist really, that only sciences or methods exist, only the play of universal predicates whose accumulation one hopes will coincide with his essence. But this essence slips away and flees like the infinite. This indeterminate being, evanescent under the crushing weight of the universal determinations that are slammed down upon it in the thwarted hope of 'fixing' it – it is this being we are asked to consider as 'man'. But man is definitively absent from the rendezvous of the Human Sciences, because he is absent first of all from that of philosophy. In both cases, one of the terms – science, or man – has to be irreal in order for the other to be real.

Perhaps we ought to reverse the terms: science must be unique and specific if it would be a real science and cease to be a techno-political phantasm; and it is man who must be irreducible in his multiplicity if he would cease to be this anthropological fetish, this somewhat drab phantom that is but the shadow of the Human Sciences, that is to say of the self-screening light of Reason.

The twofold poverty of the human sciences: As far as 'science' is concerned, they can claim no more than an indeterminate plurality, or the inorganic unity of a nebula. In either case, they demonstrate that they are but an artefact, the foam that the wave of other sciences has left behind it on the terra incognita of man.

No matter how they heap up, they still do not add up to a science, with an object and procedures that are autonomous and theoretically founded. As of this moment, they are mere imaginary phenomena resulting from the intersection of other disciplines – theoretical ersatzes or synthetic 'sciences'. They cannot be said to have any existence in themselves; they are just a vague institutional skein that survives on its plasticity, and through compromise. Having not yet discovered their foundation or their essence, they are content with being the caricature of contemporary philosophical impotence and nihilism: playing out the most diverse theoretical procedures, focusing on a mythical and fantastic figure of man whose only necessity is that of the present conjuncture.

Every science that is born strives to capture all of reality, is animated by the old mytho-philosophical ambition to identify the All with the real, Totality with the absolute. The most recent – ethnology, linguistics, biology and the science of history (in the Marxist sense) – like all the others, do not emerge without trying to moor man, considered as a residue, to their continent or to their raft. Whence a series of retroactions or anthropological artefacts in which, each time, man is declared as having been accounted for. But all these universals, even when united by the State in the nebula of the Social Sciences, do not amount to even the most modest beginnings of a specific science of man, distinct from the science of *historical* man, *speaking* man, *social* man, *psychical* man, etc. These are false sciences of man, just as there are false sciences of chemistry or of life; but false sciences that have succeeded, for reasons of self-avowed opportunism, in implanting themselves and prospering. They lack both specific theoretical foundations, distinct from those valid for the sciences of the living, historical, speaking, sexuated (etc.) being, and a sufficiently determined experience of their object.

A genealogy of the Human Sciences would indeed demonstrate that they derive from the same archaic and metaphysical presuppositions as those of *rational psychology*, which the cogito did not expurgate: in general, ontological presuppositions (those of simplicity, atomicity, substantiality, causality, etc. which are simply pluralised) combined with others necessary for their mathematization. Scraps of old philosophy, of politics, of 'rational' psychology and sociology, stitched together externally by the process and the security of a cheap mathematization. It is this generalised intersection that makes for the techno-political richness – that is to say, the real vacuity – of this bric-a-brac, as empty of theoretical rigour as of humanity (and for the same reasons). The essence of the science of man remaining unthought, its rigorous phenomenal content being forgotten, it is recomposed out of practical and theoretical elements effective elsewhere, but here selected with no necessity, under the mere arbitrary authority of the psychologist, the politologist, the sociologist, the historian, etc. There is no longer any necessary link between the sciences of man and their object, no theoretical foundation to guarantee this link and to render it necessary.

How to found a rigorous science of man, established in the rigour specific to theory as such – that is to say, in the experience of the full and phenomenally positive sense of *theoria*? One that no longer borrows its means of investigation, of demonstration, of validation, from existing sciences? It must be founded in the specific essence of its object, in the truth of its object: the discovery of the science of man and that of the real essence of man are the same thing.

As regards 'man' precisely, the concept these sciences have of him is doubly indeterminate. In the first case, 'man' is a concept indeterminate in its origin and in the Greco-unitary philosophical presuppositions that serve as its foundation. Its essence, despite the cogito and *rational psychology* (or because of them, but prior to their advent) has not been elucidated for reasons of principle. One cannot take the anthropological forms of philosophy for a science or a rigorous theory of man, since anthropology is only a phantasmatic projection of Greco-Christian ontological prejudices onto real man. Man has never been the real object of philosophy, which, for its part, thinks and dreams of something else (of Being, for example) and, at the same time, hallucinates the individual. Greco-ontological thought, with the annexed and bastard sciences that now trail along with it like so many disavowed corpses, has never been able (for reasons of principle to which we shall return) to determine radically any object whatsoever or to appraise what a finite individual is. It is not just the founding text of its psychology and its anthropology, the cogito, that it leaves undetermined in its sense and its truth; but more profoundly *the non-anthropological essence of man*. Philosophy such as it exists, precisely because it can be an anthropology, does not know man. It knows the inhuman, the sub-human, the too-human, the overman, but it does not know the human. It knows man only in surrounding him with prefixes or scare-quotes, with caveats and relations (with himself, with others, with the World): never as a 'term'. For it confuses ordinary man with any man whatever, with the universal individual of which the exemplary figure, the excellent essence, is the philosopher – the human par excellence in speaking, knowing, acting. It identifies man with generalities or attributes, with a knowledge, an activity, a race, a desire, an existence, a writing, a society, a language, a sex; and it is once more the philosopher who pushes himself forward behind the mask of these generalities – the philosopher requisitioning man in the service of his aims and his values, which are very specific but which need the cover of the universal. The essence of the individual has remained unthought by the philosophy that is content to *postulate* it, that advances a possible supposed-man while denying the conditions of his real experience with the multiplicity of authoritarian universals that it uses to filter that experience. Thus the latter remains undetermined a second time, because the Human Sciences, not being of the stature of the old philosophy, can only accentuate its original *theoretical carelessness*, and that which in reality it is part and parcel of: its want of humanity.

The cogito, and all the unitary figures of the subject and of man, remain unelucidated in their essence, because they are all without exception founded in *anthropological parallelism*, in the more or less deformed but never invalidated mixture and parallelism of man and logos, in the ruined cradle of the Human Sciences that is anthropological philosophical difference.

To begin with man, so as to draw consequences as to the State, Power, Language – the World? Anthropological difference prohibits one from beginning with man and his solitude. It begins, instead, with a mixture or a universal: man as language, as desire, as society, as power, as sex, etc. It cannot content itself with ordinary man: it does not even see him. It will thus have already doubled him, at once exceeded and devalued him, with these philosophical marionettes: the gregarious, the vulgar, the quotidian, the exoteric, sound understanding or common consciousness; and with their symmetrical terms or complements: the overman, the philosopher, the authentic man, the reflecting subject, Spirit, etc. More generally, anthropo-logical difference is the scission of the indivisible essence of man; it separates, or believes it can separate, what man can do. This is doubtless an hallucination that affects unitary thought – that is to say, what is essential to the Greco-occidental tradition, more than to the essence of man – but it explains why philosophy has never known man, and has given rise only to a mere anthropology. In place of man, in place of his real and absolutely singular essence, it manipulates anthropological or even andrological images, quasi-transcendental androids: the cogito, the ens creatum, Spirit, the *I think*, the Worker, the Unconscious, etc. – fictional beings charged with populating the desert of anthropological screens, shadows thrown up onto the abrupt walls of Ideas, inhabitants for ideal caverns.

Anthropo-logical difference is thus the postulation and the forgetting of the real or 'finite' essence of man. It is identical to its own history, the auto-destruction or auto-inhibition of the mixture of man *and* logos. It goes deeper than the 'humanism' that contemporary philosophy attacks, limiting and closing in on the target so as to be more sure of attaining it. It reigns still in unitary deconstructions of humanism. It is qua difference, not in so far as it speaks of man, that it is henceforth at issue. Anthropo-logy as parallelism and as difference (the nuance does not matter here) is *the* Greco-unitary myth that must be excluded by a theoretically-founded science of man, but on the three following conditions: that this exclusion should be not the cause but the effect of that science of man and of its positive essence; that the latter does not take up the vacant place of unitary anthropology, but should on the contrary be the instance capable of radically determining it; and finally that the rigorously described phenomenal content of man should be, *in an original identity*, *to whose non-circular essence we shall return*, at once the principal 'object' of that science and its unique 'subject'.

The human insufficiency of the Human Sciences is a theoretical insufficiency. We have spoken, against common sense, of the theoretical carelessness of philosophy. For the deficit of *theoria* does not belong originally to those weak and inconsistent sciences. It comes first of all from the Greek ontological prejudices that have prohibited the simultaneous deployment of the essence of theory and the essence of man and which, in place of a phenomenally rigorous and positive science of man, have produced a mere counter-mythology or counter-sophistics – 'philosophy' – which, in its prudence, has programmed an 'anthropology' become, under the borrowed name of 'Human Sciences', a cutting-edge discipline.

Is it still a matter of an ultimate philosophical gesture? Or is this radicality no longer of the order of philosophy? At least one is obliged here to make a clean slate of the unitary prejudices of the Human Sciences, in order to be able to found this rigorous science that philosophy will have failed to be.

2. MAN AS FINITE OR ORDINARY INDIVIDUAL

Just as it is not a matter of reopening the interminable combat between philosophy and the Human Sciences, so it cannot be a question of making man 'exit' from the enclosure that they form together as a function of their very conflict. It is instead a matter of showing that he never entered into it, that this conflict is not his affair, except from the point of view of a unitary hallucination whose mechanism must be analysed; that he is determined and complete from the outset, and absolutely precedes the phantasms of anthropo-logical parallelism. If philosophy is an anthropo- or andro-eidetics, we must systematically oppose what we call 'ordinary man', who retains in himself an inalienable essence (which above all is not to say that he is causa sui…), to the philosophical android or anthropoid – that is to say, the *homo ex machina*, a part of the philosophical machine, of Being, of Desire, of the State, of Language, etc. *Man, in his real essence, is not visible within the horizon of these presuppositions, which are also those of the Human Sciences.* Anthropology may simulate him, evoke him magically, but it is not yet a science; anthropo-logical difference is not man, but his transcendent avatar in the World. If the essence of man is not a *difference*, something like an *undecidable decision*, it is the radical subject of an ordeal which, far from alienating him, is finite, retaining him in himself and prohibiting him from ever exiting himself. Ordinary man is inalienable, which is what distinguishes him from his projections on the anthropo-logical screen – projections that are inconsistent, ir-real and devoted to history.

Man is the real object of a science once he is rec-ognised in his specificity, irreducible to the objects of other sciences, and in his reality rather than in the mere possibility of his 'figures'. This unique twofold exigency may later receive various nuances, but it holds in principle, and is undivided in its foundations. Each science has its own way of driving back the old unitary ideal of totality, and the rigorous science of individuals has its own too: it demands (but radically, at last) that the All and its modes, the universal or authoritarian predicates, should not be 'all'; that man should be, from the start, outside-all, introduced into the World, or rather outside the World – a duality of which the World, the All and their attributes are but one side. The reality-condition of a science of man is that it ceases to be unitarily closed up in totalities and unities, and that one no longer confuses the real relations of sciences amongst themselves with the Greco-philosophical forms of unity, which are perfectly mythological. It is this unitary or Greco-occidental paradigm, which traverses almost all of philosophy right up to its contemporary deconstructions, that must be abandoned, along with all its prejudices, in order to perceive the reality (rather than the mere possibility) of man. The latter is not and has never been an object visible within the Greco-unitary horizon, or even within the anthropological canton of that horizon. There is no point in renewing or even deconstructing metaphysics. What is necessary is to change the paradigm of thinking; to pass out of the philosophical paradigm (which ranges from Being to Difference, from the Same to the Other) to a paradigm that we call *minoritarian* or *individual*, and which is founded on *a transcendental but finite experience of the One as distinct from Being, the World and their attributes*. The distinction between the individu*e*l and the individu*a*l is the foundation of a science that is non-empirical (non-worldly, non-historical, non-linguistic, non-sexual, etc.): a transcendental science of individuals or of the ordinary man. Whereas the individuel is always also universal, the individual is the undivided without remainder or excess, that which is nothing-but-undivided and which precedes a priori all forms of universality. The individual problematic is thus founded on a thinking of the One rather than of Being. Being, but also Difference and the play of the Same and the Other, are always unitary. Aside from their own particular difficulties, they are incapable of doing justice to man, or even of rendering him visible; they are content with the substitute of an anthropology or (what is hardly any different) a unitary critique of anthropology.

We propose to break the alliance between man and the authoritarian predicates (Desire, Language, Sex, Power, the State, History, etc.), an alliance that gives rise to sciences that are not those of man – the alliance of man and the philosopher, master of predicates. We must change hypothesis and even paradigm: break up the mixtures, found philosophy on man rather than the inverse; venture a history of the human existent that no longer owes anything to unitary prejudices; a biography of man as solitary or celibate of the World, of Faith, of Technique, of Language, and even of Philosophy.

But this man, it will be objected, does he exist? Does man exist in any other form than the residual or epiphenomenal? *Is there a proper and primitive essence of man that is not an attribute of something else?* The human in man cannot be reduced to the sum of its predicates: the living, the speaking, the acting, the historical, the sexuate, the economical, the juridical, etc. – the philosophising – however one might calculate these predicates. That would be possible man, not real man. The latter is subject, nothing-but-subject. But neither is the subject here in turn a special predicate; it is a subject that has never been a predicate and that has no need of predicates in general, a subject that is from the start inherent-(to)-self, or sufficiently determined essence. The essence of man is retained in the One, that is to say in non-positional inherence-(to)-self, in a nothing-but-subject or an absolute-as-subject, that is to say a *finitude*. For reasons of principle that will be stated later, we identify the absolute with finitude rather than with infinite totality. Individuals are 'real' in advance of totality – they are not modes of a substance, and they do not even understand themselves on the basis of infinite and universal attributes (Language, Life, History, Sexuality, Economy, etc.). There is no point in asking whether these predicates are included analytically or synthetically in the subject 'man' or whether the latter is the difference of himself and language (anthropo-linguistic/logical), of himself and sexuality, etc. As we understand it, man is 'ordinary' in a positive sense: not a residual, shifting figure of philosophy, or of the Greek episteme. He is determined in advance of the latter, and precedes absolutely the philosophical calculus of predicates, just as he precedes each of these predicates taken one by one.

Ordinary man is thus stripped of qualities or attributes by a wholly positive sufficiency. He lacks nothing, not even philosophy. But that he is stripped of predicates does not mean that he is stripped of essence: on the contrary, this is man in so far as he takes his essence from himself or more exactly from man, immediately, without it having been, beforehand, an attribute. He does not owe it to History, to Biology, to the State, to Philosophy. There is no deprecatory or pejorative nuance to this 'ordinary' or 'minoritarian'. I am a sufficient Solitude, far too short of 'solipsism' to have to disabuse myself of it. I am not a cogito, a relation to a Site or to an Other. I am out-(of)-the question: not the question of man, but the ontical or ontological primacy of the question of man. I do not find my essence in my existence or in my questions, I feel my subjective essence before these questions arise. I am the beginning of my life and my thought. And if I thus exclude the question and its mise en abyme from my essence, it is because this essence (and essence in general) is defined by characteristics that are absolutely original, primitive, internal and without equivalent in the World: it is defined by the One or the irreflective. There is a question-(of)-Being, but the One is out-(of)-question.

What we describe here are the structures of this ordinary man. Structures that are individual, invisible in the light of Reason or Intelligence. These are not ideal essences, but finite, inalienable (and consequently irrecusable) lived experiences. The individual structures of the essence of man are describable outside of any anthropological prejudice – that is to say, outside all Greek philosophical rationality. Only these individual and finite determinations accord to man something other than a mere possibility – a determined and specific reality – and render possible a science of his relations to the World, to History, to Language, etc., relations that are not at all those hallucinated by the Social Sciences. This is the meaning of the 'biography of the ordinary man': a rigorous description of the most general experiences that govern the relations of individuals as such to History, to the State, to the Economy, to Language, etc.

The text of this science is thus no longer the cogito and its *membra disjecta* distributed across the Human Sciences. It is the irreducible kernel that one must extract from the cogito in which it is still enveloped and masked. But this extraction cannot be conceived, in turn, as a philosophical operation, since it is rather an immediate given, to which we are content here to 'sensitize' ourselves.

The foundation of a science of man consists first of all in creating a non-philosophical affect: in rendering oneself sensible to what immediate givens, what non-hallucinatory reality, what *finite transcendental experience*, there is in man; in taking that essential step without which unitary anthropology will continue to fascinate us with its conjuring tricks. There are immediate givens of man. They do not, doubtless, constitute the whole of his relations to his predicates and to their unity (World, or Philosophy); but they are the rock that permits the scientific description of his relations. They are primary but they do not, of course, exhaust this science of men and of their relations. The phenomenal given of this science, its unique text, is the One: but precisely because it is the One, it is not unique. The One is (above all) not Unity, the unitary Ideal that still reigns in the cogito and leaves its essence undetermined. The complete text of the science of man is double or dual – *dual* rather than duel – just as it is individual rather than individuel: the One and the World, minorities and Authorities, individuals and History, the State, Language, etc.

Thus it is not, properly speaking, a *Principle of Humanity* whose statue we are raising here alongside or beyond the Principles of power, of language, of pleasure... In the name of ordinary man we take care not to pander to the slaves in the Cave or, for example, to assure a defence of sheep against eagles. We describe, rather, a real essence of man *before* the animal difference between eagles and sheep, which the philosophers would have us believe belong to man and to his becoming. And ordinary man is not even the antidote to 'superior man', or to the overman – he is no more the hero of the future than the trove of the latest archaeology. It is, rather, against this heroic and agonistic conception of man that the Greeks have transmitted to us, and which shoots out new flames under the names of difference, différance, differend, that we try to render visible a man without face and without qualities. This is a treatise of Solitudes.

3. FROM PHILOSOPHY TO THEORY: THE SCIENCE OF THE ORDINARY MAN

The science of real men is thus no longer a philosophy or a mixture of anthropological prejudices and mathematization. It draws its essential character from its object: it is itself 'individual' and 'minoritarian'. It is distinct from philosophy on several counts: It is a thought that is (1) rigorously naive and not reflexive; (2) real or absolute and not hypothetical; (3) essentially theoretical rather than practical or technical; (4) descriptive, not constructive; (5) human rather than anthropological.

(1) It is not philosophy that has to become a rigorous science: it cannot do so – its circular essence prevents this. However, a rigorous non-empirical science is to be

invented, a theory that precedes philosophy and that will be the science of philosophy. To become scientific – this is the essential predicate and the telos of philosophy, an undetermined project and a Greco-unitary phantasm. *We must think science, from the outset, according to its proper phenomenal exigencies, and cease to move in the aporetic circle of philosophy that gives rise, like an irresolute dream, to the compulsory goal of scientifically exiting this circle.* Such an exit only brings the aporia back once more, in a higher form. Now, a science generally does not become rigorous except by depriving itself, for reasons of positive sufficiency, of the aporetic essence constitutive of unitary philosophising. The essence of the science of the real (empirical or even indivi*dual*) is its non-circularity, its non-reflexivity, its naivety. This principle of sciences, a principle of which we shall not especially say anything here, but which is itself founded in the One, is the *Principle of Real Identity or immanence*, a principle of which philosophy knows nothing, but which is valid for sciences both empirical and transcendental.

Upon this common basis, the characteristics of the science of man are obviously not entirely the same as those of the empirical sciences in which philosophy sees (perhaps mistakenly) an inferior naivety, an impotence and a failing. The Principle of Real Identity must receive, in the case of man, a transcendental specification. Thus the science of individuals boasts a naivety that is transcendental and no longer empirical. A naivety that, without being 'superior' to philosophy (nothing is superior to philosophy, since it is the very spirit of superiority itself), no longer owes it anything, and determines it without reciprocity: it suppresses the circle and no longer passes by way of a circular procedure of determination. Science's setting-itself-outside-the-circle in general owes to the real itself, which has never been circular, above all in its essence here given by individuals. There is no disguised philosophical operation at work here, but only the experience of the positive phenomenal tenor of individuals or of ordinary man – which is the very foundation of this science. The science of the real (the real par excellence, the human real) is a non-positional science-(of)-the-human-real. It is not constitutive of its object, but fuses with the immanent, non-thetic and finite experience it has of that object. It is a transcendental science, of course, but one that definitively breaks with *empirico-transcendental parallelism*, along with all modes of difference, and in particular anthropo-logical difference.

Whence its naivety – ante-philosophical and wholly positive, not merely ante-predicative or ante-reflexive and consequently still philosophical. The real is not a presupposition of thought; it is a presupposition at most *of* philosophy and *for* philosophy. It is already essentially thought, but non-thetic, irreflective or individual thought-(of)-self. We thus advocate, at the basis of the absolute science of man, a *transcendental naivety*, precisely not philosophical but real. An absolutely naive science, stripped of constitutive philosophical operations, operations whose naivety can no longer be, like those of empirical sciences, critiqued, reflected, overcome by philosophy and its Consciousness, differed by philosophy and its Other, and so on.

(2) It does not begin with the cogito, which was never a real beginning, since it was always preceded by idealising philosophical operations; but with individuals as transcendental non-positional experiences-(of)-selves. That is to say that finite indivi*dual*ity is not a principle either, always first according to the ratio essendi or even according to the ratio cognoscendi or even according to the unity of difference of the two. These are subtilised forms of the circle, and not yet that finite transcendental identity which is the essence of the real and which is no longer a concentrate, a condensate of the relative-absolute, logico-transcendental circle of philosophy (thought *and* the real, being *and* thinking as the Same, etc.). Such a transcendental but radically finite identity exists, and it is man in his non-anthropological experience. An identity that is neither logico-formal nor logico-real, but nothing-but-real; not at all 'logical', in the sense that the logos is always a circular relation to the real.

Here again, a science of men is wholly distinguished from a philosophy. Philosophy is a science of real possibility, not a science of reality *before* the possible. It is a transcendental logic, give or take various nuances, not a transcendental reality. Through fear of transcendental realism, which is in fact an absurdity, it confuses the real now with the Logos, now with the Other of the logos. Philosophical magic denies the authentic real in the name of a fantastic image (sometimes ideal, sometimes empirical) of the real. Philosophy is not, and has never been, an absolute science – it is only a relative-absolute 'science', with an irreducible hypothetical moment. Nietzsche, in his own way, gives us the key to philosophy: the real is an interpretation; and interpretation is the real, or represents the real, for another interpretation. It is the idealist-absolute mixture of real hypothesis or interpretation that the absolute science-(of the)-real excludes so as to move, from the outset, upon that anhypothetic terrain that philosophy has always regarded as a promised land.

(3) Greco-unitary philosophy is practical in its essence and its origin: it is a praxis and/or a techné of superior essence. For three complementary reasons that we do not have time to analyse here: it is a form of know-how that has no absolutely given objects, but only *ob-jects*, that is to say *stakes*, or which takes its own circularity as an ob-ject; one whose essence is care, concern, interest, rather than disinterested contemplation; ultimately it is a mixed, logico-real know-how, which, programming the intervention of thought into the real so as to bring it

about, prohibits itself from knowing it as such or in its 'real identity'.

As such, it is deprived of any rigorous theoretical foundation – it does not have too much theory, but not enough. It leaves theoria unelucidated in its essence. Of course it has theoretical aspects: but theoria is included in philosophy only as a predicate for activities, values, aims that are nothing but socio-political or other prejudices, that are not elaborated in their real phenomenal content, and that make of philosophy an opportunistic and rigourless activity, an antimythological strategy rather than a science. Philosophy does not need to 'become' fully theoretical – that is to say, be suppressed and realised. It needs to be de-rived or, as we say, uni-lateralised, as secondary activity, by theory deployed in its essence. Thus the theoretical can cease to be a mere predicate of praxis – it is this mixture that must be broken. Even in its Greek versions, which seem to give a primacy to the theoretical, to 'contemplation' over action, the insertion of theoria into a mixed structure is enough to subvert the irreversible real order that goes from the theoretical to the practical.

It goes without saying that these terms can no longer have their vulgar and/or philosophical meanings. Otherwise, such an order would seem a paradox, an idealist prejudice, or even a return to a Greek prejudice – a badly understood one, moreover. Philosophy, let us repeat, has always been, up to the present time, a praxis with theoretical aspects, and not at all the experience of the real essence of theoria. How is the latter to be conceived?

Theoria ceases to be a universal predicate when it is the essence of science, but an essence that has never been a predicate. Theory is a radical subject, an experience-(of)-inherence-(to)-self, whose essence is individual. It ceases to be an attribute and a unitary goal when it is identified with the radical, finite and individual immanence of the subject; when 'contemplation' is (to) itself its proper essence or when, *before* contemplating the World, the Object, Unity, etc., it is inherent-(to)-self, rigorous (that is to say, non-thetic and finite) transcendental lived experience. This is to exclude the *auto*-contemplation that is proper to Unity rather than the One such as we understand it, as 'individual'. It is to exclude, in particular, the cogito or *transcendental ego*, which are just transcendent modes of auto-contemplation through the mediation of the World, precisely because of all the philosophical operations, praxes or technés of doubt, suspense, the quest for foundations, etc., that it still circularly presupposes.

(4) Thus, brought back to its essence, real theory, not determined by philosophical operations or prejudices, is *a non-positional contemplation-(of)-immediate givens or (of)-irreflective transcendental experiences*. The latter are the materials of this science that describes the content of the finite phenomenal experience of man, of his relations

with the great authoritarian attributes of History, Language, Power, etc., and with their totality, which is the World – without intervening in them. The theory of man is not a theoretical practice, an intervention into an object and a transformation of that object. It is rather a non-positional, but also non-altering, description-(of)-positions (philosophical positions, for example, but more generally unitary positions): an immediate or irreflexive description-(of)-the phenomenal descriptions that are the real content of the life of man and of his relations with the World. A passive thought, but not *before* an ob-ject (where passivity is the counterpart of a production), doubtless because rigorous science, as will be suggested in relation to the necessary destruction of the Copernican revolution, is a thought stripped of *ob-jects* (but not of 'contents' or of 'objects' in the wider sense); a science that has no 'face-to-face' – which does not mean to say that, in the idealist manner, it is deprived of reality or of materials: it is content to describe strictly immanent phenomenal experiences *before* (and outside of) all unitary-philosophical prejudice. In particular, outside all phenomenological prejudice, it gives phenomena their status as immediate givens rather than as already-transcendent intuitions. Finite thought renounces reflection, analysis, and construction; it confines itself to the irreflexive, to phenomenality deprived of phenomenological operations. Phenomenal givens are not residues, but that which is, from the first, real, and which thus possesses the power not only to make possible, but to really found the latent phenomenology that is the essence of unitary thought.

This is why the treatise of the ordinary man will be constituted of *theorems*; theorems that, moreover, are not empirical but transcendental. They are not so much 'the eyes of the soul' (as Spinoza says of his own theorems) as the soul itself, describing itself in its individual radical immanence. They are content with describing phenomena lived by ordinary man, phenomena that are invisible, in principle, to philosophy and phenomenology.

(5) Finally, unlike the Human Sciences, which are merely anthropological, and which usurp the title of 'human', the transcendental science of individuals is 'human' for the very reason of its scientificity. The science of men should be written 'science-(of)-men': they are its inalienable subject, without any ob-ject whatsoever. The theoretical and the human have always been opposed: but far from opposing their common essence, one has been content to oppose prejudices that are transcend-ent and have no phenomenal rigour. In reality, man is the only nothing-but-theoretical living being there is; a mystical being: the irreflected contemplation-(of)-self is his essence, because it cannot be the all of his relations to the World. There is no theory except human theory: not in the anthropological, but in the individual sense of these words.

4. THE POSITIVE AND SCIENTIFIC MEANING OF TRANSCENDENTAL NAIVETY

(1) All comparison of one science with another, and above all that of a science as special as a transcendental science with empirical sciences, is dangerous, and rarely goes beyond metaphor. All the same, we have seen that the former and the latter have in common a naivety, and that this trait, *taken as positive*, is probably essential to their definition as science. The transcendental theory of individuals possesses yet a second character in common, this time, with one particular empirical science. Even if this is but a mere metaphor, it may allow philosophers better to enter into this project: quantum mechanics and its foundation in objects (let us say particles) that qualitatively escape, by definition, the earlier modes of visibility and objectivation proper to classical mechanics and thermodynamics. *At least from the point of view of the habits of thought* (if not from the point of view of the type of rigour it involves, in terms of which we cannot claim to compare an empirical science and a transcendental science for reasons, moreover, that have more than one meaning) the introduction of the individual conception of man supposes a qualitative leap in relation to unitary presuppositions, and cannot be carried out within the framework of simply solicited, renovated or deconstructed existing philosophical positions. It is another thing again than a

'revolution in thought' since, as will be suggested now and then in what follows, it is the renunciation of every 'revolutionary' manner of thinking – a renunciation that no doubt necessitates distinct (and perhaps more difficult) mental efforts from those demanded by a revolution.

Indeed, it is less a question of soliciting, of fracturing, of displacing objectivating or metaphysical representation, than of *resolutely thinking outside of it, without ever giving oneself ob-jects; which is not to say that this thinking is empty and without 'objects' – on the contrary*. But these objects are not ob-jects, that is to say realities in the slightest bit affected by transcendence: they are individuals, defined by their transcendental immanence alone, and by the experiences that they undergo in their relations with the World or the Authorities which, themselves, moreover, are not ob-jects. Individual or minoritarian thought, as distinct from unitary or authoritarian thought, moves in the sphere, wholly positive however neglected by philosophy, of an invisible radical, an 'unconscious' perhaps, but one that is, if we might say so, purely subjective – an unconscious that would be only subject, without this meaning that it is transcendent or ob-jective (linguistic, biological, etc.) and constitutive of the subject.

This is another paradigm, not yet another variation on the unitary paradigm. What we call the minoritarian paradigm supposes the abandonment of the Greek ontological habitus and its deconstruction. It opens up the field of realities that have been absolutely hidden since the origins of philosophy, and dissimulated for reasons more profound still than the existence of Greek forms of philosophy, even if these forms almost definitively killed off in the West any inclination to shake off the yoke of unitary hallucination. It is not at all a transcendental field of individuals that is proposed here as a new transcendent back-world of philosophy, but a dispersion of purely transcendental rather than transcendent individuals, individuals whose essence, consequently, is to no longer obey the laws of opening-and-closure, the always-unitary laws of a 'field', of a 'body', of a 'continent', of an 'epoch', of an 'episteme', etc. From the point of view of theoretico-mental habits, as much effort must be made to penetrate the laws of these individual, offscreen or out-of-field = outside-Being entities, absolutely unperceived by ontology, as to penetrate into the domain of 'particles'.

(2) The unitary paradigm, to identify and determine any object whatsoever, must have recourse to a variable and relative combination of two philosophical parameters: immanence and transcendence. These parameters being relative to each other, they are thus each of them partially undetermined, and will only be determined reciprocally. The space or the field is called unitary because it is formed by this circularity, the circularity of these two dimensions that are both necessary in order to identify any entity whatsoever. Suppose now that there exist entities which,

in order to be fully and sufficiently (if not completely) determined, need only *one* of these parameters, the first one. Minoritarian or individual thought is the experience of these entities that do not enter into the unitary field, and which are not determinable by that relative combination, but by one dimension only, thought truly independently of its unity with the second; and then by a combination, but a non-reciprocal, non-relative combination, of the two. They are not unitarily determinable because they are determined already by themselves, as terms before all relation or reciprocity. Finite individuals are real entities before being magically captured by the unitary field. It is a matter of thinking of terms firstly in their finite transcendental identity, before all relation, and then of describing what follows from this, as to their potential relations to the unitary World. The relation of the two fundamental parameters changes completely, and it is here perhaps that the comparison with quantum reality ends: precisely, it is no longer a relation, that is to say a reciprocity or a reversibility, a relativity in any case. We have, first of all, an immanence that is primary and stripped of all transcendence. If it is correctly conceived, it suffices for the determination of finite individuals and for the founding of a science of individual entities. The parameter of transcendence only appears with the World or unitary thought, but itself must be elaborated according to that first immanence. Unitary reality – what we call effectivity – must thus be rethought according to the individual or minoritarian real. From the first parameter to the second, there is no longer a unitary relativity/ reciprocity, but a strict asymmetry – an irreversibility or an order that breaks with the more or less decentred circles to which the aporetic philosopher is accustomed. Philosophy is relativist in the bad, Greek, sophistic and empiricist sense of the word; true relativity is founded in an absolute and unsurpassable (finite) experience – here, that of individuals as finite.

Minorities or individuals should not be confused with the micro-political, micro-psychological, micro-sociological, micro-sexual, etc. The micro always belongs to the molecular, it does not attain the truly particulate. It retains a continuity, on the quantitative, qualitative or even intensive scale, with the macro. It is not a question of suspending (phenomenologically, for example) the modes of unity that conceal an invisible world, which will then be brought into the light of reason, into the philosophical daylight. It is a question of treating, from the start, the real in the strict sense as philosophically unengendered or non-constituted. Here there is a world as immense as it is invisible, intangible, inobjectivatable; but we must realise that this world is perfectly thinkable, once it is thought, and once unitary hallucination has dissipated.

We describe here the immediate givens of the invisible. But the invisible is what is seen in the One; it is not the Other, once more an Other or an Unconscious of our World. These givens cannot be confused either with objectivated or empirical realities, or with the philosophical procedures of their objectivation. *Objectivation can thus no longer serve to verify experimentally the essentially transcendental theorems whose sole pertinent criterion is the irreflexive immanence of the One that serves them as guiding thread – that is to say, their descriptive fidelity to the real.* It is on the basis of, or through, these non-positional experiences-(of)-self that we contemplate and describe the aporias of language and of philosophy, the agitation of the World, the goodwill and the barbarousness of the State.

These principles, correctly understood, may perhaps permit the denunciation of the supposed well-foundedness of a question that we shall not neglect to pose, without being able to resist making an apparent objection to it. Given that we do not seek here, in the traditional way, a new object – a political object for example, an unprecedented cause to defend, or the possibility of a politics of minorities that would rest ultimately upon certain principles – we will of necessity be asked: Won't you at last show us your minorities, give us examples or cases, stop talking so abstractly? Is it a question of a new interpretation of the political and juridical status of national, linguistic, cultural, sexual minorities – or else, if not, on what condition does one *become* minoritarian, *become* a 'man' of the type that you claim to be describing?

These questions have become so obvious to us that the response we shall give here may appear a little flippant. We write to demonstrate that this sort of question has no pertinence for a rigorous conception of the essence of minorities or of individuals; in other words, that its pertinence is merely politico-logical or anthropo-logical, that its possibility owes to the (politico-logical, etc.) Difference that is the matrix of Greco-occidental or unitary thought. It is this type of question that we must now abandon, to accede to a problematic of minorities and to a science of man that will itself be minoritarian, rather than being an ultimate concession to the State or to Philosophy. The minorities we are concerned with receive no new political or juridical status. They are not elevated into a cause for some new revolutionary practice. However, the pre-state determination of their essence permits the carrying out of a rigorous critique of the political or the statist and of the anthropological, without denying massively their order and their existence.

Whence a thought not without precedents, but without examples. There are no *examples* or *cases* of minorities thus described. They are the object of an experience, doubtless, but an experience we shall define as strictly transcendental, and no longer as *simultaneously* empirical: they are thus not given within the universal horizon of power and governmentality, of culture, of language, of sex, etc., nor, in the contemporary manner, as the modes of this horizon. Not only do they refuse for their part to fall under categories and into types; they are that which permits the exclusion from thought of the descriptions and argumentations of examples, of the cases and facts that are always part and parcel of those great universals. They are, par excellence, the absolutely invisible of the State, of political or philosophical practice, of language, etc. This is what gives them their particular pertinence and their capacity to resist those Authorities. If they were to become visible at the social, historical or linguistic surface, they would again become parts or members, more or less constrained or integrated, of the State. Finite minorities are the definitively invisible essence of Authorities, and as such are denied by the latter. This negation must be destroyed while respecting the absolute invisibility and inaudibility of finite individuals, supposing that one renounces philosophical demonstrations of the rational type, founded upon the primacy of Unity, of Universality, of the Logos, of Being, of the State, of History, etc. and while making explicit the immediate givens of the One. Generally speaking, *there is no 'minorities question'*: the true minorities are, in History and in the World, absolutely silent. This is why, ceasing to be at stake, over and over again, they must instead become the object of a science. There is a minoritarian question only for the State; there is only a question of individuals for the World, for those who ask how to tolerate them, how to define their difference or their margin, in other words and always: how to integrate them. Minorities become a problem or a stake for philosophers and State intellectuals who claim to determine their cultural and political, linguistic and sexual specificity – a task of and for the State, which can elaborate no concept of them except a tautological and vicious one, already compromised, as soon as it makes a question of them. To say it rigorously and more succinctly: it is a question of breaking (with) empirico-transcendental parallelism (or, we could say, state-minoritarian parallelism) in the thinking of minority; the parallelism that prevents supposedly minoritarian cases, facts or givens from coming to reflect themselves in their essence, from which they draw an existence and a reality that no longer owes anything to the universal horizon of the State, for example, or to the rules of governmentality that organise this field. Individual thought in general renounces concrete representations, representation in all its forms; it defines the essence of individual multiplicities in such a way that it excludes all figuration whatsoever – as if one had passed from a macroscopic and even molecular sphere to a particulate sphere whose laws would be entirely distinct from the figurative laws of the foregoing regimes. The One is the criterion that makes the closure of representation make a definitive leap, permitting us to abandon philosophy's aporetic knowledge so as to found a necessary science of man.

We shall not subscribe, therefore, because of this refusal of all empirico-ideal experience, to the notion that minorities are a concept without reality or the object of merely nominal definitions. They are real essences, lived in experiences that are pre-political, pre-linguistic, etc. – true immediate givens. Their necessity, *if one insists*, proves to be that of an ultimate and absolute requisite of the existence of Authorities themselves, and that of the effects that their conception produces on the State, politico-logical Difference, anthropo-logical, sociological, etc. Difference – that is to say, the old Greco-occidental couplings that then lose their validity, and are no longer thinkable circularly and viciously on the basis of themselves, but must be thought on the basis of indiv*idual*ity. But the exploration of these effects confirms the reality of finite individuals, it does not prove it. This essence of the minority is positive, concrete, and amenable to a rigorous transcendental description that brings into play notions whose content and organisation are articulable and definable.

(3) The realisation of a theoretical science of man obviously supposes not just a complete change of philosophical problematic, but a change in the paradigm of thought in general. It supposes that one cease to describe, in the guise of the phenomenal givens of man, modes of *Philosophical Decision*, which are always mixed and circular (in general viciously circular) operations or procedures; and that one entrusts oneself first of all to the real in its

individuality, to that which philosophy cannot (except by way of a unitary illusion whose mechanism we shall analyse) any longer claim to determine.

All the same, a resolutely naive science cannot be tolerated by unitary philo-centrism. Can one thus abstract from philosophy, it will be said, without manifesting a very philosophical innocence? Precisely we do not abstract from philosophy, which would still be one last philosophical operation, one last, desperate attempt to 'exit'. We begin with the real that has no need of philosophy, and that determines it without reciprocity, assigning it a place that we shall later specify. The science of the real, that is to say of individuals in their individuality and in the immediate givens of the latter, precedes absolutely (a precession without counterpart) philosophy and the Human Sciences, that is to say the unitary mytho-logical sphere. All these essences (finite multitudes, and even Philosophical Decision) are immediate givens, and suppose no passage of philosophy 'to' the real, as one might pass to the Other; no transcendent and universal operation losing itself in exteriority. The irreflective real, in its veritas transcendentalis, is not a power-to-be, a 'real possibility'. It is an immediate donation more originary still than the distinction between Being and beings, beings and the Other, Being and the Other, the Same and the Other, etc. The problem of knowing whether it is possible to 'leap' out of philosophy (out of its discourse, its reason, its texts, etc.) into the real is obviously a poorly-posed problem – it is a unitary problem that has pertinence only from within the dominant paradigm that imposes itself through these types of intimidating effects.

The problem is not that of knowing whether there are any immediate givens. The latter are transcendentals, are immanent, and draw from themselves their pertinence. In any case, it is more scientific and less vicious to admit immediate givens of this type, to install oneself in them from the start, than to postulate transcendently, in unitary fashion, rational *facts*, scientific, ethical or aesthetic facts; or even semi-empirical and semi-transcendental facticities; or even the *Other*, the transcendence par excellence, the immediate donation of transcendence or of the Infinite. In all these cases, the real is only tolerated, filtered, mastered, through its falsificatory mélange with a form of possibility or of transcendence; or even, in extreme cases, reduced to the latter or to the Other. As if philosophy could, itself, leap beyond its shadow, its essence as simple possible, so as to 'posit' (only to posit...) reality. The 'ontological proof' has been nuanced, differentiated, derationalised, palliated, etc.; but it has remained the heart and the breath of contemporary philosophy: to pass – it passes and does nothing but 'pass' – from the possible, from the Other, from transcendence, to the real or to immanence, or to the mixture of the first and the second. Philosophy will have been, up until now, the mutual embrace of the real and

the possible, their non-scientific confusion, the falsifica-
tion of the essence, the absolute essence, of individuals.

The real is philosophically indeterminable, but determinable by itself, a priori, before all philosophical intervention. Philocentrism responds that this is impossible,
that philosophy is always necessary, even if only because
one speaks of the 'real', of 'a priori', of 'singularity',
etc. – all the *textuality* of philosophical discourse. Our
general response is that this objection is not pertinent,
demonstrative or scientific, because it is vicious – it is
itself circular, and it merely reproduces the exigencies
and the claims of philocentrism, which has decidedly no
reason to renounce its narcissism. The latter transforms
its fact into right, exempts it from its factual existence
and from its brutality so as to prohibit any endeavour
that would radically limit it. This argument comes down
to saying that philosophy is the all, or rather that the All
is the absolute or the real: which is the mytho-logy par
excellence of unitary philosophy. Here, philocentrism
again manipulates an argument that is a sort of displaced,
broadened, apparently inverted 'ontological proof': it
always concludes from existence to essence, or, more
exactly, *it concludes from effectivity* (the World, Society,
History) *or from the mixture of the real and the possible, to the
true real which is also essence...* from predicates to a subject-
without-predicates; from Authorities to minorities, etc.
It is this vicious argument, this founding paralogism of

unitary thought, that the individual experience (scientific in its manner) of man must reject as a superior form of mythology.

The transcendental naivety we have invoked is an a priori indifference to the philosophical such as it exists – it renders all philosophies contingent. But the real, or absolute science, are such that indifference or non-participation in philosophy do not belong to their essence, do not define it, but follow immediately from it. Indifference in the matter of philosophy, no doubt – but it is no longer entirely that indifference that philosophy secretes with regard to itself; that of scepticism through an excess of dogmatism; that of the Other = real (nihilism, and then counter-nihilism); that of the Other as Other-than-real (contemporary deconstructions), etc. Instead it is an a priori indifference, but one whose precession over that which it indifferentiates would be absolute and without reciprocity – which would permit, at last, the dissipation of the unitary magic that is Greek philosophy – and the Other...

.

Toward a Science
of Philosophical Decision
(1987)

Translated by Taylor Adkins

1. PHILOSOPHY AS THE OTHER OF SCIENCE

To introduce philosophy to science, rather than introducing science into philosophy – this task is already posited
along with philosophy, which is its realisation. It is thus
pointless to posit it again. There is no metaphysics that
does not aspire to be the science of Being, or of the
Logos, or in any case the highest form of all knowledge,
which it would thus complete and render adequate to
its essence. This can no longer be the question, with
philosophy supposed as given. On the one hand, the
scientific self-realisation of philosophy supposes that
the latter produces of itself, and manifests, the concept
of science; that it thereby modifies the empirical concept

of the sciences, imposing upon them a certain ideal of validation and foundation; and that, in this way, it devalorises and critiques the meaning and truth of the real sciences. This philosophical endeavour of appropriation and critique of the sciences calls itself their interpretation or their ontological foundation (for which the sciences would be a deficient or lesser mode of the ontological project of objectivity or of the *Idea* of science), or their epistemological interpretation (for which there would be a *fact* of the sciences, which philosophy reappropriates for itself). On the other hand, science remains in the state of an infinite dream, an impossible dream constantly deferred and played out again and again. Philosophy is not a science, because it *wants* to be one (this is its essential will): in philosophy, the will runs deeper than science. It therefore contents itself with the scientific 'form', with a 'becoming'-science, with its infinite telos, etc. And it is this that calls itself (even before Husserl) philosophy-as-(rigorous)-science.

Another project is possible: Supposing Philosophical Decision to be given, together with its natural desire to be a rigorous knowledge, is it still possible to introduce it to... the experience of science – at least if we suppose the latter to be autonomous or independent of Philosophical Decision? To school philosophy in science, not so as to make it think the latter and instruct itself accordingly (an epistemological schooling), but so as to allow itself to be thought *by* science? Perhaps in general there are two sources or paradigms of knowledge: The infinite ideal of science belongs to Philosophical Decision and to the historicity of its mode of phenomenalisation of the real; but only as an essential *attribute*, not as Decision's essence in person. Philosophy believes that its mode of phenomenalisation of the real is universal. Perhaps this is not the case, perhaps this is the artefact of an illusion and a naivety internal to every Decision of this type. And perhaps science is a radically different, more primitive mode of phenomenalisation that can leave Philosophical Decision intact, as one of its objects.

It seems impossible, in any case, to renounce the ideal of a philosophical knowledge that would be rigorous in its foundation and validation. But does philosophy itself have the relevance, force and reality necessary to assume such an ideal? It is perhaps the ultimate maxim and the ultimate consensus: a founded and validated knowledge. But its meaning is still hidden. We all seek a rigorous practice of philosophy – but is this telos so universal and so certain? More exactly, aren't its universality and certainty still posited, all too often, as proceeding unproblematically from and with Philosophical Decision? Are they not once again comprised within the philosophical circle – just as postulated by historicism, hermeneutics and even, to a lesser extent, deconstruction?

I shall suppose (a supposition whose foundation we shall later discover in science) that it is possible to avoid completely reducing this scientific postulation to its philosophical modes and forms; that there is, for example, a universality and a certainty proper to science, that one cannot confuse it with the old metaphysical *certitudo*, and that the latter can deny it only in appropriating it. Philosophy's search for a rigorous and certain knowledge may not necessarily be reducible to philosophy's need, desire or therapeutic concern, and perhaps cannot be assumed by it. *If* science 'in general' is not a mode of Philosophical Decision (of the ontological project, for example) *then* a non-philosophical science of Philosophical Decision would be possible and would no longer be a supplementary mode of the latter's quasi-'scientific' self-realisation.

Philosophy contains almost as many programmes for the reform or revolution of science as it does systems. But all of these projects postulate the inclusion of the scientific within the essence of the philosophical, and leave to philosophy, whether over the short or long term, the development of this history and this politics of 'becoming scientific'. Even, perhaps above all (although in a more insidious manner than 'grand' rationalism), when (logical or sociological) positivism claims to renounce the philosophical ideal of self-legislation, and submits philosophy to the *sciences* interpreted as *positive*. The positivist critique of philosophy is in general a false scientific critique and a true philosophical auto-critique – just one more system. One will recall that there are several cases in point of this Ideal of philosophy as science or science as philosophy; the most essential being the following (noting in simple terms the typical tendencies):

1. Two forms that *forget* the immanent scientific telos of philosophy as 'absolute science'. These two forms are dominant in the current conjuncture:

(*a*) The historicising critique of philosophy, its reduction to 'History of Philosophy', which is not only (we shall claim) a particular coded academic practice, but the presupposition of the majority of academic practices. It is understood that this presupposition (the reduction of Philosophical Decision to its texts, to its corpus, to its institutions, to its politico-textual 'unconscious', etc.) is an inherent (albeit extreme) *possibility* of Philosophical Decision, not at all an external 'happenstance'.

(*b*) The logico-empiricist critique of metaphysics, which is ahistorical and atomistic in general, or at least predominantly (since it is increasingly contested from within). Here we find still the same type of presupposition: the reduction of Philosophical Decision to an inert variety of 'ontological' points of view. No longer the textual or the signifier, but a (factual and supposedly autonomous) given, consisting of facts or logical forms. This is probably a possibility of Philosophical Decision, which has the ability to auto-deny itself as such, under the particularly alienating form of a substitution of science (interpreted as *positive*) for philosophy.

Since the first of these forms is still largely dominant in Europe, this is what we shall chiefly examine.

2. Two forms that affirm the immanent scientific telos of Philosophical Decision.

(*a*) The controlled importation of the procedures of proof and 'empirical' scientific validation (logical, geometric, chemical, etc.). The result is a knowledge which knows itself and wills itself to be mixed; which, for example in the classical 'dogmatic' way that is its most general style, affirms the co-extension of science and metaphysics, with various nuances, but without remainder on either side.

(*b*) The auto-development of the scientific telos of philosophy as the purest Idea most removed from any object or any regional and worldly scientific knowledge (Husserl): same presupposition as before, but more *purified*.

If we refuse this basic presupposition of philosophy – the co-extension of philosophy and (absolute) science – as insufficient to the task, and if we intend to keep Philosophical Decision in its integrity and not devalue it through an empiricist and positivist critique with recourse to the existing sciences, there remains only one solution: To replace philosophy as auto-legislation, but in another place, there must be an absolute science (transcendental and not empirical) that would be a science-(of)-science. Science does not fall under an epistemology or an ontology, but 'under' itself. A *science-(of)-science* is not necessarily a positivist project, if one can only 'reconcile' science and the transcendental function in a science-(of the)-real as such, an 'absolute Science'. On this basis, transcendental science will necessarily also be a science *of* or *for* philosophy.

Thus the separation of science and philosophy will no longer be *undetermined*, oscillatory and reversible. Undetermined to the extent that it is determined by philosophy, for the latter includes in its essence an underdetermination for which it compensates with an overdetermination, the play of a process, a history, a becoming, etc. The separation can then always be read or operated in both directions, being reversible according to various proportions: the whole history of philosophy consists in these attempts to constitute *mixtures* of science and philosophy. If, on the contrary, we manage to define in science a thought that is, of itself, real = absolute – a thought *index sui* which no longer needs to be externally thought in Decision in general, in 'ontological Difference', for example – then we maintain a certain reference, a pole in relation to which Philosophical Decision must be situated unilaterally.

We thus propose no longer to think in accordance with or under the law of mixtures; we propose to render the separation irreversible and to read it in the following sense: It is not science that is the Other of philosophy, but philosophy that is the Other of science, in relation to which it becomes possible to evaluate its 'specific difference'.

2. MALAISE IN PHILOSOPHY?

Can we any longer justify a science of Philosophical Decision on the basis of the insufficiencies of the latter?

Philosophy has always made its malaises known; and not only those whose affliction it has displayed, absolutely, upon itself, through its sheer existence, so that auto-critique consummated critique. It is thus vain to invoke them as justification for the passage to a scientific form capable of disabusing it of its congenital dissatisfaction. However (and this is what motivates our inventory here), it has perhaps only partially revealed these malaises, repressing them in the same gesture. But they may be more visible today, at a time when philosophy is particularly attentive to itself.

Let us be more specific. It is easy to justify the project of a science of philosophy through the senility or sterility of its *current* state, opposing it to a philosophy to come, which would be more active, more productive, less distanced from 'reality', and so on. Such symptoms and such dissatisfaction have been manifest whenever there has been philosophy, i.e. in the passage from one philosophy to another. Wishing to be universal, it would have its malaise be universal too, allowing it to be specified each time by various historical conditions. If this affect is congenital to Decision, we shall keep from *dismembering* it and from complaining about current philosophy as opposed to an older or future philosophy. We are thus obligated to displace our critique, to raise its level and its demands. It is necessary to penetrate more deeply into the *essence* of Decision itself so as one day to have the right, if not the duty, to complain about it. And, in general, one cannot 'critique' Philosophical Decision by arguing from its insufficiencies – this would be to proceed 'negatively'. It is still necessary to perceive the origin of these illnesses, an origin that is probably visible from anywhere except within philosophy. We shall therefore not attach too much importance to the inventory of reasons for practising philosophy otherwise. But does that mean we must relativise them? On the contrary – they must be *absolutised*.

For, since these malaises belong to the essence of Decision itself, we can take our complaints about them only to science – and not to philosophy, lest we worsen them. This is what allows us to give them their full meaning; and it is here, on the other hand, that the current state of thought is indispensable: current philosophy is driven, above all since Nietzsche, and to various degrees, by the need for its re-affirmation or its intensification. But it should above all not be thought that this re-affirmation of Philosophical Decision is any less naive than its primary affirmation, or that it suffices to cure the originary malaise. Reaffirmation is in a sense even more naive than the affirmation that it confirms and prolongs without really destroying. In short, it renders philosophical naivety and spontaneity all the more visible or manifest, without dissipating them at all. The parousia of pre-scientific and philosophical naivety, for example, does not really destroy the latter, and above all does not substitute science for it: the ideal of parousia is the very success of philosophical naivety, its ultimate fruit. One does not exit philosophy at all, one does not go outside metaphysics, by reaffirming them: one simply sees them function better. It is this supplement of essential sensibility, of the philosopher's pathos, which is the mark of the conjuncture and which better allows us to 'relieve' (or sublate) the malaise – no more. Even History of Philosophy, which creates the most prevalent malaise as dominant practice, along with the various forms of rationalist treatment of philosophy, are in principle and immediately positive possibilities of Decision – the possibilities of its denial or of its extenuation, the programme for its quasi-extinction. We must place ourselves at the point where Philosophical Decision manifests itself as such in its spontaneity and its most accomplished forms. We shall thus avoid overly brief or opportunistic explanations which consign themselves once more to being a part of the symptom.

3. OBJECTIVE PHILOSOPHICAL APPEARANCE

With the above caveat, we can say that the intimate affects of Philosophical Decision *as such* are those of *repetition*. In every sense of the word: repetition of the identical, but also repetition of difference or of the 'same'. The affects of the 'same' are 'superior' to those of the identical which they re-affirm, but they do not change its nature. For example, if we speak of the *nausea* attached to the practice of philosophy, it must be understood that this affect is valid for all practices – from the most identificatory to the most differentiated – that are content to will a 'superior' Identity, a universal equivalence, integrating an alterity that cannot really destroy the latter. Thus we shall have to respect the heterogeneity, but also the univocity (for us decisive) of the categories of *nausea*, *repetitiveness*, *sterility*, etc. through which we shall describe the principal affect of Philosophical Decision in general, even at its most 'affirmative'.

(1) Philosophical Decision is an operation-(of)-transcendence, anti-empirical to various degrees, but always destined to fulfil itself in a *position* or an ontological opening, in whatever mode that may be. It is a game

of positions: not only are the positions finite in number (however many variations they may be capable of), but the *positionality* of philosophy, its nature as game of positions, encloses the virtual infinity of positions into the finitude of a structure or circle. Hence its capacity for repetition, which is its very essence rather than a failing that could be mitigated by technical correctives or new procedures to ensure greater efficacy and less sterility. The accusation of sterility, repetitiveness and slow progress must follow from the recognition of repetition as the essence of Decision, rather than preceding it; in this way it will not reduce repetition to a historico-systematic accident of 'certain' philosophies.

(2) Consequences: philosophical practice is simultaneously marked – this is not contradictory given the structure of Decision – (*a*) by the reproduction of a constant finite stock of authentic information. Authentic, if we bracket the *redundancy* which forms the bulk of everyday philosophical practice, and whose only goal is to extract the benefits of power from the productions of the social field, and if we no longer consider the thresholds of emergence (themselves malleable) of 'new' philosophies; and (*b*) by a diminishing of the proportions of its output: with exploitation reaching its limit, the finitude of the possibilities originally included in Philosophical Decision is exposed, in a progressive exhaustion of the stock and a

rarefaction of 'novelty' (which is therefore nothing but a possibility or virtuality that has not been manifested yet).

(3) The combination of these two traits explains what I shall call the auto-inhibition or auto-paralysis of Philosophical Decision; the feeling that it has only ever worked by itself and upon itself, broadening its circle only so as to better conserve it; making it implode, certainly – but only so as to better reaffirm it. Philosophical Decision is the care of self that remains self, even when it is interested in the Other; that plays with itself when it devotes itself to transversality; or that remains supposedly inevitable when it is fractured or solicited by the Other. Hence its regular auto-interment in its texts, its works, its archives and its history, in its institutions and in the unconscious that it secretes or *as which it reproduces itself.*

Philosophical practice, in its most 'academic' form as in most of its para-academic forms, in the most historical forms as in the most active and diligent, is followed – and no doubt also at the same time *preceded* – by a gigantic, consoling and vigilant shadow, by a historico-systematic body that is its unconscious, i.e. Philosophy in person. We shall ask ourselves to what extent this body could correspond to a sort of *capital* of philosophy. It would be produced by philosophers who are more and more obsessed with and blinded by it, revering it as the element that gives them life, being and movement, and thus stimulating the surplus value of thought that will then be attributed to it – whereas it would use its energy to convince them to work for it. Furthermore, there is barely any philosophical (especially Continental) practice anymore that is not haunted by this phantasm of a constituted, undetermined and tutelary philosophy, *the fantastic foundation of the philosophical community*. It corresponds, if not to the motor, at least to the (always immobile) motive of practice. It is a stock of knowledge, a willing of decision whose accumulation *seems* necessary to Philosophical Decision; to its reproduction, in any case, but also (and this is perhaps the height of alienation) to its production.

The preeminence of this horizon, impeded to the precise extent of the opening that it seems to procure for Decision, is not an accident. Even if its increasingly incommensurable dimension marks our conjuncture and even if it dominates the present, it belongs nonetheless to the essence or the will of philosophy. We shall call it the *objective philosophical Appearance*, the element of the manifestation of knowledge that is *given* and *received* as necessary by the labourers of thought who deem it necessary for the founding of their community. This is philosophy's intimate seductive force over 'philosophers', its means of commandeering them to its service, of having them devote themselves to questioning it, of leading them to the most spontaneous and naive practice...

Corollary: the affect of the 'death of philosophy' is indeed real. It is lived by concrete philosophers, at least qua subjects of philosophy; but it is partial. It is only one of the two sides of a more complete affect, which is that of auto-inhibition or auto-stalemate. Instead of grasping that every stalemate of Decision forms a system with a supplementary opening, this system displacing itself toward a relative-absolute limit, simultaneously external and internal to Decision; instead of understanding that philosophy removes nothing, takes nothing away from itself without giving itself, but in a sense gives less and less to the extent that it is increasingly given itself as such; instead of maintaining the *philosophical balance*, we have isolated or abstracted its most negative operation, its (voluntarily and/or involuntarily) suicidal nature. In reality, *there is indeed a suicide of philosophy, but it has lasted as long as philosophy's own history* – and one should never count philosophy's chickens before they are stuffed and mounted. There belongs to any essential Decision the possibility of the impossibility of philosophising. It still must not be separated from the possibility of thinking that conjugally animates it, even if this couple's life is often hell.

(4) The combination of the finitude of the philosophical circle, its circularity, and its unlimited displacement *within* a relative-absolute limit, signifies a permanent state of conflict. War, an essential war, belongs intimately

to Philosophical Decision. Every philosophical *position* is also a virtual struggle against another position. The board for this game of positions is meagre, imposing a mutual inhibition, a reciprocal attraction and repulsion. And it is *meagre* because, if there is a structural rule of Philosophical Decision, it is that of the *Unity of contraries*, of the Coupling of the opposed, whatever the modes of this 'transcendental Unity' might be. This type of Unity, devoted to the tasks of synthesizing a diversity (Being and Nothingness, for example) and which must be divided between contraries all the while remaining indivisible, is by definition in short supply, and afflicted by intestine wars. The history of philosophy, or more precisely *objective philosophical Appearance*, functions as a paradigmatic dimension of every decision that selects from it its game of positions; and also as that dimension, syntagmatic or 'historical' in principle, that allows for the organisation of a philosophical discourse. It is ultimately necessary to tie together repetition, auto-inhibition, conflictuality – and historicity...

4. THE MOST APPARENT SYMPTOM: HISTORY OF PHILOSOPHY AS DOMINANT PRACTICE

The ultimate and most manifest symptom of the malaise linked to the spontaneous, naive and 'compulsory' practice of philosophy is the increasing primacy of History of Philosophy (HP), which has become the dominant practice of philosophers.

We shall not rehearse the critique of HP as an academic practice, which has been pursued elsewhere.[4] This critique must be limited by recognising that the HP is a *possibility* included in Philosophical Decision, whose de jure historicity can always be reified (by means of the mechanism analysed above which puts into play *objective philosophical Appearance*). Indeed, HP is in this sense the moment in which the malaise 'takes' or 'congeals' into a particularly pervasive symptom. However, for the same reason, there is something too easy in the critique that claims to dissociate and oppose Philosophical Decision and its dominant academic practice. The argument is too quick because it miscognises philosophy's vocation to sediment itself in an inert objective Appearance. And it demonstrates a certain bad faith. The dissociation of 'good' historicity from 'bad' History of Philosophy functions to produce certain, completely short-sighted, 'benefits':

1. It dissimulates the risk-free transference of HP, corrected or amended, into other institutions. Its marginalisation is not its suppression; rather, it conserves the essential qualities of philosophical spontaneity and naivety. One might correct and at times compensate for HP through Marxist practices, archaeological practices, deconstructive

---

4   Cf. F. Laruelle, *Pourqoi pas la philosophie?*, Volume II, *Les Crimes de l'Histoire de la Philosophie* (privately published, 1983).

practices, etc.; in doing so, no doubt, one modifies and 'works' the watchwords of historicity and history, but conserves them as an essential optic upon the essence of Philosophical Decision. Above all, one respects the essentiality of its will to the auto-application and auto-legislation (more or less differed) that are the ideals of its naive practice.

2. It spares one the trouble of re-opening the question of a violence deeper than that of the academy, and which nourishes the latter, rather than the other way around. All the 'defaults' of the academic practice of philosophy have their roots in Decision itself. It is therefore the latter that ought to be reevaluated, at least in its spontaneous form. But the interest in history, and ultimately in objective Appearance, excuses one from the scientific examination of Decision and its essence. One is content with leaving it to itself, or at best to phenomena of alterity, opening, solicitation, etc. which make inroads into it, exacerbating the 'game', but only the better to save it in the last resort. Philosophy, always more philosophy!... To make it a weapon against politics, against technics, against society, against the human sciences, etc. As if *spreading* the malaise could suppress it... as if dividing up a naive practice would not multiply the naivety through this very amelioration.

3. The systematic recourse to HP, under various more or less indirect forms, enables the establishment of a

consensus (if not a community) discreetly and at minimum expense. Through its (supposed or apparent) factuality, for one thing. But more profoundly, we only invest so much in HP because it is a half-measure, a compromise between spontaneous philosophical Faith and an equally intra-philosophical suspicion and auto-critique. This third way allows those contraries that had prosecuted intestine wars at the heart of Decision to reach an harmonious accord; and attenuates the auto-destruction of philosophy by realising it in controlled forms. The psychological and affective importance of HP stems from its essence or its provenance: it reassures because it furnishes an apparently certain ground – that of science, supposedly, a science now confused with the old metaphysical *certitudo*. History is the pseudo-scientific, all-too-philosophical alibi for the forgetting of the 'scientific' essence of philosophy. Instead of a veritable science of philosophy, one prolongs the visceral suspicion of itself that the latter had fostered in its savage state; one brings it back to the poorly understood ideal of science, the ideal of certainty and facticity, the 'modern' ideal that 'everything is historical' and will be held to account by the tribunal of history. These practices have but one goal: to threaten philosophy with itself, all the better to save it in extremis. It is always the same logic, that of hypocrisy: History is a consensus against the basest forms of philosophical war, but it is the consensus for a better-managed war. History is the means of strategising, mastering, subjugating at a distance and even *through* distance, and dividing-to-conquer. It is primitive philosophical violence pursued by other means. For there is an 'economy' of philosophy: exchanges, debts, conflicts, a whole market of critiques and violences more or less disguised as peace treaties, but which are nothing but sheets of paper, textual games or language games. History is the consensus of these struggles. Even local agreements and contracts between philosophers register relations of dominance, renew hierarchies and are at the basis of the equilibrium necessary to movement. The *pax philosophica* is a snare for those weaklings who would ignore the heroic essence of the philosopher. To surpass, to overcome – these are not accidents, this is the essence of occidental thinking. 'To philosophise is to dominate' (Nietzsche) – here is the key to the community of philosophers.

5. FROM PHILOSOPHICAL FAITH
TO SCIENTIFIC KNOWLEDGE

We therefore do not address our critique especially to 'current' philosophy, but to the current good conscience that believes it has resolved its problems with philosophy (problems which in reality are born of the latter) by taking refuge in history understood, once more, philosophically: a vicious circle... More radically, beyond any current state of affairs, we cannot reproach contemporary philosophers for doing too much history: they do what they can, and this can be neither corrected nor reformed. We suggest that they know not what they do, and that they passionately submit themselves to a *transcendental Illusion* that affects, beyond 'metaphysics' or 'representation' alone, Philosophical Decision as such. To the same extent as their predecessors, perhaps with more critical vigilance, albeit biased because still of the same order, they *confuse two heterogeneous modes of phenomenalisation of the real*: the philosophical, which implies Decision or Transcendence as its major operator; and the scientific, which excludes from its essence such Decision, and phenomenalises the real by retaining it in its most realist and most immediate 'naivety', in its immanence most deprived of any exteriority whatsoever. This initial confusion is naturally followed by another: every knowledge is ultimately reduced to an historical knowledge, i.e. to the deployment of a transcendence.

This unitary amphiboly is the very soul of philosophy, and not simply that of its dominant practice in an academic setting. Whence that belief, contained in the spontaneous philosophical Faith which it prolongs, that it is through history that one might accede to a science of philosophy – as if this would not lead to another vicious circle. Philosophical Faith is itself the same thing as the transcendental Illusion and the negation of science, the same thing as that belief that philosophers have varied, enriched, displaced and altered, but without destroying: to think = real; to philosophise = real. The belief-in-self-as-in-the-real, or as in that which can co-determine and co-produce it, even in manifesting it. Such is the unfathomable depth of philosophical Faith.

The intimate connection between historicity, war and repetition remains visible in the mechanism of Decision, and forms an indivisible whole. It must in turn be linked with the savage, pulsional auto-practice of philosophy. If it is impossible to sceptically dismember Philosophical Decision, to cleave it, split it or choose – to operate a supplement of decision – as philosophical critiques habitually attempt to, then it is Decision taken globally that must be reevaluated, along with the Faith that feeds into its spontaneous practice by philosophers, and even into the Ideal (as we have seen) of philosophy-as-rigorous-science. This ensemble formed by Faith, the structure of Decision and its operation of transcendence, spontaneous practice (the philosophy of philosophers) and finally history, must be bracketed-out, by means of a non-philosophical science of philosophy.

That science allows for the liquidation of historicity, i.e. the simple vicious auto-application of philosophy, is a potentially dangerous observation. Let us suppose a standard or statistical Anglo-Saxon style, exemplified in the case of logical positivism: it, also, will claim to bracket, if not all of history, at least the historicity of philosophical problems; it will develop an analytical, ahistorical and atomistic optic in its formulation and solution of those problems. However, even though this style is a possibility of Philosophical Decision (or precisely *because* it is one), it is difficult not to see in it a negation, still philosophical, of the native historicity of Decision. Here we find a weak destruction lacking in history and submitted to re-interpretation through this more powerful experience of Decision represented by the standard 'Continental' style. If we really want to eliminate the mediation of (Marxising, archaeologising or historicising) history in the treatment of Decision, it is Decision itself that must be suspended, without recourse to the means that it seems to offer for this operation.

This supposes that science in its most specific stance is *a knowledge of the real that does not modify that real*; in which the observer can modify the phenomenon without modifying the real implied *in* and *by* the immanence of the scientific stance. Science would not form a circle with it like philosophy does, when the latter claims to be not only a knowledge of the real but a co-production of it. The latter is what is correctly called ob-jectivity – a confusion of the real that is known with the object of knowledge (which is always modifiable). Hence the distinction: philosophy is the theory and practice of the ob-ject and of ob-jectivity, it has ob-jects or confuses the real with the ob-ject or its representation; whereas science has a real 'object', i.e. has no ob-jects in the philosophical sense; it maintains a relation with the real which is no longer that of *objectivation*. There are two heterogeneous modes of phenomenalisation that philosophy – always unitary – would conflate, whereas science seeks the autonomy of its own way of thinking the real and the distinction of these two modes.

So as to found in its reality (not only in its mere real possibility), the scientific phenomenalisation of the real which we have thus far only supposed or called for, and so as to distinguish it definitively from that of philosophy, we shall ask if, and under what concrete mode, we possess a sufficient experience of this phenomenalisation – an experience in which we can recognise science's autonomy of thought and, in the same stroke (a consequence of this duality), its greater primitivity, its anteriority to Philosophical Decision and its essential features (repetition, auto-inhibition, war and historicity).

Of course, it would be contradictory to claim once again to accede to the essence of science through the processes and technical procedures of philosophy. This means that neither (transcendental) *reduction* nor *meditation*, nor the analytic and regressive type of *foundation* nor the search for ultimate limits, etc., are any longer viable or legitimate. Even less so the epistemological 'reflection' upon the so-called 'fact' of the sciences, which is nothing but an artefact of philosophical objectivation. Through what other technique could we accede to their essence? *Through no technique – for every technique co-determines its ob-ject and co-produces it, as philosophy does. No technique is necessary in order to re-place oneself into the most general stance of the sciences with regard to the real.* The technico-experimental apparatus is a means ordained to the essence of science, it is not this essence itself. The latter resides only in the positivity, the quasi-'ontological' consistency, of a realism and a certainty that are *naive* and without 'decision'. Of course, it is not a question of the local 'objects' and 'representations' produced by the sciences, but of that which every 'scientific' stance immanently postulates as to the real it relates itself to as such – a question of scientific 'intention' and its *transcendental claim*, if you will.

Philosophy will always look for and posit science too late: at the end of its 'reflection', at the end of its 'project' of objectivity, at the end of its 'dialectic' – in general, at the end of the transcendence that founds all of its techniques. Now, it is precisely transcendence that science excludes at least from the relation (of non-relation) that it 'maintains' in the last instance with the real. Hence its naivety, its irreflectiveness, its realism, its 'blindness', which are so insupportable to philosophical ob-jectification that the latter never stops denigrating them, reducing them, falsifying them – this is what goes

FROM DECISION TO HERESY

by the name of 'epistemology' and is the very *epistemo-logos* in every epistemology.

By 'non-relation'-(to the)-real, we mean that *there are* – they are their own criterion of reality and truth, and are thus transcendental criteria – *givens which are radically or non-thetically immanent-(to)-self*, and which thus refuse the philosophical artefact of ob-jectivity. Science is the only a-positional and an-objective mode of thinking, and this is why philosophy, which *wants* this a-positionality but *cannot* acquire it, denies science's autonomy. It is not only Kantian or 'neo-Kantian' idealist epistemology that refuses the existence of radically immanent givens or of a non-thetic self-phenomenalisation, precisely so as to oppose it to *categorical ob-jectivity*. All of philosophy, as Decision or Transcendence, is unable to accede to the essence of science, and thus produces as a backlash this 'reactive' symptom called 'epistemology'. If the programme of a rigorous science of philosophy must in any case pass through the 'destruction' of epistemology, it is indeed because the traditional unitary relation of preeminence between Science and Philosophy is reversed – more than reversed, since it cannot be a question of a reversal of hierarchy and a passage to anti-philosophical 'positivism'. To sum up these simple indications, we shall say that science does not receive its essence from Philosophical Decision; that it possesses a positive and specific essence; that this essence allows itself to be thought neither as mode of Being nor as avatar of the ontological project, nor as exploitation of the properties of Being; that in general its non-relation to the real does not pass through philosophical-type objectivity, and that it does not fall under the legislation of ontological Difference.

The positive reason for all these phenomena, that which explains this (non-)relation-(to)-the-real as transcendental experience-(of)-the-real, we can sum up in this term: the *One*. The element of science is the One, not Being; which implies a general usage of language, and of the 'categories', that is completely heterogeneous to that of the 'logos' that philosophy uses to constitute or unveil = realise the real. Science is a non-thetic reflection-(of)-the-real which does not change the real in manifesting it. Whereas science changes the order of its representations instead of the order of the real, philosophy *claims* to change the latter with the former – whence its transcendental Illusion.

6. THE IDEA OF A PURE SCIENCE OF PHILOSOPHY

No doubt it is always possible to continue traditional philosophical practice, with its traits of repetition and circularity, conflictuality and historicity, its will to appropriation and auto-inhibition. It is tailor-made for continuation, it postulates its own unlimited or interminable nature. It is always possible to add a 'new' system; to carry out a new variation on the 'limits-invariants' that form Decision; to define, for example, a 'new' experience of the Other and, complementarily, to define a new form of the old metaphysics, its 'logocentric' form to be 'deconstructed', etc.; to proceed to new cut-outs or disarticulations. These are all operations of decision, possibilities included (more or less immediately) in the power-to-philosophise. And it is even still possible to desire an Ideal of philosophy-as-rigorous-science. But all of this, all these exciting and conflicting endeavours, change nothing in regard to philosophical Faith or to the mirages of objective philosophical Appearance. This *repetition* only confirms it in its essence, destroying only its 'inferior', 'transcendent', 'gregarious', 'natural', or 'worldly' (etc.) forms. And above all, this is to prolong, purify and amplify the aspect of spontaneity and violent savagery that belongs to Decision when it is left to itself. What we call the naive practice of philosophy is not a simple possibility of Decision. It is the very mode of its existence (conflictuality, historicity), and there is no 'historical', 'political' or 'philosophical' reason to arrest it.

What is more, the programme does not consist in *putting a stop* to philosophising (for once in its life...) or in *interrupting* the continuum of philosophical decisions. This would then be a simple negation. It consists in feeling the Philosophical Decision and its authority over itself to be already and actually suspended, by science such as we have defined it. Not its authority over the World and effective actuality, where, in a certain way, with all its risks and dangers, it incessantly battles to enjoy its full validity. But its authority over science and over the real to which science accedes; and thus also, *from this point of view*, over the rigorous knowledge that can be acquired of it. Spontaneous philosophical Faith, its unitary belief-in-itself-as-in-the-real, its transcendental Illusion, etc. – none of this is destroyed in the worldly or effective sense of the term. In that sense, everything is conserved, but only qua object to be examined. On the other hand, it is destroyed or invalidated from the transcendental = immanent = real point of view. From this point of view where the real = One, this relation-(to)-self of Decision, its circularity, no longer relates (to) itself. There is a 'dual' dissociation of the object of science (Philosophical Decision) and of the science of this real object. Science is not a segment or a fragment of its corpus, a moment of Philosophical Decision. No part of the World, and no part of philosophy, are conserved in the One – in the real and in the science that gives it in a primitive way. The reality of a Science of philosophy is founded in this way.

If there is a programme – and this is tentative – it is that of the passage from the spontaneous and naive practice of philosophy to its pure science, to a theoretical examination of Decision transcendentally founded in its own reality. Philosophers have vilified science – its 'naivety', its 'technicism', the 'deaf' and 'blind' nature of its thought, its 'operativity-without-thought' – quite enough. From the science that 'dreams' (Plato) to the science that 'does not think' (Heidegger), there is a loop that is none other than the philosophical circle. It is perhaps time to tell the last stragglers of epistemology and the 'philosophy of the sciences' that the sciences do indeed have a consistent and specific thought, but one that is not exhausted by the philistinism of the 'fact of science'; that science thinks, but, simply, that it does not think like philosophy; that it only objectifies its representations, not the real; and that, consequently, it has a more primitive and more essential *naivety* than the 'secondary' naivety that pertains to philosophical practice even in its most exacerbated operations of critical vigilance. This secondary naivety is a residue, an ignorance – a negation, in the last instance, of its source, which is the naivety proper to scientific knowledge.

It is not exactly an operation of turning back or reversal, as if one turned back onto philosophy itself the argument of the naivety and spontaneity of its immemorial practice. Philosophy owes that form of naivety, which still affects its 'reflection' or its 'critique', to a more originary experience of thought, that of science; to a naivety in a sense more well-founded and non-thetically certain-(of)-itself, albeit muter and frailer from the point of view of the 'logos'. But this naivety does not falsify itself, does not deny itself (being too self-inherent) as does philosophical naivety. Only Science boasts the probity of its naivety; philosophy falsifies the latter, separates it from itself or detaches it from its transcendental essence. Philosophy thus makes it the complement of reflection (general Transcendence), with which it is summoned to form a system. It projects an image or an anti-reflexive or pre-reflexive (ante-predicative, etc.) version of this naivety, a rather crude version, destined to be refined. This is how it accomplishes its unitary operation of conquest over science.

Will we manage to extract ourselves from this hallucinatory ploy? Such would be the effect of a science of Philosophical Decision.

Revolution within the Limits
of Science Alone
(1987)

Translated by Christopher Eby

That the era of revolutions is over, but less so than the
age of great revolutionary narratives (or whether the
inverse is the case) matters little. A revolution exists only
across a narrative that is too congenital to it merely to
'accompany' it. This undecidable conjugation of the event
and its virtually philosophical sense can, on the other
hand, do nothing other than endure. Certain premature
axioms, then, are invalidated: 'Revolution is dead – long
live liberalism (liberal revolution)!'; 'Revolution is dead
– long live the philosophy and history of revolution!'
We have become too profoundly Hegelian to become so
once again and one more time. We are too revolutionary
'at heart' to still 'have time' for revolution. Revolution is
metaphysics pursued by other means. The problem of its

possibility or effective reality – a problem of the reciprocal support and effacement of event and narrative – is no longer an interesting theoretical problem, and we now consider it settled.

On the other hand, new questions can be formulated: (1) Is a science of revolution possible that would not be a history – that is, a disguised philosophy? (2) How, by way of such a science, can we preserve the material and political acuteness of revolution and prevent its dissolution into either the historian's network of infinitely specific causes or determinations, or the philosophical categories and operations of 'sense bestowal'? How can we rediscover its real determination and protect it from these enterprises of confiscation: history (with its too-diminutive explanations for the event) and philosophy (with its too-grandiose explanations for the event)? Can revolution in turn enter the space of a scientific continent and, if so, which one?

It is not a matter of a revolution in the way in which we think revolution, but of both a 'change in terrain' and a 'transformation' of the way in which we think it. The problem is no longer, are revolutions still possible? Anyone will admit that they have populated the past and that de jure there are still more to come. Rather, the problem is, what within them is real? 'Real' in this case no longer designates historical and political effectivity, but those components of revolution that a science can access.

For the classic problem – the eminently political and philosophical preoccupation with *effectivity* – of how to produce or render possible a revolution, we substitute a problem of reality – that is, of science. For the 'ontic', even 'ontological', perspective of its production and manifestation, we substitute a scientific perspective that we understand nonetheless in a transcendental manner: what aspects of revolution can legitimately fall within the purview of a science?

These questions suggest another, as yet incomprehensible one. For rather than asking, *what is man such that he is capable of revolution?* (a question indebted to the revolutionary humanism of philosophy, which levels man by way of an uninterrogated, empirical concept of revolution), we must urgently 'invert' the question: *what is revolution if man is capable of it and, especially, if he is capable of thinking it under rigorous scientific conditions?* The real critique of German Idealism and, beyond that, of all philosophy and of *the essentially revolutionary humanism that the latter always retains the power to secrete*, passes through a science of revolution. Indeed, it is this realisation that was presaged by the only two somewhat rigorous attempts that have been made, although in a problematic form, toward a science of revolution: mathematical Catastrophe Theory (CT), in general and in the branch that applies it especially to this object, and Historical Materialism (HM). However inadequate these two attempts may presently seem, better an inadequacy than an appearance or an illusion. It is the latter that characterise philosophy, which (as we shall see) is capable only of being revolutionary in essence, a philosophy *of* revolution, and thus leaves no chance of gleaning from the latter the least morsel of rigorous knowledge.

From this point of view, 'German Idealism', the collection of vicissitudes to which an 'a priori Critique of Revolutionary Judgement' is susceptible, did not introduce revolution into philosophy, in which it already was, as we shall demonstrate, an invariant structure of Philosophical Decision. This Idealism is only the coming of revolution in its manifestation as the essence of that thought known by the moniker 'philosophy', the essence to which revolution was already beholden. The sanction that a science grants to philosophy thus cannot be the one which Nietzsche and even Heidegger give to 'great' idealism; for here, it is given not so much to a philosophy, to Philosophy, as to its inveterate claim to exhaust the *essence* of every thought and every reality. The end-without-end of revolutionary narrative can now be the simple, indifferent material of a science. As for the 'post-modern', it is the micro-revolutionary auto-dissolution, and thus auto-conservation, of the 'great' revolution. Through it are laid bare the miseries of philosophy – at least, its most naive scepticism – which still attempt to interest us. Yet revolution is not dead; we are simply no longer interested in it.

THE EIDETIC CONTENT OF 'REVOLUTION'

Perhaps a science requires a dual donation of its object, or a dual object, a duality that conceals the fact that the 'same' word is used to designate these two objects in unitary thought – that is, in philosophy. First, as quasi-experimental 'given' (or 'fact'), which one associates with structures, models, and laws, and from which one produces an 'object of knowledge'; then (and this is quite different) as the 'real object' to which these laws are related, but only 'in the last instance', and which constitutes what reality there is in revolutionary effectivity. A science does not describe or explain facts, but the real. However, it uses these (theoretico-experimental) facts to describe the real.

Thus, the first task consists in elaborating what can be meant by 'revolution' from the perspective that makes it the object of a science. When historians and politicians speak of revolution or suppose its existence, of what object exactly are they thinking? Starting from this point, an initial correction of their representation is necessary: rather than taking an empirical and inductive approach proceeding on the basis of phenomena, supposed and spoken of as 'revolutionary' without any proof, and from which are then abstracted a vague, generic concept, it is necessary firstly to undertake a description of the a priori structures of every revolution, of the eidetic content, as it were, of this concept, of the system of invariants without which revolutionary phenomena cannot exist. It is on this point that the philosopher, provided that he carries out his work to the very end, is more rigorous than the historian. The latter loses track of his concept of revolution, or else preserves it only as a local abstraction from a continuum of historical and political phenomena. The eidetic content signifies the undecidable unity of facts and interpretations, of the event and its narrative, of forces and representations – not the dissolute accumulation of alleged 'facts', but the mixtures of these facts with horizons or lines of interpretation from which they are de jure inseparable. The first scientific given for a truly human science that would not be the mere transfer of techniques crafted for other objects, can only be this indiscernibility characteristic of theoretico-factual phenomena.

It is a matter of an imperative prohibition against all empiricisms and positivisms, a rule grounded in three reasons: (1) In a human science, it is always possible, and even necessary, to introduce the philosophical dimension or 'form' into the phenomena themselves; to number the many virtual philosophical decisions (of which man is capable and by which he appropriates these phenomena) within the ranks of the givens of that science. To put it in more misleading and external terms: 'ideology' is an effective, 'uncircumventable' dimension of human phenomena and must be taken *with* the object of science, rather than dismissed a priori by the latter. (2) The concept of revolution, in particular, has never meant very much outside of philosophy. The latter, insofar as it is Philosophical *Decision*, is firstly an operation of overturning, of re-starting from the zero point, by way of the edge or the milieu. The idea that philosophy could *not* be revolutionary is a revolutionary idea lost by philosophy. In reality, philosophy is the site par excellence of revolutions, never ceasing to revolutionise the subsisting state of things through new decisions. (3) Finally, in order to be rigorous, a human science requires the *Principle of Philosophically Necessary and Scientifically Insufficient Interpretation*: because a science cannot itself be an interpretation but must take into account, as human (and perhaps not only as human), all possible interpretations of its object, it can do so only by numbering the latter, in their entirety, among the initial experimental givens. It is here and only here, and only within these limits, that their claim can be heard. Hence, when confronted by any commonplace human phenomenon, it is necessary to derive, as consequences of it, all of its possible interpretations – at least their principle or their philosophical invariants – and to 'equip' oneself with them. Philosophy is the always-possible *universal form* of phenomena; and because it is always possible, it becomes necessary to 'realise' philosophy locally in every case. In a rigorous science of man, this rule is the equivalent of the experimental production of phenomena in certain sciences of matter. Thus, the quasi-experimental object of this science shall be the complete or developed concept of revolution, an *eidos* or an invariant.

If revolution is not a fact but a system of invariants, then it must be possible to describe its eidetic content.

1. It is the moment of strongest affect in a process – an affect that bears witness to the Other or the real. At times, the irruption of the real; at others, the real as pure irruptive force. These two formulae cannot be conflated: the irruption of the real is always less potent than the real itself, which recaptures it and re-interiorises it, while the real as irruption is less potent than the irruption itself. The latter announces itself, then, as a supplement of reality that sporadically transforms what was initially given as the real into mere representation and fantasy. To the first, more attenuated circumstance corresponds a continual becoming-revolutionary; to the second, a revolution that interrupts becoming itself, a generalised or absolute inhibition that prohibits the setting back into motion of the ancient machine of power relations, even if, effectively, it still 'continues'.

2. It is the moment of the reversal of existing relations, a specific operation that is impossible to avoid. It comprises several embedded structures (we ought to distinguish:

inversion, reversal, overturning as re-version, or indeed repetition of inversion), and several dimensions that affect all events (whether topographical, topological, dynamic, economic, etc.). This operation de jure touches *all* power relations, de facto only those that resist less or are more exposed.

3. Together, these two characteristics render revolution profoundly unintelligible, even doubly unintelligible: to the codes of theoretical and political appropriation of the recent past, which revolution invalidates, tears down, diverts, etc.; and more radically, to any rationality whatsoever that humanity might have at its disposal. Overthrowing, inverting, turning, is a problem of force and only of force, a problem of additional external energy. As the moment of irruption of the real, and even more so of the real as irruption, revolution falls by definition outside anterior legitimacy and the sphere of authority. Its necessity is operatory and structural – it is, if you will, the necessary reason of unreason. It surges forth from within rationality, but as its obscure, primary and semi-unconscious moment, a moment of images and forces, of myths and acts of violence. There can be no revolution that does not begin with the refusal to be spoken in the old language (supposed, out of habit, to be rational) or in any language whatsoever that is denounced as recuperative.

However, this unintelligibility is not necessarily lived as negative, except in relation to anterior rationality. It is not a problem for revolutionaries themselves. And in any case, this ir-rationality as absolutely positive eidetic structure perhaps escapes certain given forms of rationality, but not (or not always) philosophy – at least provided that the latter ceases to adhere to a dogmatic and conservative rationalism and realises the scope of its proper functioning (which concerns space and topography, force and dynamics, just as much as discourse), realises the specifically revolutionary character of its procedure. Terror is an essential law or an eidetic necessity of every revolution. That revolution should fall partially but necessarily outside of language, sense or discursivity, that it should become locally a problem of force (i.e. of fracture and division, decision and inversion), that it should be, so to speak, not fully philosophisable and even a riposte to all philosophy – but necessary for it, forcing it to think according to this limit – only certain modes of thought, which are historically post-revolutionary (Nietzsche, Heidegger, and deconstructions in general), can accede to this phenomenon, recognising it more easily than did 'Idealism', which wanted too immediately to transform Revolution into a factum and get it philosophizing, by inscribing it within operations that corresponded to a more 'metaphysical' phase of philosophy.

From this point of view, revolution corresponds to the moment of *decision* in a philosophical process – not the decision of a will but decision as willing essence of every will. Hence its profoundly 'arbitrary' nature, in the sense that this decision, saddled as it is with the task of founding a new political, social and theoretical rationality, can itself only be on this side of reason and thus devoid of every right and foundation, except that of believing once more in the magico-metaphysical virtue of instantiated auto-foundation. Being 'by right' without legitimacy, and maintaining what little reason it has only through its force, a revolution necessarily commits itself to an interminable process of legitimisation that is at once anticipatory (the future, the new values) and retrospective (the repetition of the past, the re-starting at point zero) – a process that only another revolution can portray as simultaneously necessary and forever incompletely fulfilled or impossible to carry out under such conditions. Every revolution must enlist the aid of another revolution, albeit a phantasmatic one, to reveal the instant of a quickly fading fulguration, as opposed to the ground of violence and arbitrariness of the real; the very real as this ground of violence, arbitrariness and war.

4. As we have just described it – in terms of eidetic content – revolution is still abstract. In actuality, there are two topologically *neighbouring* concepts of it that belong together, as its abstract and its concrete sense. Revolution

as an overturning and force of scission of the real – such is its abstract sense. It necessarily inscribes itself within a more vast process from which it is inseparable: the concrete and complete concept of revolution – as over-turning *and* displacement, as inversion *and* re-institution, as destruction *and* reproduction. It is an essential law that revolutionary reproduction exists as much as revolution itself; it is the effective complete reality within which irruption is inscribed and, most of the time, 'contained'. The totality of 'Revolutionarity' is rather a continuum into which is inserted the force of the inversion of values and powers, to the extent that every revolution grafts onto it – at least imaginarily – an anterior (the unfulfilled or the poorly executed, which must be repeated-rediscovered) and a posterior (in order to fulfil the present).

Rather a continuum: The revolutionary continuum does not exclude inversion, on the contrary; nor is it completely excluded by it. An inversion is also a dynamic and even phoronomic operation, a change and also an inversion of directions. A society passes continually from one regime to another through the discontinuity of a revolution – just as, elsewhere, it passes from a stabilised regime to a revolutionary 'regime' or 'non-regime' – to the extent that continuity tolerates a bi-directionality of values, decisions and tendencies. The most stable societies are perhaps intimately structured or crystallised by a revolutionary 'fold'. More exactly, since all such societies are acquainted with revolution, and since we are not speaking of a 'fold' contracted by societies like an historical bad habit, it is revolution itself which *is* the fold or which 'folds'; just as, inversely, the fold is a minimal articulation, the elementary (but perhaps not the only) catastrophe of every history. Revolution is in principle universal and transcendental; it is thus not a fold that history could contract, seeing as it is the contraction itself, the originary folding, that creates the space of history. Revolution, understood in its entirety, is the disjunction that opens the time and the space of societies.

If the revolutionary fold is the invariant catastrophe of the philosophical way of thinking (and not just that of certain philosophies) as well as of the becoming of societies, then there are several versions of it, depending, first, on whether the dehiscence that 'makes' the fold and puts side (by) side two social groups or two partial classes is more or less accentuated, 're-marked' as irreducible to the immanence of the entire process; and, conversely, on whether the totality or the concrete of the process prevails over the revolutionary 'abstraction'. These philosophical variations clearly comprise part of the eidetic that constitutes the givens of a *science* of revolution. They are always possible in principle, and one could distinguish, for example, two poles, according to whether (this is a question of hierarchy and proportions) the revolutionary fold is instead a refolding, a continuous immanence, or even instead an un-folding, an Un-foldable, an alterity which still folds, but according to the supplement of that which refuses every re-appropriating and normalising folding.

THE EXISTING SCIENCES OF REVOLUTION

When faced with our inability to know whether the history of historians is actually a science, and if one eliminates the usurped claim, propagated by philosophy in general and particularly by philosophies of history, to be sciences (they are such only in the metaphysical sense of the word 'science'), one will admit that there exist two rigorous attempts to constitute a science of revolution – Historical Materialism (HM) and Catastrophe Theory (CT) – and that the latter applies, explicitly or otherwise, to historical revolutions. The approach presented here is obviously not reducible to the preceding eidetic description, which is only the lesser half of it, and it is different still from these two theories. For reasons of principle that cannot be recounted here, it necessarily borrows elements from them, but *by radically transforming them on the theoretical front*. More precisely, it encounters their problems and ambitions on an entirely-other theoretical basis: that of an 'empirical' science of man, a science which is empirical by virtue of its object but which would be instituted, founded and recognised in terms of its transcendental scope, that is, in terms of its satisfied a priori claim both to originate in the real itself, that is, in the *essence* of man (and not in human *phenomena*) as in a last instance, and to relate the knowledges it elaborates to this real of last instance.[5]

This is therefore not an external heteroclite synthesis, as philosophical syntheses sometimes are, but a science which founds itself on its own object, which respects the latter's specificity and takes as immanent guiding thread the following question which the existing Human Sciences can only keep at bay a priori: what aspects of revolution and of its so diverse eidetic content can be given to man and known within the limits of man as object of science – that is, as we posed it above, within the limits of science insofar as man in his essence is its *real subject in the last instance*? Every other way of proceeding is heteronomous, transcendent, and violent – appropriate to non-human objects but inappropriate to man. This is clearly the case in the Human Sciences, but also in HM and CT: all these sciences are still too philosophical, they all simply postulate or decide the essence of man, or *suppose* their object, as given, without having elucidated it according to the undoubtedly unique way in which it can be given to them independently of Philosophical Decision. Because in the end, there will be a rigorous science of man that is not a mass or an aggregate of techniques designed for

---

5   On the theoretical problems of a first description of a human science of man, see *Une biographie de l'homme ordinaire* (Paris: Aubier, 1985) [from which chapter 1 of the present volume is drawn – ed.] and *La décision philosophique* no. 7 (Paris: Osiris, 1989).

other objects, only when the mode of presence or specific manifestation of its object is elucidated – a task that any philosophy whatsoever will always prohibit, since, qua this manner of thinking, it has already *decided* upon what it *must* be.

CT and HM do not escape this rule. CT transfers to history – that is, to an at least partially human phenomenon – what has been mapped out spatially by way of dynamic geometry. The geometrisation of the human is always possible, but, as a venture in philosophical finality, it will ever remain merely one of these interpretations that belong exclusively to the object of a science of man. It cannot take the place of the latter, which constitutes itself instead by responding to the question (which CT does not even pose) of the relation to man as subject-(of)-science. HM is more explicitly and more specifically a science of human phenomena. But it still conceives the latter on a truncated level, thus reducing man to this new attribute – history – while 'forgetting' to describe his specific essence as such, which is ante-historical and ante-economic. In addition, it carries this out in a transcendent manner, *historicising* the human where CT *geometrised* it.

The rigorous approach consists in founding these historical and geometric methods – insofar as they must here refer to man – on the prerequisite of a precise elaboration of his radical being. CT and HM are epistemological transfers of methods and objects, transfers typical of philosophy and which, as I have shown elsewhere,[6] assume this character according to the law of the 'idealist triad' and its amphibolies: a particular region (nature-space or history), along with its regional knowledge (I), is *identified* as or *confused* with a new science as such – Science of Man (II) – and necessarily with the very essence of all science (III). There is no reason why a science should constitute itself in this very philosophical way, through confusion or circular identification between objects and procedures. The transfer to man of bodies of knowledge developed through work on other objects, and now reputed or supposed to be his attributes, is an enterprise without rigour that has decided once more to ignore that of which it speaks, or to speak only of that about which it is content to know nothing.

The essence of man must cease to be simply postulated or supposed, in order to be recognised as given or included within the science of man and within the scientific stance in general. We will thus avoid what in every way obstructs these enterprises and makes them lapse into complacency: being an interpretation rather than a knowledge, a tautological and vicious 'explanation' in which one finally explains revolution through itself, and in which the only real content of the latter becomes the autoposition of Philosophical Decision. Precisely because

---

6   See *La décision philosophique*, no. 7.

philosophy is revolutionary, it cannot be a knowledge founded on revolution, but only a mere hermeneutic or even deconstructive 'commentary'. It is preferable to exhibit beforehand all the ultimate requisites of science and philosophy so as to avoid the speculative games of auto-interpretation between them. Both 'sciences' in question are indeed sciences with respect to their theoretical procedures, yet they fall short of the name with respect to the clarification of their object and of the relation of knowledges produced therein. So much so that they take the form and ambitions of philosophies, and can then no longer remain within the limits of their object, but unduly transport it elsewhere and attempt to incorporate into it man understood as an unthought mass of predicates.

The *apparently* inverse move (for it is real rather than inverse: precisely, it is not a philosophical revolution, but a science that founds itself in its object) consists not in claiming to revolutionise man once more, but in 'humanising' revolution, in the sense that man is the transcendental or immanent thread of his scientific treatment. By relating revolution to man as well as to its real basis, we immediately include him in the conditions of revolution's entry into the scientific order. We do not decree the knowledge of man a priori; giving ourselves man as real immanent foundation is 'the contrary' of deciding knowledge of him a priori. Indeed, we do not confuse his essence – necessarily given in a radical, rather than a priori, manner, in the form of an absolute, immanent lived experience, which is 'the seat' of man – with knowledge of man; it is philosophical idealism that fosters this confusion. On the other hand, by giving up on the prospect of viciously revolutionising revolution once again, we give ourselves the means truly to transform it, that is, both theoretically *and* practically. Until now, we only revolutionised revolution in various ways; the point is to change it. And only the 'correction' of the philosophy-(of)-revolution by a science of revolution can demand and fulfil this task.

CORRECTION AND TRANSFORMATION OF REVOLUTION

A science as such knows that it is distinct from a philosophy by virtue of its concept of knowledge and its concept of the real it seeks to know. It spontaneously or a priori makes a triple distinction: on the one hand, there are its givens, the material that it must work in order to produce knowledge therefrom: in this case, the theoretico-factual mixtures of revolution, the entirety of revolution('s)-representations-interpretations. On the other hand, its *object(s) of knowledge* (OK) – that is, the result of the preceding work, an object that constitutes itself according to certain rules or procedures. In the material sciences, these procedures are those of modelisation and experimentation, whereas in a rigorous science of man, these procedures express the transforming or determining causality of the specific object it seeks to know – not matter and its regions, but man in his essence. This causality, which expresses itself via procedures that are themselves specific and distinct from those of matter, is thus founded in the object and can be elucidated only on its basis. In fact, a science distinguishes its *real object* (RO) – in this case, man rather than his attributes (among which are included history and revolution) – to which it relates, in a very particular mode, the knowledge produced. What is essential is this distinction between the two objects, a distinction that science immanently demands between the representations of revolution and revolution as real object.

This distinction is 'radical', but what does this term mean? As distinct from a philosophy, which always posits an identity or a similarity between OK and RO, which forges from representation or knowledge a part of the real it seeks to know, a science announces the dissolution of this identity or circle of mutual belonging, and places between the *terms* a 'radical' discontinuity – that is, an asymmetry or a unilaterality of determination, a static duality in which the second term (representation or knowledge) is absolutely contingent in relation to the first (to the real) and cannot determine it in return. This duality which unilateralises representation is the condition of a science, and distinguishes it from the philosophical operation.

Thus, it demands in this particular case that *revolution in its essence or reality is absolutely nothing 'revolutionary'*. Nevertheless, it clearly does not suffice to posit, in the ambiguous manner of deconstruction, that the essence of revolution is nothing revolutionary or is the inhibition of revolutionary representations. It is even necessary that this *non-* derives from the very reality, from the positive reality, of 'revolution' as *real object*. The real of revolution, at least within the limits in which the latter is an object of science and ceases to be auto-fantasised by philosophy, is nothing that appears within the horizon of revolutionary projects or objectives. A science 'dually' distinguishes, without any *mutual belonging*, reality and objectivity. It does not place reality at the terminus of objectivity, but must *suppose reality to be given* a priori *without being known* a priori, *precisely and solely in order that it can be known 'subsequently' and that the representations which comprise knowledge can be related to it alone*. This 'relation' itself is clearly more fundamental than any operation of 'verification' or 'falsifiability', for it founds such operations and makes them possible. Thus, a science does not consist in the 'objective reality' (Kant) of knowledges, but instead, and first of all, in the donation of its RO (not its knowledges) and subsequently in the 'relation' of its knowledges to the latter. Against *objective reality* a science sets the *real objectivity* of its knowledge. Insofar as it is postulated immanently by a scientific stance, the object 'revolution' is first characterised by its reality – that is, its self-inherence, its radical immanence, its real and no longer logico-real identity. What reality there is in the revolutionary phenomenon – that is, what is accessible to man within the limits of science – can only be a unique identity, unknown to Philosophical Decision, which I describe elsewhere as non-decisional and non-positional identity-(of)-self.

The procedures of knowledge in a science of man are constituted, then, from rules of transformation which express this duality of RO and OK but which cannot be examined here. The contingent revolutionary representations, which all are 'unitary' and impregnated with philosophy, are in this way worked according to the specific reality of the RO. The results of this transformation, itself non-revolutionary, are knowledges – that is, new representations becoming capable of rigorously and truly describing *the real content of the human phenomenon of revolution insofar as the latter is not conflated with its (philosophical, political, etc.) effectivity*. The effective revolutionary phenomena (of rupture, terror, inversion, repetition, the imaginary, etc.) are now mere theoretico-experimental material inserted into the specific structures of the OK and defined by these procedures. This is all that a science of man can do, and this constitutes its proper type of universality. For it is not content to execute naively these transcendental and non-empirical procedures, which comprise a science, upon the material of empirical or theoretico-experimental procedures. This immediate or irreflexive execution is instead the feature of other sciences that possess all these transcendental structures (RO/OK). But as science-(of the)-subject-(of)-science (of every science) – of man – a science of man pays special attention to these structures and the procedures that put them to work. It thematises – albeit still and always in a mode equally irreflexive or non-decisional-(of)-self – these transcendental dimensions of every 'empirical' science, insofar as the science of man is the science of all sciences, a science that is also clearly 'empirical' by virtue of its object. The real transformation of representations into knowledge amounts to an 'experimentation' proper to the science of man. Moreover, it is not experimentation that is real in the sciences of matter, but the necessity and contingency of experimentation, such that they are included in the science-essence of each of these sciences.

We cannot describe here those procedures charged with transforming *effective* revolutionary representations into *real representations* or knowledge – into, more precisely, representations-(of the)-real. We can, however, give an example of the work to be done: *Terror* as one of the modalities of revolutionary phenomena is not given only as a fact, but undecidably as a (virtual or explicit) philosophy and a politics, as an *effectivity* rather than as a fact. From this point of view, terror forms part of a systematic multiplicity of possible interpretations, *of which one*, *among others, might be that of terror as the inversion of regicide.* Once we recognise this eidetic diversity of terror (which is thus not only a fact but, as 'fact', is inseparable from this eidetic dimension), we will be able to transform these representations *into knowledge that is clearly not 'historian [historienne]' or 'political', but specific to a science of man* – into knowledge 'about' revolution, knowledge valid within the 'human' limits of its science. This real transformation consists then in making this inversion seem like a *still transcendent* mode or form (limited to the transcendence of political and 'ideological' space, etc.) of an entirely other experience of exteriority and transcendence itself. Indeed, terror, in its requisite or ultimately eidetic sense, is practice and proof of objectivity, of a *new* social, political and philosophical objectivity which terror, as a result of its overwhelmingly philosophical character, clearly confuses with reality itself. But a science must work this objectivity of effective terror in its determinations as the simple mode of another *real* or immanent experience of objectivity, *as the symptom of an objectivity that is non-decisional and non-positional-(of)-self.* Terror is then understood as the political and philosophical call-*to* – and the repression of an objectivity that is impossible and of an entirely other nature: non-negotiable, for example, from the standpoint of its political forms.

This work is apparently simple, but the correction of revolutionary representations is necessarily limitless.

One will recall firstly that a science of man does not replace history, political theory, or the Human Sciences in general, but uses them as material; and secondly, that it contents itself with finally putting them into relation with their real object – man in the last instance – and transforming them through this putting-into-relation.

THE NON-MARXIST GENERALISATION OF REVOLUTION

Every philosophy of revolution – even HM and CT, which *function as* philosophy – is founded upon a restrictive and unremarked postulate of philosophers, a postulate that is contingent for a science, necessarily implying its suspension. *This is the postulate, itself revolutionary or philosophical, of science as revolutionary* – the postulate of the reality of revolution as Philosophical Decision or auto-affection. It dictates that the theory of revolution itself can only be revolutionary (the confusion or amphiboly of practice and revolution). Yet, far from thereby opening up thought and practice to this phenomenon, it instead simultaneously closes them or encloses them within the limits of a revolutionary practice or decision, thus denying them the radical opening-up of science. This postulate takes the following precise form in contemporary thought: *to every fixed form of power, understood as a 'relation', necessarily corresponds – via an essential relation – one and only one*

131

other power relation, which takes the form of an inversion of the first. The inversion belongs to the essence of power and precisely defines its relational nature. Both Foucault, with the motif of the 'permanent ground of struggle', and Deleuze, with the theory of forces, radicalise this explicitly 'Nietzschean' postulate, which is already present in Marx in a less clear and less explicit form; they give it multiple affirmation but do not render it contingent as postulate, as a science would demand.

Only a science, with the 'non-revolutionary' pragmatic of revolution that ensues from it, can liberate the practice and theory of their 'revolutionary fold', which constitutes the Marxist and Nietzschean space of power and closes it to a more rigorous theory. In reality, for a science of man there can be no necessary correspondence between an event or real affect of power and a determinate type of revolution or inversion *or*, moreover, a multiplicity of revolutions of the same philosophical type – that is to say, supposed capable of determining in turn that event. What corresponds to the event, instead – now in a 'dual' or non-necessary relation – is an open multiplicity of philosophically diverse types of revolutions, a limitless multiplicity of possible effective revolutions, all contingent or equivalent in relation to it. What science determines in revolutions can be called the *Equivalence Principle of Revolutions with Regard to Man and Science.* This principle directly suspends another one, the *Principle of Sufficient Revolution*, which is clearly the same thing as the Marxist or Nietzschean postulate of revolution as the essence of thought (in all thought, revolution is at stake; in every revolution, thought is at stake).

All contemporary imagery (at least since Nietzsche) of the revolutionary essence of thought, of the fold as its elementary catastrophe, sanctions this restriction, this internal closing of the space of thought, this contraction-(of)-self of occidental thought and the Greco-revolutionary narcissism that prohibits its true transformation. The fold is no more necessary for thought than revolution is necessary for truly transforming history. It is clear that neither can be denied its effectivity. Yet precisely because they define the breadth of transcendent thought and are the engine of history alone, they are mere objects and are not necessary as a perspective on themselves. In this way – with revolution reduced to the state of *effective* real-representation and thus not real itself – we establish a limitless, non-revolutionary pragmatic of revolution, an opening more radical than that of Marxist 'practice', which is still limited from within by a philosophical decision.

The Transcendental Method

(1989)

Translated by Christopher Eby

1. A DIFFICULT THOUGHT

That method called 'transcendental' is characterised by a remarkable plasticity – to which Kant, Fichte and Cohen have already drawn attention – but also by an equally well-documented difficulty.

There are three reasons for the difficulty of the 'transcendental' and the philosophical style that defines it. The first stems from the manner in which the notion is introduced. Sometimes it is presented in scholastic form, through definitions drawn from Kant but isolated from both their effects and the manner of thinking that gives them their concrete meaning; sometimes it is confused with doctrinal systems, without its own features being identified, forming mixtures with objects and goals that are not necessary to it: Newtonian physics (Kant), ethics and right (Fichte), the phenomenological description of the world (Husserl, Heidegger), etc. To avoid these extremes, we shall delimit the characteristic and stable features of the transcendental 'gesture', the invariants that make it a style and which are found, in distinct concrete forms, in the doctrines of thinkers ranging from the scholastic to the contemporary. In our presentation of this gesture, we wish no longer to confuse it with the uses or appropriations that have been made of it in order to address problems of empirical origin (epistemological usages, for example); or, worse still, to confuse it with its original authors. Kant's work is a major but nevertheless local turning point in a tradition that concerned itself with recapturing the meaning and continuity beneath, first, the heteroclite of objects and aims and, second, the artificial oppositions and exclusions that these provoked.

First objective: to purge the transcendental of its transcendent models (science, logic, perception, right, etc...) and to extract its unique aim, that of the autonomy [*Selbständigkeit*] of reason, perhaps, and certainly that of philosophising thought.

The second reason stems from the overdetermined character of this term, whose meaning is not summarised by the definitions given by Kant, however decisive they may be

– these definitions, moreover, are themselves heterogeneous. There is a history and a fluidity in the meaning of the word, not only from one to another philosophy labeled 'transcendental' (or not, as in Leibniz and Heidegger), but within each of them, principally according to the functions that the word assumes in relation to another notion that is generally closely related to it but with which it does not merge: that of the a priori (the universal and necessary structures of knowledge, of perception, of language, etc., which have their seat in the 'subject'). 'Transcendental' can thus designate any of the following: singular philosophies (Kant, Maimon, Fichte, the young Schelling, Husserl), trends or problematics that pervade a dispersed group of works (transcendental idealism) or represent a temptation and a reciprocal objection (transcendental materialism, transcendental realism), a style or 'allure' (Bénézé) of thought; or even a necessary ingredient of every philosophy: not every philosophy can be called transcendental, but the transcendental inheres in any philosophy (whether avowed by the author himself – Sartre, Merleau-Ponty, Deleuze – or not – Nietzsche – or detected by historians – Descartes). For philosophising is always a decision or a 'transcendence'. Finally, more profoundly, 'transcendental' indicates a *method* that generalises Kantianism (Cohen, Natorp, Cassirer), but indicates also each of this method's moments, operations and stases (deduction, analytic, dialectic, aesthetic, appearance, reflection, etc., *transcendentals*).

> *Second objective*: So as to avoid the trap of this overdetermination – its absurd and unintelligible inventory – and the artificial figures that it would impose, to place oneself at this methodological level and identify its invariant operative moments.

The third reason is more obscure but its stakes are more decisive: the transcendental tradition is traversed as such by a division, a distribution that is generally repressed. To allow this tradition its full extent, we must discern two branches, and a concomitant risk of rupture. Firstly, a major or dominant branch, illustrated by Kant, Fichte, Husserl and nearly all contemporary thinkers: that of empirico-transcendental parallelism, of a co-belonging and parallelism of the transcendental condition and the conditioned, sometimes open and broken, but always maintained. Secondly, a minor or minoritarian branch (one dominated by the first, in any case) which, against the unitary conception of the transcendental and the empirical, asserts more or less clearly their duality and the irreversibility of the former and the latter. It is true, however, that this remains more often a proclivity (Descartes, Maine de Biran, Sartre) than an explicit thesis (Michel Henry).

Third objective: to avoid the ordinary reduction of the transcendental thematic to its dominant tradition, a reduction essentially influenced by German Idealism and the problematic of self-consciousness and Difference.

Finally, several limitations must be lifted: the limitations to one author (Kant); to a certain type of philosophy – theories of cognition (Kant, Fichte, Husserl); to a theory of the subject, moreover one misconstrued as a subjectivism (Kant). The transcendental is just as much that which founds objectivity (Kant, neo-Kantianism, Husserl) or that which founds the question of authentic ontology (as Heidegger insists), even in Kant. Kant is the author who gives the transcendental its philosophical credence, who distinguishes its meanings and fixes its stakes, but he himself recognizes, in the existence of a 'transcendental philosophy of the ancients', ontology in person. It is necessary, therefore, to remove this confusion of the transcendental with aims that are partly foreign to it. Even the aim of a critique of the speculative power of Reason does not belong to the essence of the transcendental, but employs the latter in its service, whereas, after Kant, it will pass into the service of the Absolute. But, more profoundly, one must wonder if its destiny is definitively connected to that of ontology – that is, of transcendence.

2. FIRST DISTINCTIONS: THE TRANSCENDENT-TRANSCENDENTAL CORRELATION

Distinguishing between these two terms is a specifically philosophical conquest; it depends not only on Kant's difference, for example, from both empiricism and dogmatic rationalism, but more generally on philosophy's autonomy in relation both to the confusions of common sense, and to science and theology. But their correlation and the foundation of this correlation is another kind of distinction: never an exclusive distinction, but a relation of conditioning which can take many forms, like the empirico-transcendental circle or parallelism, of which it is the equivalent. This relation can be strictly reciprocal or reversible (Nietzsche, Deleuze); or reciprocal despite everything, in spite of the facticity of the empirical (the differently-accented psycho-transcendental parallelisms of Kant and Husserl); or non-reciprocal and irreversible, as in the work of certain contemporary thinkers (Henry). This correlation is, at least within the dominant tradition, the concrete element of the transcendental.

'Transcendent' denotes a disruption of continuity that is said in various senses (including the mathematical sense): epistemologically – as a claim of knowledge beyond experience (Kant: the illegitimate or speculative usage of the principles of understanding beyond the limits of possible experience); ontologically – as a thing separated, by virtue of its essence, from the subject, and irreducible to it (Kant: transcendence of the 'thing in itself'; Husserl: transcendence of the object or the invariant and irreducible object-sense); theologically – as a sublime order of reality or an infinite being which hierarchically exceeds the finite being of man (Descartes: through the perfection of its understanding and its will; Levinas: through its exteriority and its exalted status as 'Other'); and finally, transcendentally – as the 'objective' correlate of the transcendental (we shall see how), but then the transcendent object is transcendent *for* consciousness or the subject, included in an ideal immanence (Husserl).

However, this correlation can again become a simple identity and then give rise to a terminological, if not theoretical, confusion. Kant himself employed the term 'transcendental' as equivalent to 'transcendent'. In this case, it is a matter of a certain *usage* of representations – a transcendent usage opposed to the empirical or immanent usage of representations.

> A concept is used transcendentally ... if it is referred to things *as such and in themselves*; but it is used empirically if it is referred merely to *appearances*, i.e., to objects of a possible *experience*.[7]

---

7   I. Kant, *Critique of Pure Reason*, trans. W. S. Pluhar (Indianapolis: Hackett, 1996), 305 (A238/B298).

In this sense, even a non-empirical, metaphysical reality or a reality existing 'in itself' is called 'transcendental' – a transcendent reality (the 'transcendental object' is thus the 'thing in itself', the cause of the phenomenon, but not itself phenomenon). That which is transcendent in the Kantian sense and transcendental in the scholastic sense is always that which exceeds the categories – that is, for Kant, the domain of possible experience. Be that as it may, 'transcendent' is a term with a deprecatory nuance in transcendental thought (in Kant, the speculative illusion; in Nietzsche, the transcendence of values, the creation of the weak). Its connotation is more positive, on the other hand, in the works of others (the extreme case being Levinas, who posits exteriority or transcendence without any transcendental to posit it).

'Transcendence' is simultaneously said of the state of a being separated from a subject of reference and of the operation of separating it (either the subject separates it, or it separates itself from the subject), thus implying the verbal origin of the word (transcend-e-nce and transcend-e-ntal) and the activity or operation of 'transcending' (the Bergsonian neologism), i.e. of going beyond oneself toward the transcendent. Whence a reversal of object and subject in which the transcendental power proper outlines itself. Transcending is henceforth an operation assignable to the existent-that-transcends or even to the subject that produces or 'objectivises' the object, thus conditioning the transcendent. To be able to distance the object, the subject must in reality distance itself from itself or be affected by transcendence, by way of a schism, an opening up, or even a nothingness. In contrast to the supposedly given object, we shall call *objectivity* the set of conditions that only appear to separate the transcendent from the subject because the subject in reality separates itself from itself through them. This is no longer an empirical separation; rather, it is a priori, in relation to the empirical as such.

'Transcendental' will be said, then, of the cause, within the subject, of the transcendent's transcendence – a cause that is not transcendence itself or the a priori, but distinguishes itself from them as the essence (or the a priori real) of the a priori. The transcendent (the object or World) is the *correlate* (Husserl) of the transcendental subject; the transcendental is what *relates-to*... the transcendent (the 'transcendental relation' – for example, 'being-in-the-world' in Heidegger, or the principles of the understanding in Kant). The transcendental subject is no longer a separated substance (Descartes); it is either an internal experience or an originary functional unity – in either case, 'objective' – that relates to a given. It is the originary *difference* of subject and World, a difference that precedes them. The common distinction between the psychological and the in-itself is shifted and transformed. There is a 'phenomenological' redistribution of transcendence (of objective sense, no longer of the in-itself) and of immanence (intentional and no longer psychological): transcendence within and through immanence. Husserl, who returns to transcendental experience beyond Kant, but not to Cartesian substantialism, puts it as follows:

> By phenomenological *époché* I reduce my natural human Ego and my psychic life – the realm of my *psychological self-experience* – to my transcendental-phenomenological Ego, the realm of *transcendental-phenomenological self-experience*.[8]

Whence the most general schema of the transcendental method as composed of three essential regressive moments: (1) the transcendent, indicating the given or the empirical, that is, the continua of common experience or experience which is scientific, perceptual, linguistic, etc.; (2) transcendence, indicating the a priori conditions of the given or its objectivity (not empirical but 'ideal', of the nature of the *ens imaginarium*, even); (3) the transcendental, as the subjective cause or essential possibility of the object's objectivity. This order is the one that the 'transcendental' analytic follows, but it receives a recurrent necessity from the subject whose reflection (precisely 'transcendental') accompanies, as its element, the decomposition of the continua of experience. Hence a progressive enriching of the functions

---

8 E. Husserl, *Cartesian Meditations*, trans. D. Cairns (The Hague: Martinus Nijhoff, 1967), 26 (§11).

of the transcendental: the third moment of the method assembling the preceding moments in recurrent fashion. The articulated unity of these moments forms the concrete content and the full meaning of the famous Kantian definitions:

> I call *transcendental* all cognition that deals not so much with objects as rather with our way of cognizing objects in general insofar as that way of cognizing is to be possible a priori.[9]

> We must not call just any a priori cognition transcendental, but must call transcendental (i.e. concerning the a priori possibility of the a priori use of cognition) only that a priori cognition whereby we cognize that – and how – certain presentations (intuitions or concepts) are applied, or are possible, simply a priori.[10]

Thus the transcendental has a dual function: foundational or explicative (of knowledge) and critical (of metaphysics). That the transcendental conditions the transcendent is the condition for responding to the question of the possibility of a knowledge in general and, in particular, of a speculative knowledge or one that transcends the limits of experience. The transcendental withdraws from experience (the 'Analytic': Kant, Husserl, Heidegger) only in order to better return to it (the 'Transcendental

---

9 Kant, *Critique of Pure Reason*, 64 (B25).

10 Ibid., 110-11 (A56/B80).

Deduction') and close the field of experience (the 'transcendental field'). This is a decision on behalf of experience and *for* its knowledge. Whence a circle and a double game which comprise empirico-transcendental parallelism – the dominant branch of the tradition. One of Kant's texts (the *Prolegomena*) sums up this twofold pertinence:

> The word 'transcendental' ... does not signify something passing beyond all experience but something that indeed precedes it *a priori*, but that is intended simply to make cognition of experience possible. If these concepts overstep experience, their use is termed 'transcendent', which must be distinguished from the immanent use, i.e., use restricted to experience.[11]

3. THE TRANSCENDENTAL AS METHOD

Thus, a method is called 'transcendental' when it is able to capture each of the last two moments outlined above, which a more discriminating analysis shows, in actuality, to be three. Each is accompanied by techniques that differ according to the author, techniques specified by the type of reality under analysis, which varies from one thought to another, but which is always Reason itself, more or less restricted to the sciences, or extended to all

---

[11] I. Kant, *Prolegomena to Any Future Metaphysics*, trans. J. W. Ellington (Indianapolis: Hackett, 2001), 373.

experience (Reason as mathematical physics, moral judgement, perception, language, formal logic, etc...). Each of these three moments can be called 'transcendental', even if the last is such par excellence:

1. The analytic extrication, or the 'inventory of [local] a prioris' (Dufrenne) on the basis of either experience, or the type of reality whose conditions of possibility one seeks. Kant called this operation – the exhibition of the forms of intuition and the deduction of intellectual forms – 'metaphysical' rather than transcendental. This theoretical rigour (the a priori is taken to be the universal and necessary moment, meta-physical in the literal sense of the word) will not always find a corresponding historical rigour (Kant, in accordance with the scholastic tradition, will still use the term 'transcendental' to designate the a priori); but the substitution of *a priori* for *transcendental* in this function and the distinction between the two are both necessary to ground the transcendental method as such.

2. The gathering of the multiple and local a prioris into a 'universal a priori' (Husserl), a whole determined by that Unity called 'transcendental' (and not 'categorical': the latter is a particular a priori governed by the transcendental or superior Unity of experience). This moment merits being called transcendental for reasons even more profound than those of the first: it corresponds to an ascent toward the real or absolute condition of possibility of experience. This higher condition is always

a Unity – there is no philosophy without the task of determining the real through thought – that is, through a Unity which is not itself entirely synthetic or produced, but which must be supposed as the ultimate reality of a thought under whose authority experience is unified and thinkable. This Unity is 'transcendental' in the sense that it must surpass experience in a mode that is no longer only meta-physical – like that of the a priori (which remains multiple and diverse because it is connected to experience) – but *absolute*, a surpassing carried out, in other words, in and through the mode of Unity.

Thus, this superior unity transcends beyond the specific, generic and categorical distinctions – beyond the diversity proper to the universal – but it must be supported or conveyed in turn by transcendental entities that vary according to the author (Kant: the *I think* and the apparatus of the 'faculties'; Husserl: pure psychism). The passage from categorical to transcendental is a fundamental and necessary operation, and comes about through the mechanism of an *Aufhebung* of the psychological and transcendent apparatus of the faculties. This operation can be more or less successful (less successful in Kant's work, according to Husserl; even less so in Husserl's work than in Kant's, according to the neo-Kantians). In any case, it remains an *Aufhebung*; it does not manage to break the empirico-transcendental circle and ground experience in an absolute knowledge, but it *believes* itself capable of doing so.

This second moment rediscovers, in its own way, the scholastic treatment of the *transcendentals*. Before designating a style of thought, 'transcendental' designated certain philosophical objects: the most general terms or predicates of being, those that transcend categories or predicaments as well as the natural genera. The transcendentals (*transcendentalia*, or even *transcendentia*) were recognised by Aristotle and thematised by Albertus Magnus (*Quodlibet ens est unum, verum, bonum*), Saint Thomas Aquinas and especially Duns Scotus. In general, Being is the most universal; the others are its attributes or 'passions', either simple and convertible with Being (the One, Truth, Good) or disjunctive (Contingent/Necessary, Actual/Potential). Whatever may be included in these variable and open lists, these 'transcendental properties', distinguished only by their 'point of view', provide a surplus-value of generality that makes them as valuable as the permanent and necessary 'categories' of all philosophical discourse as such. They do not bring to the *res* any supplementary reality, any generic content, any *real* predicate or property (even if 'transcendental' can just as well be said of an 'in-itself' and 'absolute' reality [Kant] as of an ideality). Indeed, the 'transcendental terms' could even designate, as unknowns, the letters comprising the figures of the syllogism. They always, however, designate essential relations.

Hence also the 'transcendental relation', a relation of essential or constitutive dependence of one being upon another, whose meaning, between the scholastics and Kant, became inverted, or at least became unilateral, so that it distinguished a constitutive, verifiable, or conditioning power in its relationship with a conditioned.

3. The third and most fundamental moment is the systematic unification of the essentialities or a prioris of this Unity, with Unity understood as relation to experience – the unification, consequently, of the a prioris and empirical givens under the authority of transcendental or originary Unity. The nature of experience may vary (sensation, perception, present being, etc...), but this operation, which Kant christened 'Transcendental Deduction', lies at the heart of the method. It leads to these great circles, these concrete and autonomous unities: 'Unity of experience' (Kant), '*Lebenswelt*' (Husserl), 'Being-in-the-world' and 'Care' (Heidegger), 'General Perception' or 'Flesh' (Merleau-Ponty), etc. It is the synthetic moment and no longer the analytic one, the moment when the unity of all experience succeeds its dismemberment. In this way, 'transcendental' receives its complete and concrete meaning, at once originary and ultimate, of *veritas transcendentalis* (Baumgarten) – that is, reciprocal immanence between being and thought.

What has happened? The analytic of the structures of experience generally deduces a prioris that are more and more universal, or qualitatively different, up to a very particular a priori endowed with the specifically transcendental ability to pivot, 'turn', and bend itself toward experience: the 'I think'; the pre-reflexive cogito; self-consciousness as a reflection of object-consciousness; but also Heideggerian (de-subjectivated and de-objectivated) 'Turning' and the 'eternal return' of the Will to Power in Nietzsche. In general, one passes from the transcendent to the transcendental (recurring, moreover) through a 'turning', and the analytic is extended continuously in the major operation of a Transcendental Deduction, a legitimisation of the a priori in view of possible experience and depending upon it. Transcendental reflection did not remain 'in thin air', that is, in the supposed vacuum (cf. Kant) of transcendence, Ideas, or meta-physics, but reoriented itself toward experience and put the a priori in the service of the latter. Here, the transcendental is foundation and essence (where essence = possibility of experience). It does not explain the empirical reality of knowledge but the reality of its possibility, of *possible* experience or experience considered in that fundamental and universal legality upon which its validity is grounded: ultimately the non-empirical effectivity of science. Yet it is also directly critical, and de-limits metaphysical divagation. It is opposed to both the empirical (bearing on the a priori, its relation to subject and object) and the transcendent, that is to say the a priori liberated from the limits of experience (it turns the a priori toward experience and fixes its empirical usage). Transcendental Deduction is a science, a science of the limits of the a priori usage of our knowledge; in this way it de-limits the appearance and illusion of transcendent judgements.

The originality of the transcendental method bursts forth in the Transcendental Deduction. With that in mind, we must refer to the well-known manner in which Kant posed the problem of the possibility of knowledge: neither the rational-analytical nor the merely empirical can account for this possibility or its indubitable reality. Its sufficient reason is to be found in the milieu or synthesis of these opposites – of a priori analytical judgements and a posteriori synthetic judgements. Kant retains the a-priority of the first and the synthetic power of the second, and reveals their unity as an autonomous principle at work in the operation of the Deduction. *A priori synthesis* biases this sterile operation in some way, and demands itself; Kant can then elevate it to the status of method and argument. The specificity of the 'transcendental proof', which argues (about the de facto existence of a priori concepts, about their function in knowledge and the restriction of their domain to the latter) according to the exigencies of 'the possibility of experience', is nothing other than that auto-exigency of a priori synthesis, whether or not it bears its limitation within itself. Of course, this auto-exigency, specific to the transcendental in its dominant tradition, does not always receive the juridico-critical and rational form it assumes in its Kantian version; but, just as the latter can take on an ontological sense (Heidegger, in his discussion of Kant), one should seek to rediscover its universal scope – its invariant functions – across the whole of the transcendental tradition.

The telos of the transcendental is fulfilled by the Deduction, and this telos is the real: not in the empirical and contingent sense, but in the 'higher' or specifically philosophical sense of the synthetic concrete Unity of the empirical real and the possible or ideal a priori. In fact, there is always a partitioning of reality, which is said in various senses:

1. Reality in the strict sense, that which founds 'real possibility', and which Kant distinguished from mere logical possibility:

> For the deception of substituting the logical possibility of the concept (where the concept does not contradict itself) for the transcendental possibility of things (where to the concept there corresponds an object) can trick and satisfy only the unseasoned.[12]

The real, in an even less logical sense, was eventually said (by Husserl and Sartre) of the subject or the cogito that stands in proximity to itself, in a non-empirical presence,

---

12   Kant, *Critique of Pure Reason*, 309 (B302).

in a con-crete proximity to itself that prevents it from floating in exteriority and transcendence.

2. The empirical reality of the transcendental given (sensation, being, World).

3. The ideality of the a priori, the material of knowledge or thought which, however, remains ideal and possible, and consequently is under threat of collapsing into empirical contingency and requires a real ground, a concrete (i.e. singular) foundation (Transcendental Unity).

4. A synthesis of these determinations. On the one hand, Transcendental Unity (already supposed, or anticipatory and recurrent) becomes what it is on its own basis, without being synthesised from scratch on the basis of opposing terms (empirical/a priori); it presides over the synthesis but does not derive from it. Yet, on the other hand, by uniting itself a second time with them (the Kantian 'Transcendental Deduction', the Nietzschean 'Reaffirmation', the Heideggerian 'Turning', etc.), it produces not the real (which cannot be produced) but *effectivity*, the synthesis of all determinations. Particularly in the dominant branch of the tradition, Unity alienates itself despite everything, and becomes; it conditions a process in which it finds itself put at stake. The transcendental is requisitioned to the service of science, art, language, etc. Even as a simple reflection that can seem to be lost in exteriority and in the correlative transcendence of the fact (of science, art, morality, etc.), the transcendental does

not operate without the initiation of a concrete becoming, if only that of the thought of science or an a priori factum (from the perspective of *veritas transcendentalis*) and that of illusion's critical delimitation. The authentic transcendental subject, delivered from the risk of simple transcendence, gives rise to process, to immanent auto-production, and becomes concrete: perhaps there was never a process-without-subject at all, outside of a thought that falls into the most absurd transcendence. On the other hand, the minor branch of the transcendental tradition conceives of a *subject-without-process* – inalienable in effectivity – after having conceived, as we shall see, a *transcendental-without-a priori*.

These three moments are operative invariants that we can isolate in non-Kantian forms in the works of the majority of authors, all of which have otherwise different conditions: one or several sorts of a priori: a rational or indeed historical a priori; a formal or material a priori; a more or less universal and encompassing a priori, limited, for instance, to physical science (Kant), logic (Husserl), perception (Fichte, Merleau-Ponty) or indeed to the ontological difference between Being and being (Heidegger); and a transcendental unity diversely understood through its psychologico-transcendent support and even through its functions. Transcendental can then be said distributively of the three moments to the extent that all concern the a priori and suppose a 'reflection' upon it.

And it can be said of them collectively, since it designates the global method of philosophy. Yet their distinction and articulation are fundamental for the very notion of a 'transcendental method'.

Indeed, neo-Kantianism has made specific but pointed use of this title, intending, in the spirit of Kantianism, to move against any ontological interpretation (in this case, the substantialist and reifying interpretation, that ontology that Heidegger also deconstructs by other means – and within which he includes, moreover, neo-Kantian epistemology) and to generalise its operative and episte-mological content. Against the metaphysical and dogmatic interpretation of the a priori (that of Fichte and Hegel) made possible by Kant (on anthropological grounds, it is true), neo-Kantianism emphasises its local and above all functional nature, its procedural status in the service of an objective determination of experience. In order to do so, the psychological entrenchment of the a priori had to be surpassed in favour of its function, its natural contingency surpassed in favour of its transcendental truth; the a priori had to be placed in the service of the scientific work of the conditioning (the genesis, even) of the given. This interpretation fulfills the project of logicising and functionalising the *Critique of Pure Reason* (the primacy of logic over aesthetics, category over intuition; the reduction of the latter to the indexed state of the given; the limitation of finitude – as a result of the reception of the given – to intuition or sensibility; the infinite opening of Reason beyond knowledge, etc.), restoring it to immanence through an infinite productivity of science and knowledge in general, which surpasses the opposition of subject and object in the higher unity of science as an authentic 'transcendental subject'.

This interpretation is distinctive and historic only by virtue of its insistence on the primacy of logic over the intuitive, of infinity over finitude; and the narrow epistemological signification that it assigns to Kantianism. Therefore, it belongs not only to the 'Kantian heritage' (Vuillemin) but to the most traditional philosophical heritage; it is universal, and emanates, along with the Kantianism of Plato (Natorp), the inevitable Platonism of both Kant and of the transcendental in general (at least in its dominant tradition). It rediscovers the functional but higher sense, which is that of the Platonic *agathon* and of every philosophical decision.

4. THE TRANSCENDENTAL AS SUBJECT

Transcendental is usually said of subject rather than of method; this theoretical error is almost ubiquitous in the dominant tradition; it is also the symptom of an unresolved problem. The subject's coming onto the scene is indeed ambiguous and brings out an aporia or a real duality of the tradition that the 'all-method' conceals.

In the minor branch, concepts appear that are inconceivable in the major: a transcendental-without-a priori, a subject-without-process, an experience-without-method – in short, a transcendental as radical experience and no longer as syntax.

It is obvious that, in terms of the reality of doctrines, these are only two trends, which are mixed and intricated in diverse proportions (cf. Kant's transcendental Idealism and that of the young Schelling; the neo-Kantian subject as object consciousness and Henry's radically subjective transcendental Ego, etc.). Yet one sometimes dominates the other, which is enough to define, depending on which one dominates, two globally concurrent branches in the transcendental phylum.

Why does the dominant tradition fail to take account of the experience of the subject as such (of its being – the being of the cogito or the 'I think' which is left uninterrogated, according to Heidegger) at the very moment that it invokes this experience within the transcendental framework? It habitually supposes, more or less explicitly, a dehiscence between the subject and the transcendental instance, a supplement of transcendence of the latter in relation to the former. It is precisely in Kant that the two are most separated: the subject is understood either psychologically as inner sense, or, at best, as transcendental apperception. Yet even in this case, it is not the bearer of the ultimate transcendental condition that is formed by objective principles ('principles of the understanding'). The subject, the seat of the 'human' a priori, is only one function in the sheaf of conditions of possibility, a means in the service of the transcendental conditioning that encompasses and surpasses it. Husserl, for his part, reconciles the Ego and the transcendental, but at the cost of an ultimate residuum of 'parallelity' or 'difference' between pure psyche and the Ego which the transcendental and its autonomy initiates. The supposedly transcendental subject will have been nothing but a subjective-type condition within the system of conditions of objectivity, which themselves form a structure endowed with a superior 'objectivity' (Heidegger). Transcendental Unity surpasses and sublates that of the subject, which is dismissed into the psychological finitude of inner sense. Correlatively, transcendental reflection, that of Reason which, as 'authentic' subject, takes the place of the anthropological and finite subject, remains profoundly objective; it floats in transcendence, released from the moorings of the real subject, which is conflated with 'self-consciousness' and then condemned to the designation of 'object-consciousness' (Cohen).

Hence the traditions' divergence around the stakes of the transcendental subject's radical autonomy and its eventual intrinsic finitude – that of a subject-without-process: 1. In the dominant branch, objectivation or transcendence is a power that belongs to the *essence* of the subject, a subject that is transcendental only because it can go beyond itself toward World (or as World) or Being, can maintain itself at a distance from itself yet remain itself throughout this estrangement. Its division either is its very ipseity, or belongs to it; its alienation is a loss of its essence, but this essence possesses the ultimate power of losing itself; therefore, it is also inalienable, and the subject defines itself by this mixture of *inalienable alienation*. This structure is invariant whatever the variations of transcendence: negation, nothingness, nihilation, difference. It is preserved in the passage from the subject as *consciousness* (Kant, Fichte, Hegel, Husserl) to the subject as *difference* (Nietzsche, Heidegger, Deleuze), from a phenomenology of consciousness to a topology specifically called 'transcendental' (Deleuze), from alienation and re-appropriation to the 'good neighbour' (Nietzsche, Heidegger). From the point of view of this mixture, the opposition between philosophies of consciousness, sense, or the 'transcendental signified' (Derrida) and the more contemporary philosophies of their deconstruction loses its relevance. Ontological or epistemological deconstructions of the transcendental subject (Heidegger, Derrida) content themselves with relaying Nothingness and ordering Being through an experience of the Other capable of exceeding Being. They modify the experience of transcendence by radicalising it, but, in the same act, they confirm their very membership within the tradition that they render triumphant. This is the sole worth of the famous Kantian definitions of the transcendental, when it is said of a reflection and a relation (of the a priori to the subject, and then to the object). Hence its real weakness: it needs to be attached to the a priori's transcendence, which thus acts as real earth for the originary 'archi-earth' (Husserl). Undoubtedly, this is an indivisible connection (Transcendental Unity), but one that requires a *support* all the same, just as Transcendental Deduction requires an Analytic that precedes it.

2. In the minor branch, transcendence itself does not belong to the essence of the transcendental subject itself; the former must undoubtedly be founded in the latter, but does not condition it in return. The correlation between transcendental and transcendent – i.e. intentionality – holds only for the former, not the latter (Henry). It is a matter of liberating the transcendental subject from this ultimate residuum of Representation – intentionality and its Heideggerian radicalisation as 'opening', 'ekstasis', and 'project' – and of founding its absolute autonomy with regard to the World upon its most intrinsic finitude – that is, the powerlessness to self-alienate. The subject is transcendental neither as the immanent cause of transcendence nor through the operation of objectivisation, but by itself and in advance of the latter. At this point, the transcendental is no longer a transcendence *for* experience, but an immanence given *in* a specific experience.

Transcendental experience is sometimes called 'inner' experience (Maine de Biran, Henry), at other times non-thetic self-experience (Sartre). This solution – sometimes faintly outlined (as in Sartre, where it is once again part and parcel with consciousness and intentionality), sometimes radicalised (in Henry: the ontology of radically subjective transcendental Life) – does not at all imply a simple experience, ante-predicative and even cogitative, of 'presence to self' (Merleau-Ponty), but a dissociation from the transcendent-transcendental circle or parallelism.

Kant already seemed to condemn this attempt – a condemnation relayed through the Nietzschean critique, and then the Heideggerian 'destruction', of the cogito. But if this condemnation is valid for the cogito, qua intuition of an intellectual 'nature', it is no longer valid for a radically pre-cogitative transcendental experience stripped of all transcendence and representation. For Kant reduced all experience to intuition – that is, to a mode of *repraesentatio* and to a donation of the object. Now, this transcendental and non-thetic experience-(of)-self lacks any transcendence or position. It has never *been* an intuition – still less an 'intellectual intuition' – that would still relate to Representation. Transcendental, non-thetic experience-(of)-self, as a radical experience of the individual distinct from that of totality, is also distinct from every intellectual intuition grounded in monism and pantheism (Schelling, Emerson and New England 'transcendentalism'), as a radical experience of the individual is distinct from that of totality. Nor is it a mode of the subjective *certitudo* and presence deconstructed by Heidegger. The equation Self = Self – that is, the formal identity assumed to be real, undoubtedly summarises or concentrates the transcendental Illusion of metaphysics (Fichte); but finite transcendental experience, the radically non-thetic self-subject, is not a return to this amphiboly: it is an immediately transcendental or real Identity that was never acquired, as was metaphysical Identity, on the foundation of 'general logic'.

This solution resolves the aporias of the dominant tradition and those of the Kantian heritage in particular. The transcendental is henceforth a finite but absolute lived experience; individual and inalienable, it is a real that no longer merely comes to crown ideality – an experience 'in itself' rather than a usage of the a priori in view of a transcendent experience. Transcendental conditioning and the most radical subjectivity are reconciled by avoiding the path through exteriority and circularity, which are proper to the dominant Philosophical Decision, not to subjectivity. On the one hand, subjectivity becomes unconditioned, but not along the lines of metaphysical *certitudo* – ultimately, it falls outside the 'history of Being' (Heidegger); on the other hand, the transcendental conquers a consistency and a reality, releasing subjectivity from its logical and metaphysical support.

The Copernican Revolution is radicalised, i.e. destroyed: the transcendental subject ceases to be 'revolutionary'... because it ceases both to obsess over the emergence of the object and to be thought through the mediation of the object (of World, of History, etc...).

5. THE ESSENCE OF 'VERITAS TRANSCENDENTALIS'

Instead of devoting their energy to the transcendental itself and mapping it out in its unique essence, philosophers often preoccupy themselves with aporias and undecidable distinctions between the empirical and the a priori. Hence the innumerable superfluous parts that encumber the *Critique* (in particular). Our rule has been to privilege the internal history of the transcendental concept, its immanent telos, over its external and local definitions, over the objects, themes, finalities and trans-cendent models it historically conveys; to substitute a taxonomy of operations and techniques for the more or less external architectonic of the *Critique of Pure Reason*, which is founded upon a psychology of faculties and an epistemology of physics simply sublated [*aufheben*] into the transcendental mode. A concept always has several overdetermined senses, but they eventually converge under a rule of distribution. Such is the case with *veritas transcendentalis*. Whether truth is transcendental in the last instance is perhaps a particular philosophical decision

– this is still doubtful; perhaps it is even a matter of philosophising itself. In any event, it is the highest concept of the tradition we are examining. *Veritas transcendentalis* is the manner by which philosophers name two essential problems: that of the autonomy of Philosophical Decision and that of its reality. These two problems intersect in the problem of *immanence*. For the transcendental designates (in Kant, for example) the highest usage of a faculty, i.e. its a priori power. Yet, more profoundly, it designates a higher and foundational usage of the a priori itself. The second stage of thought is that of immanence: it distinguishes itself from the first stage – transcendence, or the a priori. It puts into play Transcendental Unity, that is, the autonomy of a thought (if not a subject) that drafts the rules of its veritative functioning from its own grounds.

There is a latent conflict between immanence and transcendence here. We must review its origins. First, we can elucidate two modes of transcendence: (a) a surpassing in the direction of genera, or the surpassing of one genera by another; (b) the surpassing of all genera and distinctions in the direction of Being, which is not a genus but a 'transcendental'. The latter in turn bifurcates into a 'horizontal' transcendence toward Being as universal and a 'vertical' transcendence toward Being-as-being, as 'One' or God (the bifurcation of Heidegger's 'onto-theo-logy'). The transcendental is thus superior to the transcendent – the transcendental is transcendens par excellence – but remains bound to it through a correlation. To 'go beyond' onto-theology itself would suppose an originary transcending which Heidegger will call 'absolute transcending' since it surpasses the transcendental itself. Thus, a dual historical solution is outlined here: either the transcendental is itself submitted to transcending, or transcendence is submissive to the transcendental, whose concept must then be revised in turn.

Therefore, immanence is the telos or the engine of any history of the transcendental. Yet it is also, to this extent, an aporia of the dominant tradition. How do we render philosophising truth autonomous with regard to the sky and the earth – between which it is suspended (Kant) – without grounding ourselves in a theology, or reducing ourselves to experience? How could the philosopher produce from himself his own laws if, on one hand, the a priori is traced from the empirical, then the transcendental from the a priori, and if one thus returns, turns back [*Züruckkehr*] to the foundation on the basis of experience instead of actually possessing it immediately and entering only into an descending dialectic? And what if, moreover, this *Aufhebung* of the psychological condemns the transcendental to becoming the guardian of the a priori, to care for the *meta-* (physics) of the metaphysical and to re-assert the a priori as such? Or if the entire *veritas transcendentalis* is reduced to 'repeating' meta-physical Difference (Nietzsche)? Or if one passes

THE TRANSCENDENTAL METHOD

from meaning to value, from the a priori to its ground, with the latter remaining ordered by the former even as the ground in turn is fractured as non-ground (Heidegger)? How could the transcendental not be in the service of ideality and the break it introduces into the real – that is, in the service of transcendence in general, regardless of its modes (Nietzsche and Deleuze: Difference or the re-affirmed distance in a transcendental topology; Heidegger: ontological Difference, into whose essence it is necessary to 'reenter' after a 'withdrawal', and which continues unfailingly to be part and parcel of that which it leaves so as to enter)?

The autonomy of truth is never as rigorous as is hoped for, which makes it easy to challenge its 'auto-nomy' and to deconstruct the rational usage of the transcendental (Heidegger). Yet it is still the exigency of the 'transcendentalis' (at once, of transcendence, alterity or withdrawal and, despite everything, of immanence), that reveals itself in this 'Turning' (*Kehre*, Heidegger). The invariant of the dominant tradition is that the transcendental instance remains defined by its functions or usages (Kant: conditioning; Fichte: genesis; Nietzsche: genealogy; Heidegger: appropriation-expropriation [*Er/Ent-eignis*]; Derrida: exappropriation; etc.) with regard to an empirical given. It exhausts itself in a fundamental operation: a demarcation line in general, a critical line of separation (Kant) or gathering (Heidegger), a line either topographical (Kant) or topological (Nietzsche, Heidegger, Deleuze). More generally, this essence of the transcendental in its dominant version is governed by the more traditional task of Greco-occidental thought: to ensure the unity of opposites (in this case: empirical and a priori, singular and universal, object and subject, illusion and truth, metaphysical and physical, etc.). Here, it is instead denounced as experience and asserted as method (Kant, Cohen), process (Nietzsche, Deleuze), syntax (Heidegger, Merleau-Ponty), paths (Heidegger), endless labour (Derrida), etc.

Here we also find, of course, well-known remedies for the exteriority of transcendence and the empirical contingency that together threaten the transcendental. Yet like all remedies, these register, differ and temper the pain; they interiorise it, relieve it, fracture it, but preserve it all the same. The pain – the *amphiboly* of the transcendent and the transcendental – afflicts the entire dominant tradition and explains its history, full of crossings, regrets, perpetual recommencements, and imbued with a limitless effort; a history of oscillations from the triumphant will (Nietzsche: the Bacchic transcendental) to the sobered-up will, and to failure (Heidegger: the disenchanted transcendental). By force of will and then of not willing a transcendental authority, the dominant or unitary philosophy forgets that the transcendental can be the object of a specific experience, and that it also possesses phenomenal givens which must be described. The unitary forgetting of the proper essence of the transcendental grounds its historicity or its errancy.

The essence of Transcendental Unity – the imbrication of the Absolute with the transcendental function – is the problem that divides the two traditions. The principle of the dominant tradition is as follows: the undivided kernel, which is the *real* element in the transcendental, is simultaneously a relation, and thus needs an empirical, and then a priori, support. The Absolute is conceived as being this transcendent support, analytically obtained on the basis of experience. A meta-physical Absolute which can itself be conceived and imbricated with the transcendental functions in various ways. In the dogmatic metaphysics that Kant critiques, the transcendental is effaced and denied by Unity as causa sui or infinite Auto-position. In Kant, the introduction of finitude limits Auto-position or transcendence; it discovers and makes manifest in the latter the precisely transcendental nucleus of the relationship necessary for experience, but which remains hidden. Yet the doublet of the transcendental and finitude (the latter appearing in the form of the 'thing in itself', which resists the illuminating opening of the a priori) again gives rise to (cf. neo-Kantianism) a rational principle and an auto-position of finitude itself: the auto-limitative principle of the Unity of Experience, which explains that it is still Reason that *makes itself* finite. In Heidegger, Reason *is* undoubtedly finite, as Being ordered with respect to the given or to a fate over which Being does not have control. But Reason is still not completely dismissed: Auto-position – the means by which transcendence can become absolute – subsists qua residuum of 'Representation' or the 'Metaphysical', de-limited only by an 'absolute transcending' or a 'Turning' that conserves the essential – namely, transcendence – even if it conserves it henceforth *as* One ('Withdrawal').

The real destruction of this account is presented, and can be found, in the minor tradition. What is its proper telos, beyond its inchoate realisations? To carry out a fundamental reversal, to cease putting the transcendental at the service of transcendence, meta-physics and the absolute forms of which they are capable; to subordinate the absolute to the transcendental by directly imbricating the latter with the finitude of the subject without availing itself of the services of transcendence. To reconcile them without passing through the mediation of meta-physics, which is perhaps a pointless manoeuvre. This is, in relation to Kant and the old metaphysical conception of the Absolute (to make a risky but suggestive comparison) much as the Relativity Revolution is in relation to the Copernican Revolution: There is a *finite absolute*, which is the subject as radically finite transcendental experience – that is, inalienable or non-positional experience-(of)-self and experience-(of)-World. The Absolute is intrinsically finite; it is no longer affected from without, as is the case in Kant and in Heidegger, whose 'finitude' and 'withdrawal' generalise the Kantian hypothesis of the 'thing in itself' to apply to all possible metaphysics. Here, finitude is absolute as such, no longer merging with a form of transcendence or 'critical limitation'. This nothing-but-immanent-absolute completes the liberation of the transcendental element (that is, radically immanent subjectivity) whose existence Kant had discovered only to reinter it in the metaphysical and Auto-positional sands, by settling for the compromise of the Copernican Revolution – which, oddly, passes for a philosophy of the subject, even though it constitutes the contrary and the impossibility of such a philosophy. This new, nothing-but-subjective conception of the absolute, frees the latter from the infinite and from the Copernican aporias of the finite and the infinite. It establishes the transcendental upon the ruins of transcendence, of metaphysical hierarchies and of the pre-established harmonies (between faculties, between subject and object), euphemistically dubbed 'adequation' (Heidegger), that were necessary for them. A new, non-Copernican path to the transcendental can now be opened up.

The 'Non-Philosophical' Paradigm

(1991)

Translated by Nicola Rubczak and Anthony Paul Smith[13]

CHANGING THE PARADIGM OF THOUGHT

The ordinary of culture is that relentless struggle of philosophers that leaves philosophy intact. To occupy attention and to distract it from the principal problem – what philosophy can do in itself and globally – is the very function of this interminable combat. Nothing, especially not the 'critique' of metaphysics or its 'deconstruction', is strong enough to obligate us to reconsider the validity of this paradigm come forth fully armed and complete, the scale of this already-established horizon, the depth of this fold in which our least interrogable

13 The translators wish to thank Iain Campbell for his assistance in translating this essay.

space of thought is contracted. Nothing can solicit this authority, this philosophical authorisation of thought, unless perhaps the obstinacy, the strange obstinacy that has always belonged to the sciences, and the misunderstandings of an obvious and, all things considered, incredible dialogue between philosophies at once garrulous and deaf, and sciences which are mute but which think nonetheless. 'We shall force them to philosophise!' – but the sciences themselves have nothing *philosophical* to say to the philosophy that puts the epistemological question to them. And if their mutism is perhaps not merely the effect of their operatory obstinacy, if it does not prevent them from thinking otherwise, then it is this entirely other paradigm of an experience which is non-philosophical but not necessarily positivist that needs to be disinterred from its burial beneath the heap of philosophies-of-science and epistemologies; to be elucidated in its originality and its *force-(of)-thought*, to be opposed to philosophy qua norm of thought and of humanity anterior to all culture. We have thus found it necessary to limit philosophy in order to make room for science-as-thought.

Such is the origin of what we call, for reasons already clarified elsewhere, the 'non-philosophical' paradigm: it is obtained in the form of the auto-description of which the *essence* of the sciences is capable. But it finds elsewhere its *occasion*, the material to which it cannot be reduced but which renders it usable: first and foremost the philosophical, but also the crucial phenomena of our time, the points of effervescence and the sharpest edges of the contemporary. A line that would pass through all points of this disordered experience, that could do justice to the most 'aberrant' deliverances of the media, to the most specialised executions of technology, to the wagers of the visual or musical arts, to new political fictions and affects ... such could be the effect (the effect, rather than the condition or the essence) of this stance of thought undoubtedly more elementary (perhaps minimal) and more universal than the philosophical. Instead of deploring in these phenomena the decline of metaphysics or of culture, and confusing the end of man with the decomposition of humanism, it would find in them its necessary impulsions. Impulsions rather than determining contents, materials rather than structures, occasions rather than effects: neither a positivism of actuality nor a 'postmodern' auto-decomposition of metaphysics. We no longer believe – but this disenchantment took place long ago – that the diagram of Philosophical Decision has some real importance or other *for man*, even if he profits from a relative techno-ideological efficiency, and despite his regular rebirths through his cultural mediatisation. And again, the human and scientific obsolescence of the philosophical paradigm is nothing new – even if it is becoming a more and more crucial task to *save the phenomena from their devalorisation and complementary overvalorisation by their philosophical counterparts.*

SOME GUIDING IDEAS ON SCIENCE

Science is not ordered, in its essence at least, by philosophical or cultural paradigms: the latter may overdetermine it, but they do not determine it. Rather, it constitutes by itself another specific experience of thought. It draws from itself, from its 'cause', which is to say man-as-One, the power to accede to the real or to phenomenalise it in an original mode, distinct from the philosophical. While the latter proceeds through decision or transcendence, science proceeds by having recourse only to a non-decisional immanence-(of)-self, at least when it comes to defining the *real object* of a science – that to which it relates the *object of knowledge* as to a reality in the last instance, absolutely distinct from knowledge, without conflating them philosophically. It thereby locates calculation and technique, the operatory and the manipulative, in the object of knowledge alone, excluding it from the real. That which is nothing but an encrustation of epistemological acts – positivism, but equally all epistemology – abstracts it from its subordinate status and elevates it unduly to the status of *essence*. This abusive operation is the spontaneous idealism of the philosophers, not an opposition to the 'ordinary' realism of scientists.

Rather than one diagram among others, or a syntaxico-semantic schema, science restored to its essence is thus something like a *real base* or an *infrastructure*. Let us say: that which remains of the real or of the immanent, of the non-metaphysical, in the function (often crudely understood) of infrastructure. While philosophy effaces this radical distinction in hybridisations with transcendent phenomena (the real content of the superstructure) and wants it to disappear in favour of mixtures, science ceaselessly restores, against Philosophical Decision, this primitive, ahistorical duality which has never been a decision and which works according to a non-philosophical causality. Marxism has identified this – yet understood it still philosophically – as 'determination in the last instance'.

THE NON-PHILOSOPHICAL PRACTICE OF THOUGHT

Rather than denying them, then, we must limit the validity of the gestures that seem more than evident to us, and which have never been reconsidered as such; along with the necessity upon which philosophical consensus is founded, and which decides upon our legitimacy and our belonging to the community of philosophers. We wish to speak of all these operations that exploit transcendence and take it as given without having elucidated their right to do so, which is to say the theoretical pertinence of this exploitation in the last instance: reflection, decision, interpretation, dialectic, difference, analysis, synthesis, etc. These gestures we continue to carry out; this belief we continue in a certain manner to subscribe to – but, from now on, according to the limits within which we are constrained to consider them: as simple givens that we shall work on according to other rules, not as the very rules of thought. And what can we no longer do? We can no longer think in terms of reversal and displacement, of differences and mixtures, of game and of world, in terms of unity, of reconciliation or of the co-belonging of opposites, as philosophy does and as its deconstructions continue to do. In terms of decision or analysis, of synthesis or of the undecidable.

These gestures of philosophy, which we renounce in order to think, but which we still require as *occasions* of this activity, we can only penetrate right to their most secret mechanism if we begin with an inkling of what a scientific thought is: by *dualysis* rather than *analysis*. That is to say: firstly, to take the prototypical case of the science of the One, according to the real which is the cause-(of)-self of science: it is rigorously 'individual' in its foundation and 'individual' through immanence alone, stripped of all constitutive representation. Next, according to what we call the 'Uni-verse', which *comes after* this real of science, which is the type of radical unlimited opening that the cause-(of)-science brings to the World from somewhere prior to the World, and which will betoken the end of philosophical authority. On one hand, in terms of an immanent stance rather than of a decision which is mixed, at once immanent and transcendent. And on the other, in terms of the identity of knowledges: the identity, radical in all senses, of materiality and of ideality. In other words: we think firstly in-One and then in-Dual, or in-Duality determined in the last instance by the One, rather than by hybridising the One and the Dyad (as do philosophical amphibologies) and thus impeding thinking, working, and pleasure.

For example, the first operation, instead of transcending or idealising the real, deciding and positing it as ideality in the philosophical manner, devalorising it and overvalorising it, civilising it and redoubling it, now consists in re-materialising, as manifold and *data*, all that gives itself as generality and totality, as attribute and being, as a priori and essence. Rematerialising the ideality of essences by reducing them to the status of inert singularities stripped of the power of transcendence, treating them as passively offered right down to their innermost secret reserve, withdrawal or invisibility: *all philosophy can and must become the object of science or identity*. Because man as cause-(of)-science is the secret-being, or the being of an absolutely invisible real; all the rest, that is to say the All or Being, ceases to be for him a secret, and becomes visible to him.

The second gesture (but it is identical in the last instance to the former) now consists not in making use of philosophical objectivity itself, of broaching or opening it, or even in over-objectivising this manifold, but in *simplifying* it, removing the fold that turns it onto itself. In minimising or reducing it to its ingredient of pure universality or transcendence stripped of things, rules and universal forms. A field of a priori objectivity, unlimited but devoid of rational entities or philosophical syntaxes charged with dividing and redoubling it; devoid also of all the transcendent forms of the Other, and filled only with this materiality of singularities – this field is *the Universe* in its transcendental sense, that which is the correlate of 'simple' transcendence or the science of the One.

Here, in the most general terms, is how science does not think: by dividing and under-determining the identities of the real by means of generalities and totalities which are equally and circularly charged with resynthesising and redetermining it. And here is how it does think, in a non-philosophical manner: by giving itself (but renouncing the division of) these identities of the real: inscribing them in a Universe-space, disencumbered of its generalities and its totalities, absolutely and actually unlimited, the *data* of the World and of Philosophy reunited; in treating the latter, finally, as a material according to identities which are the only 'law' of the last instance, the only phenomenal content of the rational norm. No longer Reason as reason of singularities, but Identity as that which determines reason in the last instance.

What is the advantage of this paradigm? If philosophy is the knot of the general and the total, the fold through which they impede one another and diminish their capacity to describe experience, if it traces limits and pronounces decisions, science deploys an already unfolded space, or one devoid of any fold. A transcendence freed from its hybridisation with transcendent objects; an absolutely uni-versal opening structured by original a prioris, but purged of any regional as well as any philosophical-transcendental distinction, of any ideal model that applies without exclusion to all possible phenomena. While philosophy inhibits thought in the Cosmos-function, deploying it there only to alienate it, science is accompanied by the Universe-function which is the radically universal space, free from decision, and which it provides to singularities. While philosophy ceaselessly knots and re-ties, crossing and mixing, in order to enrich a real impoverished by decision, science unbinds once and for all and dissolves the composites, freeing singularity and universality from one another so that they are now strictly identical rather than in a relation of mutual belonging. No mystery or withdrawal can any longer escape from this universal materiality of singularities. And everything is identically, without any difference at all, manifested as it is without remainder.

While philosophy surveys identities and accompanies them with its interminable procession of models and operations that are 'universal' but nonetheless *restrained* (interpretation, decision, reflection, critique, semiology, deconstruction, communication, etc.), science frees them from their supercilious guardians charged with dispensing the geniality of sound thought and the norm of the tradition, and makes them shine for themselves – with a dull, almost bland lustre, no doubt – rendering them unto this objectivity which is pure and stripped of the false linings of objective things.

It is humiliating but necessary to hear this: there is more *real and really universal* thought in, let's say, Riemann and Einstein (but they are not the only ones) than in Heidegger or Hegel. For the problem between science and philosophy is not that of novelty, but that of *reality*. And in these figures, there is the kernel of an experience of thought other than the philosophical. We need only extract this kernel, real rather than rational, and give it its place in the cause-(of)-science, in order to see the claim of philosophy – if not philosophy itself – instantaneously dissolve like vapour in an infinite space. As such, we no longer need the philosophical authorisation to think, which gives and removes the forbidden-to-think...

As far as philosophy is concerned, the only problem is now that of its *usage*. The philosophy of philosophy, this spontaneous auto-legitimation or hallucinatory auto-pragmatism, we replace with its finally immanent pragmatism, and that is to say: in terms of science, for it, and from its sole point of view. Non-philosophers are not anti-philosophers. They are without doubt more Spinozist than Spinoza, more Nietzschean than Nietzsche, and perhaps also more Heideggerian than Heidegger, etc. But it is because they have found, in the immanence of the One, this Archimedean point that philosophy, for its part, has always sought and always lacked since it has sought it in itself, or, if need be, in a particular science, rather than seeking it where it was, which is to say in science as such in its identity. Non-philosophers invent an occasionalism of philosophy, freeing themselves from the violence of its auto-affirmation and its spontaneous idealism...

What Is Non-Philosophy?

(1997)

Translated by Taylor Adkins

Non-philosophy cannot be born quite in the same way as a philosophy. When philosophers present their doctrine, they invoke a system of questions, influences and autonomous decisions, but also of accomplishments and innovations that conform to the essence or authentic telos of philosophy. There were many influences and decisions at the origin of non-philosophy, and there will be new ones along the way. But they do not determine its essence, nor are they capable of explaining it. Rather than influences, there is firstly a conjuncture reevaluating the essence of philosophy itself, and not just some previous position or other to be contested, extended or completed by the new philosopher. Rather than an original decision, there is the constraint of a discovery – within whose horizon, however, decisions can be grasped in a continuous way. However, the correlation of a conjuncture and a discovery is still a phenomenon that might seem philosophically intelligible without further elucidation. It can only give rise to a non-philosophy when the discovery radically exceeds this conjuncture, to the point of granting it only the causality of an 'occasion' which motivates the thought of the discovery without determining its essence as discovery; or the causality of a 'symptom' whose discovery would allow us not merely to interpret but to explain, in the strongest sense of the word, the mechanism of philosophy and thus its essence. A 'new thought' must be a novelty in the real, rather than a thought; and rather than registering the conjuncture, it must reduce it to the status of a symptom, i.e. to that which manifests the essence of its object, philosophy in person, capable of an explanation that emerges without any possible representation in its object. Properly speaking, a philosophy cannot be discovered – it can only be invented within certain limits, because it can never treat the philosophical tradition in its entirety in this way. On the other hand, since it is condemned to the primacy of decision and the inability to explain itself when faced with a discovery anterior to all decision, philosophy of itself can only give rise to new philosophies, never to a non-philosophy.

THE PHILOSOPHICAL CONJUNCTURE

A philosopher never presents her thought without prefacing it with a complaint concerning the philosophical poverty of the times, nor without opposing it to the urgency of the true and the authentic 'modern' philosophical decision, which is simultaneously coherent with the critique of the age, its real demands and (big surprise!) the originary meaning of philosophy... Following the discovery that lays down the law for it, non-philosophy cuts out and delineates a conjuncture, using it as a material through which to treat philosophy – not its 'all' but its identity. Of course, nothing in the phenomena that constitute a conjuncture is really new or emergent. A conjuncture is not a radical emergence – it is a new twist, the new face of an essentially old situation that dominates the present rather than actually appearing; nor is it a purely factual constraint: it is we who decide, in a certain way (without arbitrary voluntarism), on what constitutes a conjuncture. From this point of view, three phenomena, three singular points, are knotted together, overdetermining one another, so that their correlation seems to constitute the current philosophical situation.

On the one hand, there is a doxic dilution of the philosophical tradition. The traditional aspect of Philosophy has always displayed some sort of doxa or superior and knowledgeable form of doxa. But once attempts at rigorous science, from Plato to Husserl, are foiled, this doxic origin reappears, transformed into a universal market of philosophical flows. Since the Platonic, Kantian and Husserlian 'scientific' revolutions were nothing but breaks and therefore not radical enough, philosophy returns to its sophistic source in the contemporary form of its usage by intellectuals, scientists and the media – essentially appropriated, we say again, by a will-to-speak taking philosophy as an object. An extended doxa or sophistry, it crudely admits what it has always been: an aid to political or everyday decision, continuously plunging into the technology-all, the ambient technologism. Nevertheless, several theoretical, pragmatic and institutional regimes of philosophy coexist. In one aspect, philosophy can be treated as a quasi-natural activity with invariant properties which would be interesting to explain as such – not least since its becoming-mediatised grafts itself onto this perceptual, representative, imaginary and thus hardly spiritual nature. But of course, as exceptions to this becoming-mediatised, there are the 'serious academic philosophers' – quite deadly serious, indeed mortifying – who can only save it by 'embalming' it (Nietzsche); or the 'serious critics' and the 'hermeneutic engagement' of phenomenology, which are local activities or subsets of the grand tradition, and which can neither modify the bases of the latter nor renovate its general style, i.e. its metaphysical presuppositions. They discover their true signification in functions that are at best those of 'respiration' or of the 'possible', of non-creative critique or critique as alibi, functions that they fulfil within the academic world. This is to say that the apparent exceptions to this process, through which it grows and enriches the noble part of the tradition – for example, deconstruction or any other philosophical endeavour to which a proper name can be affixed – are nothing but effects of resistance to this dilution, as it comes into contact with those reified and institutional forms – dead forms, in short – that constitute 'academic philosophy'. Like any other market, the market of philosophy thus comes up against sites of resistance that present themselves in the name of the 'tradition' and the 'serious', but they are no more new than the sophistic grounds and mediatised will animating the oldest philosophy, with which they never cease to turn, in a vicious circle. Kant said that metaphysics was an ocean without shores or lighthouse: what does this say about the element of waves, flows and communication, mobile and turbulent, this element of the market that subsumes, in new forms, the metaphysical ocean? Giving itself philosophy as its point of application while modifying its conditions and its objectives, non-philosophy resumes the Platonic project: no longer philosophy as science 'overcoming' opinion, but a non-philosophical science taking philosophical opinion itself as object. The norm of truth – which philosophy seeks and a priori attributes to itself without possessing the proper means to do so – is discovered by non-philosophy, by reducing its claims of metaphysical origin, in the form of a simple 'transcendental' theory (but one that is identically scientific and philosophical, which changes everything) – a theory of philosophical systems, rather than a new system of philosophy.

The second trait of the conjuncture is a powerlessness of philosophy with regard to 'new problems' – a powerlessness that is nonetheless not new, but which the conjuncture renders particularly visible. Philosophers' universal complaint concerning what there is to think, when this would be nothing but philosophy itself, is symptomatic of a posture of delay/anticipation which they affect to believe is accidental and the fault of the preceding philosophy, but which is so structural that it is one of the most certain criteria for recognising a philosophy. We shall call 'philosophy', beyond any given doctrine's claim to this title, any thought, explicitly 'philosophical' or not, that postulates that it holds within itself its ultimate validity for itself and consequently for the Real – and thus its radical non-subordination to the latter. This postulation is more precisely the *Principle of Sufficient Philosophy*. But this statement suffices to reveal philosophy's deep-seated malaise, i.e. its in-principle inadequacy to the present of the conjuncture. The 'actual present' of philosophy has only a divided depth, and is not a conjuncture. It sediments old conjunctures for which are valid only philosophies that have no actuality other than a retained one (a retentional actuality) or else a claimed one (a protentional actuality) that is nonetheless maladapted in principle. It thus manifests in regard to regional experience and its problems a claim, an empty and general meta-regional anticipation, and it pays for this anticipation with finitude and anxiety – such is its constitutional malaise. Philosophy and experience form nothing other (or barely so) than a vicious circle, so that the former is incapable of explaining the latter and is confined to commenting on and 'interpreting' it. Except from the point of view of knowledge, philosophy is not sterile properly speaking, for it works to adjust man to fleeting experience or to some particular knowledge or another, or more precisely to make it tolerable for him. It is a practice with local theoretical aspects, a pragmatics and a therapeutics for humanity. It is perhaps the victim of a poorly posed problem, but one that now forms a part of its own clinical situation.

The third element of the conjuncture is the new philosophical terrain upon which non-philosophy is born and from which it departed. It is at this point of the conjuncture, as minuscule and invisible as it may still remain to philosophical doxa, that the discovery proper to non-philosophy took place, without being reducible to philosophy – indeed, it exceeded philosophy, but undoubtedly was only able to do so with the aid of philosophy. It is worth relating once again that a conjuncture and a discovery are not the entirety of thought, and that a certain philosophical common sense constitutes an extension of what is essential to the normalised activity of thought. But the conjuncture is precisely also this point that is destined to change the face of thought and, following this, to enrich philosophical doxa. Of what does it consist here? It has produced a double change of the transcendental terrain of thought after and independently of Heidegger, a mutation that renders obsolete not the horizon Heidegger posited and called the 'end of metaphysics' – a horizon as 'avoidable' as the famous 'unavoidable horizon of Marxism' (Sartre) has become – but more exactly the claim to posit this horizon as unavoidable for all thought. More decisive not so much for Heidegger's thought as for his claim to delimit all thought, there is, on the one hand, Michel Henry's substitution of the One for Being, of radical immanence for the transcendence of the world. And, on the other hand, and symmetrically, Levinas's substitution of the Most-High, if one can call it that, for the Same, of infinite ethical transcendence for philosophical immanence. By catching Being – the pivot of traditional philosophy – in a 'pincer movement' between the two extremes of immanence and transcendence, this allows us to show at least that it is technically possible to treat philosophy otherwise than through itself – even if these authors have not found a serious or positive 'scientific' recourse other than the phenomenological for this treatment.

It is possible, with certain caveats, to baptise the Real, which posits a certain non-philosophical 'identity' of transcendence and immanence, under the old transcendental name of the 'One' so as to bring forth a new cycle of thought, a new general economy beginning with Being, from the Greeks up to Nietzsche, continued by the Other, from Freud to Levinas through Wittgenstein, Heidegger and Derrida as mixed positions between Being and Other, and ending – perhaps provisionally – with the One itself placed in a position of priority, but this time radical. It is impossible to gauge the extent of this change, and it is thus a 'force' whose most innovative effects will still take a while to be 'drawn out'. But it is obvious that its presence alone relativises the 'end of metaphysics' because it proposes for it a new, much more radical end through another usage or its transformation. It could be that 'radical immanence' in its transcendental and auto-affective form (Henry) is still nothing but a half-solution, i.e. a philosophical solution. A strange ambiguity traverses Henry's recent work and becomes symptomatic: that of auto-affection, the essence of immanence, and that of identity, the new theme called upon to correct the transcendental register, and which is at least as classical as 'auto-affection', but reinforces it because it remains oriented around a 'trinitarian' thematic despite this appeal to identity. In other words, in the majority of its current uses, radical immanence seems to continue to belong, if not to the most worldly transcendence of the Greeks, at least to one last residue of religious transcendence conveyed by the act of philosophising as such, and not simply by certain of its ontological presuppositions. Henry did not have the theoretical means to 'reduce' them, and some of his successors even less so. Radical immanence, auto-affection or 'Life' imply the critique of 'Greek presuppositions' and the 'philosophy' which the latter delimit, particularly those of ontological intuition. But it is also obvious that these presuppositions are broader than those of intuition alone, and that 'radical immanence', such as it has been understood until now, has been understood on the broadest terrain of philosophy and transcendence insofar as the latter is (and remains here) the principal organon of philosophy, giving rise to the pathos of 'Life' and its perpetual coming to itself or 'auto-generation'. As for Levinas, his infinite absolutisation of transcendence has the effect of an ethical and Judaic provocation, which confirms that his thought is on the way toward a reevaluation of the authority of philosophy. What do we make of this ultimately religious double contestation of philosophy? Among others, one of the objectives of non-philosophy is perhaps to show how these extremes can be brought into agreement if we discover the means to suspend philosophy, which separates them and thus opposes them in an irreconcilable way.

All the more so given that it remains to explore the transcendental of the One, which had been as forgotten as Being, and was still forgotten when the meaning or truth of Being had been drawn out from the forgetting. Still remaining a philosophical root to be brought back to the surface of thought, the One returned to thought in this ambiguous register of the radical immanence of 'life' on the one hand, and the Other identifying the ego on the other hand – ambiguous because it was able to orient the investigation (indeed, this is what happened) toward the idea of a subjective interiority, no doubt 'radical' but still posited in opposition or 'immediate negation', i.e. in the neighbourhood of transcendence, thus risking once again the loss of *the generic and complementary 'identity' with philosophy within unilaterality, through which the One is One and does not exhaust itself in an auto-affection*. This was, in any case, a novelty and a progression, a happy invention: while the philosophical tradition consumed itself with chatter that is simultaneously academic, intellectual and media-friendly, while phenomenology thought its recommence-ment in a historical mode, while the 'end of metaphysics' was posited as the delimiting condition of any renovation of thought, and while deconstruction pored over critique and textuality, a true discovery occurred silently elsewhere and was destined to remain unperceived for a long time within the current configuration of philosophy, where it would seem (and will always seem to the majority) but a contradictory oddity. In presenting itself as phenomenology and as an offshoot of Cartesianism, it would not at all do itself justice, thus testifying to its unstable combat with philosophy. The best thinkers who use it, in fact, maintain a strained relation to philosophy without having discovered the principle of this tension, the 'force-(of)-thought' wherein the One – as real or immanent drive, not as transcendental and phenomenological – exerts and confirms its purport. These philosophies of radical immanence are condemned to an aporia created by their own originality, but from a half-originality insufficient to legitimise itself – how, by what right, does one use philosophy and its Greek presuppositions so as to speak the immanence that escapes all concepts? Ambushed, more or less directly, by a negative henology, they have no response to the combined objections of metaphysics, scientific phenomenology and deconstructions. So long as it is not clearly posited, outside philosophical sufficiency, with adequate and novel theoretical means, radical immanence remains a rough approximation. These ways of thought have not freed themselves from philosophical sufficiency and thus have not freed philosophy itself and the 'Greek' in philosophy.

Non-philosophy is apparently born, in its first form, in the immediate neighbourhood of these philosophies of immanence, but from the start under the tutelage of the One. Responding to the demand for a thought that would finally be adequate to the One rather than to Being or the Other, it has progressively specified and limited its own objectives by laboriously developing its own techniques and concepts. Considered from outside, it can seem like the solution to the preceding aporia (how to 'speak' the One, how to 'conceptualise' radical immanence?), justifying the recourse to philosophy as inevitable, and its transformation by 'dualysis' – the practice of 'unilateral duality' – as the only possible procedure. But the invention of the method of 'dualysis' and the solution to the aporia would suppose an understanding of the radicality of immanence as a special form of identity rather than as the immediatised mixture of an auto-affection. This alone could make us admit that, if it is impossible to exit philosophy, the true question is that of knowing whether we ever entered it; and that, in any case, only a force-(of)-thought as vision-in-One can free itself, not from philosophy in its materiality, but from philosophical sufficiency. Vision-in-One is therefore neither an abstraction of the metaphysical triad of One, Being, Other, nor even a neighbouring concept. Consequently, if the identity of immanence has never been thought by philosophy, which has thought nothing but a transcendent One (or a transcendent and immanent One as in later Platonism), this powerlessness cannot constitute a determining motivation for non-philosophy. Non-philosophy has passed through the philosophies of immanence momentarily in order to discover their impulse, but will no longer cross paths with them except to discover in them an 'occasional' cause. It also speaks of radical immanence, laying claim to it, but it means by this concept something different than these philosophies, and proposes another usage of it than that of any possible philosophy. This is its specific discovery of 'vision-in-One' or the 'One-in-One'. Thus we leave the conjuncture, to approach non-philosophy itself.

FROM THE TRANSCENDENTAL ONE
TO VISION-IN-ONE

The discovery (the meaning of this term will have to be elucidated) that founds non-philosophy is that of the One such as it is, i.e. in its radical autonomy, as One-in-One or vision-in-One. Philosophy knows the One as convertible (with several nuances, ranging from dissymmetry and disparity to differe[/a]nce) either with Being (the transcendental philosophy of the Ancients and Moderns) or with the Other (contemporary, semi-transcendental philosophy and 'deconstructions'). That the One be precisely convertible, or simply associable, able to be paired with something else and ultimately with thought – such is the ultimate principle of philosophy, regardless of all doctrinal and thematic diversity. But this convertibility has a specific meaning: it signifies the powerlessness of philosophy to think the One strictly reduced to itself, the nothing-but-One. It only thinks identity in general and a fortiori the One itself in and through its amalgamation with Being, the Other, and sometimes beings; as accompanied by other transcendentals and within the universal horizon – a completely predicative and logical, even logocentric horizon – constituted by these predicates. From this point of view, which we provisionally suppose, non-philosophy's thesis might be as follows: the One in its solitude is unthinkable, but the sufficiency of philosophy consists precisely in wanting to, and believing itself capable of, thinking it such as it is; whereas it only thinks it as it is, as such. Non-philosophy then can seem like thought abandoning the One, thought letting go of this claim and this contortion around the object which is ontology, no longer wanting it, i.e. wanting to think it. Thought could therefore always be indebted and obligated to the One without still claiming to determine it as it would an object, be it the most secret or most high. However, this interpretation of non-philosophy's origin, aside from the fact that nothing would force it to conclude as to the positivity and specificity of the One as in-One and vision-in-One, still remains on the terrain of philosophical motivations – it is altogether in the Heideggerian style, even if it relates to the One (a henological Difference). It ends up in a simple anti-philosophy and always relies on philosophical sufficiency, i.e. the supposedly relative-absolute autonomy of thought. How do we restore to vision-in-One the radical novelty of its discovery?

A new approach, no doubt still insufficient but already more accurate than the preceding, consists in positing that vision-in-One exceeds a solely philosophical type of discovery; that it is simultaneously, even identically, motivated by philosophy and science – not by a particular philosophical doctrine or scientific theory but by the essence of the former and the latter, insofar as it is possible to grasp them on the basis of their immediate claims, yet only in a sense we accept (as material, at least). Vision-in-One is not an 'arbitrary' invention, a new ultra-philosophical or mystical decision, for it only has meaning in so far as it is produced on the basis of (but also beyond) thought in its two major forms which are science and philosophy. This is a discovery that indeed takes place in thought, and thus always somewhat with its assistance. But it is such that, if it must be able to identically explain the phenomena of science and philosophy, it also radically exceeds them, together with the horizon they form, an horizon that can no longer integrally determine it. As a result, it becomes capable of giving a veritable but a priori explanation of what philosophy has always been, a philosophy to science or of science, a mixture of the two – an epistemo-logical Difference.

But if vision-in-One is a discovery carried out in thought, and, in part, with the concurrence of philosophy, if it must also be capable of explaining the latter, we still do not know the possibility of the essence of discovery, or that which 'in reality' explains its explanatory force, and which can and must no longer have any relation to philosophy. The radical autonomy of the One, the plane or element of non-philosophy, once again and this time without the residue of an ultimate relation to thought, 'exceeds' the discovery itself and its operation. How do we 'pass' from the latter, which is always relative and without primacy, to the One of vision-in-One insofar as it is radically autonomous 'in relation' to it and determines a veritable non-philosophy instead of a 'negative philosophy' or even an 'anti-philosophy'? So as to simplify the givens of the problem, let us posit that the One discovered in and by thought is by definition a radical One distinct from the 'transcendental' One of philosophy, since it must indifferently relate itself to any form or autonomous type of thought whatsoever and must, in particular, respond to a scientific type of explanatory requirement. The latter stipulates that this radical One not be confused, even in part, with the difference of philosophy, with the body of phenomena to be explained: that it be heterogeneous, but within the limits in which it by definition involves an (explanatory) relation with thought. Thus to explain thought (as epistemo-logical Difference) is an ambiguous formula, because the radical One must relate itself by essence to the thought to be explained, but without exhausting itself in it. Vision-in-One, if it indeed possesses this capacity proper to discovery a fortiori, is no longer definable by it and does not exhaust itself in it. This is the meaning of its radical autonomy, immanence through and through without the slightest fragment of transcendence; not an autonomy that is absolute or is due to an auto-position using transcendence, re-positing the latter as is the case with the great entities of metaphysics. Thus it no longer involves any de jure positive or negative relation with thought; neither positing the latter with it nor expelling the latter from it, it is really indifferent to transcendence.

Once again, how do we 'pass' from the transcendental One to the real One, how do we bridge the gap between the former and the latter, if these questions at least still have some meaning, i.e. if this instigation of the 'philosophical recovery of foundations' is more than a mere semblance and constitutes (as hardly seems likely) the non-philosophical method? *The real One is given with and by the transcendental One, but without being alienated by this givenness or constituted by it.* In order to speak of these relations, we introduce the thematic of cloning: The real One is given in the sense that the clone supposes what clones, where givenness is second like the clone in relation to the cloned, but transparent to the latter. It gives the real

One completely, and precisely it gives it in its integrity without commencing it, deferring it or conditioning it. The principle of the solution is therefore as follows: the radical One of vision-in-One can only be discovered in and by thought as a force that is identically explanatory and transcendental, identically scientific and philosophical, discovered by thought as that which it is; if it is already discovered or already given such as it is, as such, to thought without its aid (as the transcendental would be). As such: discovered in flesh and blood in its immanence, given without an operation of givenness. Discovery only finds its full phenomenal meaning if it itself depends upon a Discovered-without-discovery that radically 'precedes' or determines it. The One is the Real or the given 'in itself': not as an in-itself outside thought, but as the in-itself-(of the)-phenomenon itself, which precedes or determines thought, an in-itself that is neither ontic nor ontological but seen-in-One through and through. It is on this condition that it can be given-(to)-thought, i.e. without the aid of thought, without its determination by the latter. More heteronomous to thought than the transcendental One, it is primarily indifferent rather than heteronomous, and this indifference determines the heteronomy of the transcendental One to thought.

This is the phenomenal or real content of the formula: 'non-philosophical discovery of vision-in-One'. The process might evoke the ontological argument, but its being applied to the One or the radical phenomenon rather than God or Being totally modifies its character and pertinence. Once it is reduced to its theological content and pinned to the three corners of the trinity or Philosophical Decision (of which it is an inevitable mode), the essence of the ontological argument signifies that the self-evident necessity of passing from thought (qua being) to being (qua thought, for example in the cogito) necessarily supposes a One-thought-and-being whose function is then maintained by God. The One, as much 'being' as one decides it is, and precisely because it is only 'being', remains a transcendental One without attaining to a real One. In this approach, non-philosophy seems to infer the latter from the former, but this 'conclusion' is not one that is structured by Philosophical Decision, for it is precisely not any kind of inference or 'passage' whatsoever. In any case, the vision-in-One-(of)-the-transcendental-One (in whatever sense we take it) is definitely not a continuity or a leap: a leap of thought into existence, a continuity of thought with being, assured by the transcendental One. The non-philosophical relation requires other formulations. We shall say that *the transcendental One in the new or transformed sense is that which the real One clones from thought or the World*. From the cloned to the clone, there is neither leap nor excess, neither supplementary 'transcending' nor even that half-leap, that gentler leap that is the 'turn', but a reflection-without-reflected, unless the radically immanent One is reflected and alienated in its image or its transcendence as in a mirror. We shall say that thought is determined-in-the-last-instance, via the 'mediation' of the transcendental One, by the real One; or that thought is determined by the Real not directly, but simply in the last resort ('in-the-last-instance'), and directly by its transcendental essence. There is no conversion or reversion, just a completely immanent 'turn' between the transcendental One and the vision-in-One which forms the real content of the new transcendental subject but which remains in the Real without alienating itself in this subject. In the transcendental One, we do not see the real One in the transcendental, intentional and phenomenological sense of vision, in the sense in which one would see it or even turn into it. But this transcendental One is only given if it is itself seen-in-One or cloned. There is no difference between the real One and the transcendental One insofar as they are 'seen-in-One', i.e. given in the mode of the real One. Hence the real One is already in the definitive state of 'givenness' when the transcendental One is given. It suffices to think in the mode of this transcendental One – this is thought itself reduced to its non-philosophical essence – in order to think not the real One but *according to the real One* and according to its radical autonomy of the Real in regard to the transcendental One itself. The transcendental One, the subject, is simply the first position (and the essence of the position-in-thought) of the real One. If the real One is like a Last Instance or a Prior-to-priority, the cloned subject is the essence of its position or its first givenness, and it is through the latter that the One determines thought or transcendence 'in-the-last-instance'. The 'last instance' is not simply the last, first-and-last, cause of metaphysics, but instead annihilates the latter and its transcendence as being nothing but a backworld. There is no longer any backworld, because the Real is completely given without an act or operation of givenness, and because the phenomenon or the Real, in its essence, is radically worldless. Nonetheless, there is a cloning by the Real of the transcendental instance or the subject.

Thus, for positive phenomenal reasons rather than anti-philosophical reasons, non-philosophy renounces any attempt to ultimately think the Real or the One, which has no need of it and is indifferent to it, sufficing as vision-in-One. If there is some thought that is not philosophical or scientific, separately and/or inclusively, it exerts itself in the form of the transcendental One, and thus according to the One without still claiming to be a 'science of the One' in the metaphysical manner. The true non-idealist limitation of thought has been obtained. Understood as One-in-One, radical immanence can no longer be obtained or produced by an operation of radicalisation, purifica-tion or auto-affection of transcendence, an operation that enslaves it to the task of founding transcendence, an eminently and definitively philosophical task. In general, thinking is not a passage or becoming between contraries, the excessive leap of the 'ontological argument' or the half-leap, the little jump of the 'turn'. There is no becoming of thought, of the World toward the One, of the One toward the World – no amalgamation or dialectic – there is only the immanent performation of a structure. Whoever has 'seen' the transcendental One has already seen the One-in-One...

REMARKS ON THE CONSTITUTION OF NON-PHILOSOPHY

Between conjuncture, discovery and invention (philo-fiction), while progressively thematising them, non-philosophy has undergone, since Philosophy I, three or four mutations of its object and its parameters (rather than its grounds or terrains), designated as Philosophies II, III, IV and, currently (2009-2011) V, along with a great deal of analytical work, specifications and corrections carried out between any two of these stages. Philosophy I as a whole is still governed by the Principle of Sufficient Philosophy, despite including several themes capable of invalidating philosophical systems (the One as identity of the individual, the transcendental, the theoretical domination of philosophy), which it will suffice to turn in all directions and bring into play as one of the factors driving breaks or lines of weakness and leading to a reevaluation of the authority of philosophy. Without belonging to non-philosophy, it certainly announces several motifs of the latter. Even the discovery that inaugurates Philosophy II and a general reworking of these themes – vision-in-One as human, 'ordinary man' announcing the future theme of 'generic humanity' – is itself an ongoing process in its formulation and is no doubt still not completed, supposing it ever can be. The elaboration of the stakes, effects and limits of vision-in-One has been a lengthy task, since it long remained captive not only to philosophical formulations, but also to philosophical limitations. It was necessary to take together, on the one hand, the strict unilateral order that goes from the Real to thought, from the vision-in-One to theory, an order that passes through the transcendental as clone seen-in-One; and on the other, the rectification or reciprocal deepening of the formulations of vision-in-One and those of the thought called 'non-philosophical' precisely stemming from the One. Many hesitations and resistances have been encountered by non-philosophy, with many more to come, arising from the confusion between the unilateral but de jure complementary order of the instances (of the Real, the transcendental, force-(of)-thought, philosophy-material) and the anarchy of invention or theoretical research, always more or less in the grip of philosophical authority and its vicious circle, always threatened with losing the dignity of theory and falling into the games with which philosophical sufficiency occupies itself. It is obvious that if we began with the acquisition of vision-in-One (Philosophy II) before perceiving its validity for the philosophical field and the inevitable suspension of philosophical authority, first positing the radical One as simple requirement repressed by philosophics themselves (particularly those of Differe[/a]nce) and before inferring thought by induction and deduction on the basis of the One and philosophy complementarily, this is because philosophical sufficiency still held us fast with many undetected ruses. A reciprocal action of vision-in-One upon philosophy (what are the consequences for its authority?) and of the latter upon the former (how do we adequately think the One or according to the One?), little by little drove the point of departure for non-philosophy back outside the vicinity of philosophy, science always assisting in principle. It took all that time to correctly grasp the requirements implied for thought by such an experience as that of vision-in-One as 'foreclosed' or indifferent to thought; and in order to limit the total-power of philosophy so as to make way for the radical given such that, in reality, it comes of itself 'futurally', or sub-venes and operates this limitation by determining thought in-the-last-instance. Now that the essential bases have been acquired, Philosophies II and III seem like a work of variations – of specifications, explanations, analyses – upon non-philosophical structure. Philosophy II theoretically establishes the entirety of the schema. Philosophy III is dedicated to various ethical and Marxist themes. Other accents have appeared little by little, such as messianism and the meaning of Christ for thought (IV). Lastly, Philosophy V, which is still underway, reprises a theme already present in the beginnings of non-philosophy, a rather paradoxical theme – namely that of a privileged affinity between vision-in-One and science. It also introduces more systematically a major liberation of this structure from philosophy, by suspending the transcendental postulate and actually positing the scientific differential as generic, through a certain use of quantum mechanics.

Non-philosophy is so continuous, diverse and monotonous in its themes that its being divided between II, III, IV and V will prove rather artificial if taken as a claim to linear evolution. It is more a question of kaleidoscopic views, all similar yet rearranged each time, on the game of non-philosophy. Each book in a sense reprises the same problems 'from zero', again throwing the dice or reshuffling the cards of science, philosophy, Marxism, gnosis, man as Stranger and Christ. The essence of non-philosophy would be, let's say, fractal and fictioned.

WHAT IS NON-PHILOSOPHY?

THE UNIVERSALITY OF NON-PHILOSOPHY

Non-philosophy is a radically immanent practice, and this is precisely why it is heteronomous to philosophy. It considers and treats the latter in terms of its universality and its traditional 'all', not in terms of the diversity of its problems. There are two ways in which this is done: (1) From the point of view of its material, it is examined in its most singular concepts and philosophemes, but on condition that this philosophical given not remain in the state of an amorphous assortment of objects and statements (there would be no possible science of this non-object), but that it be susceptible to a preliminary formalisation, and that its factuality be provisionally reduced to a structure, that of Philosophical Decision (of the mixture, the empirico-transcendental doublet, etc.); (2) From the point of view of that in it which is non-philosophy's object and no longer its material, it is reduced by the Last Instance which determines its 'all' and its 'being'. Non-philosophy phenomenalises the real identity-(of)- or (for)- philosophy, an identity that is valid for the new a priori structures (unilateral duality, cloning, material) capable of explaining its various properties. This is why, both from the point of view of its material and that of its object of knowledge, it is truly a theoretical practice of philosophy and not a particular doctrine or position to the exclusion of others. For example, it

211

is a non-Marxism or a non-phenomenology in virtue of its philosophemes and its statements which specify or effectuate the structure of Philosophical Decision and obviously subsist at the core of its own discourse as the materiality of its own statements. But it is insofar as it is non-philosophy that it is non-phenomenology, for example, and it guards against limiting its own relevance merely to the initial decisions of phenomenology, considering them only qua already reduced to their own philosophical universality. Thus a multiplicity of presentations of non-philosophy is possible, and this testifies to its plasticity and its universality rather than to a formalism. In this sense it would instead be of the order of an organon. For example, because of this new (generic) universality, that of real identity, it cannot assume one hypothesis of the *Parmenides* over another, except as mere material. The hypotheses of the *Parmenides* are retained entirely within the horizon of transcendence or the ontological predication of the One, even as they deny its Being or predicate it directly or indirectly (by supposition) of the Other or the Multiple. This horizon is that of the philosophical co-belonging of the One and Thought, Being and Thought reciprocally mediating themselves alongside the One. Whence all those 'hypotheses' which are merely modes of the One's convertibility with Being, non-Being, the Other or the Multiple, and which allow philosophy to deploy its intelligible heaven, traversed by so many storms. If the history of philosophy can seem like a perpetual dismemberment and traversing of the *Parmenides*, henceforth it can no longer assume the all of the latter, even if this all is decided by a transcendental 'One' which is simultaneously internal and external, immanent and limiting to it. It only assumes this 'all' as real in-the-last-instance and as determined by vision-in-One rather than by a new philosophical decision. On the one hand, non-philosophy only posits the real One as inconvertible or non-commutative with all transcendentals, even with the transcendental One as simple clone. This indifference, nevertheless, cannot mean that it is exclusive of any relation or that it cannot enter into any 'rapport', for it can 'enter', without alienating itself, into that radical relationless relation of immanence which is its cloning of thought. On the other hand, it reserves for thought a non-Platonic or non-philosophical status of hypothesis: not a relative-absolute or an-hypothetical hypothesis, but hypothesis as clone of its object, as a position 'cloned' by vision-in-One. This change in the status of a transformed *Parmenides* supposes a re-elaboration of non-philosophy's style of 'hypothesis'. If philosophical hypotheses on the One give rise to a system, auto-closing themselves into a One simultaneously immanent and transcendent to them, non-philosophical hypotheses cannot close the Real and even less close themselves and roll up into a relative-absolute system; instead they remain as, definitively, hypotheses. From this perspective, the *Parmenides* and the neo-Platonic attempts to prolong it in some, indeed all, of its hypotheses, can at most designate the system of possible philosophies or lead to a 'negative philosophy', which is everything philosophy can do to itself, but which cannot generate a non-philosophy.

The discovery of a 'radical' capable of suspending the principles of philosophy could undoubtedly only do so in the vicinity of the greatest objects of philosophy, the transcendentals, but henceforth on condition of ordering them according to the real-One and reducing them to the state of givens or positions cloned or determined-in-the-last-instance by the Real. What can sometimes seem like a protraction of neo-Platonism, following Damascius, for example, by postulating an 'ineffable' One whose transcendence and immanence are reciprocal, is an unavoidable philosophical appearance. What is more, this appearance is necessary, since in general such appearances motivate the philosophical resistance and sufficiency that non-philosophy requires. Non-philosophy's 'principle' is the ultimate status of the One or the Real, no doubt reduced to immanence, but indifferent to any suspicion of reciprocation with transcendence, at least such as is used by philosophy. So that the One it uses has never given rise to a negative henology, an auto-negation or an auto-limitation of the logos. If there are aspects of such an auto-limitation or auto-suspension, they are not even simple means of non-philosophical discourse, but objective philosophical appearances of this discourse.

This generic universality of non-philosophy explains its style of reference to philosophies. A conjuncture already possesses its own universality; it must be cut out and delimited as a singular set of singular points. But in its lengthy elaboration and constitution, non-philosophy has used, and will always use, as what it calls its 'materials' rather than its 'influences', Marx as well as Husserl, as much Descartes as Kant, Derrida just as much as Deleuze, etc., without giving rise to a syncretism (which would have no meaning for non-philosophy since it is not a philosophical position). This is the force of its weakness (or the other way around, as a philosopher would argue), of its ultimate status and its radical poverty: as a stranger, it speaks in all philosophical languages without recognising itself in any of them or claiming to belong. From this perspective, our conjuncture is not simply the doxic drift of philosophy – its becoming-commodity through its scientific, political, artistic appropriation – it is not merely the 'philosophical ballet' wherein philosophy fails by trying to 'dance'; it is also the 'noble' philosophical tradition constituted by singular statements and several proper names. But these exceptions can signify only that a thought that would be adequate to the identity of the real should take these singular points into account as rigorously as possible within the conjuncture.

What would be the point of a non-philosophy that didn't register all the enquiries posited and carried out by Husserl, Heidegger, Wittgenstein, Derrida? That would not be valid for Deleuze, Henry, Badiou and perhaps also the 'analytics'? Such a broad calculus would be dubious for philosophy, obviously; but it is necessary for non-philosophy, lest it reconstitute a new metaphysics on the basis of its themes. It is indeed philosophy, insofar as it is structured as a metaphysical sufficiency, that must be thought and consequently excluded from the sole essence of non-philosophy. Non-philosophy is vested in philosophy and does not believe, through naivety and new sufficiency, that it should be simply written off, above all in its contemporary forms which are most attentive to the philosophical gesture. No doubt philosophical resistance prefers those who reject philosophy (it knows that they participate in its belief) to those who explain it and come to it as to a destiny to which they are nevertheless essentially strangers.

NON-EUCLIDEAN AND NON-PARMENIDEAN

Let us put these indications into rapid effect, through a statement of Parmenides himself; one, moreover, that is decisive in demonstrating the universality of non-philosophy. Parmenides announces a universal axiom for what philosophy has become: 'The Same is Being and

Thinking'. This axiom is directly that of the structure of Philosophical Decision insofar as it posits the correlation or convertibility – give or take various specific differences, folds or refoldings – of Being and Thought. We obviously oppose this axiom to that of non-philosophy, which is that Being – at least insofar as it is understood as the 'Real' – determines Thinking without reciprocity. In reality, we oppose it to two forms of the same axiom according to the level of the instances in play: (1) Being, in the sense in which it would designate the Real, determines Thinking in-the-last-instance or without reciprocity – this is the 'force-(of)-thought'; (2) More completely, as the radical identity of Being and Thinking, force-(of)-thought determines thought in-the-last-instance as non-philosophy. Moreover, what matters is that, on the new basis of vision-in-One, which is neither Being nor thought but perhaps the generic Same, this is a 'unilateral' relation which establishes itself between these old oppositions or, better still, between the real One and their relation of opposition and sameness such as it is posited by Parmenides. On the one hand, the real One is positively non-Parmenidean – it is the Discovered or the radical Manifested; but it alone allows us to posit really non-Parmenidean axioms or axioms which are not auto-critiques of philosophy, and to remove philosophy from its own enclosure. Being and Thought are no longer, separately or together (according to the various doctrines), co-constitutive of the Real, but only, and in-identity, force-(of)-thought as vision-in-One. It is thus a question of a limitation of philosophy, of its interpretation of Being and Thought, rather than of the latter themselves. On the other hand, the axiom of unilateral determination is fully and positively non-Parmenidean, or uses the Parmenidean axiom only in order to suspend it, not to posit itself and validate itself on its basis through a sort of auto-negation.

Hence thought gains in universality what it loses in the will to power and domination. Because it posits the One as convertibility with the Same, philosophy must posit that to each determination of Being (i.e. also to the Real, in the sense that philosophy can understand it as 'total' or system of the Same) there corresponds one, and only one, determination of thought, reciprocally or bi-univocally. But now, with the real One as indifferent to the dyad of Being and Thought separated, to each determination of the Real One there corresponds no single or privileged determination of Being and Thought (indifference of the Real); but instead an infinity of these determinations, each equivalent in regard to the Real, either because these thoughts are philosophical decisions which are in every way without adequate relation to the Real or non-exchangeable with it, simply being in a relation of transcendental illusion; or because these thoughts are non-philosophical effectuations on the basis of determined philosophies, which are then adequate in-the-last-instance to the real-One in their multiplicity but always without being able to co-determine it bi-univocally. Or, in 'non-Euclidean' style: philosophy is the general thesis that with the Real there corresponds one and only one thought (one philosophical position or system). Non-philosophy suspends the validity of this limiting postulate, which is overly empiricist and can only lead to theoretical impotence and to a state of conflict. It generalises or universalises philosophy a priori by freeing it from a postulate that is foundational within certain limits, but which conceals from thought the vision and practice of its most transformative form. It is obvious that the suspension of the Parmenidean axiom as syntax is accompanied by a modification in the objects or terms at stake; and that the One, Being and Thought change meaning and relation in their modified usage. With the dawning of a syntax of unilaterality, non-convertibility and determination-in-the-last-instance which affects the philosophical assemblage of the One, Being, Thought, the Other and the Same, these transcendental entities are reduced to the state of simple non-philosophical a prioris, and are taken as identities of a new type: through cloning (the One as transcendental subject), in-the-last-instance (Being and Thought or the Other) or as object of experience whose a priori identity is sought (the Same, the All, the Mixed, etc.). All these operations employ a philosophical material but are unintelligible within philosophy itself.

Apparently, from within philosophy alone *they can seem like subtractions*: from the One is retracted or subtracted its usage of the Same, from Being its claim to the Real, from Thought its claim of co-determination of the Real, from transcendence, which is always double, its redoubling; from the Same its function of quasi-totality or quasi-system in order to be reduced to the state of simple material of non-philosophy, then more specifically, of simple support in itself of non-philosophical a prioris. But this is an intra-philosophical interpretation that somewhat betrays the spirit of vision-in-One, for these are positive subtractions, subtractions of-the-last-instance.

Ultimately, the emergence of a non-Parmenidean thought is not that of an anti-Parmenidean philosophy, but firstly supposes the introduction of a new 'point of view' or experience-(of the)-real that can never be obtained by philosophical operations, that must already be given, and to which thought's only task is to render itself adequate. Non-philosophy is therefore not a modification of philosophy nor, in particular, another attempt at a re-commencement within the space opened up by the retreat of metaphysics in its essence and its end. We thus cannot imagine any ongoing transformation through which the old One would become the One-in-One. From the One-Being to vision-in-One or One-of-the-last-instance, there is neither passage nor even 'identification' and 'radicalisation'. There is the *radical* discovery of a given which has not been given by philosophy but which opens an 'infinite' field of possibilities. Discovered-without-discovery or Revealed-without-revelation – above all without revelation – vision-in-One establishes a universal thought as generic, a thought that uses philosophies only as materials and models. Which explains why the usage of the 'non-Euclidean' model only became possible at the theoretical origins of non-philosophy due to the primacy of the One-in-One 'over' all philosophical forms of the One. Of course, it is still the subject who, as cloned agent, posits for the first time – prior-to-priority – what is held within indifference to thought. But one can now question whether the relation between non-philosophical thought and its 'object' (the One-in-One) is any longer of the reversible or philosophical type, for example a relation between two consciousnesses, one phenomenological and naive, the other philosophical, one the non-Self and the other the Self = Self; instead, it is a relation of cloning and determination-in-the-last-instance. The Real and knowledge are not transcendent to one another like the terms of a philosophical dyad. In non-philosophy, it is still 'ordinary' or 'generic man' who thinks and explains the philosopher.

THE BEING-FORECLOSED OF THE REAL
AND THE NON-PHILOSOPHICAL SOLUTION

The different relations of philosophy and even non-philosophy to vision-in-One are gathered under the general title of the Real's foreclosure. Here the term does not have its strict psychoanalytic signification, although it maintains certain affinities with it. We shall distinguish between two meanings of this term, both of which register the absence not of every relation but of any relation of reversibility between the One and thought, the indifference of the former and the effects in the latter. There is a foreclosure that we shall call secondary, perhaps not exactly a repression: the foreclosure of the Real, of Identity, by philosophical-type thought. Since the One is neither thinkable nor unthinkable on this side of the philosophical antinomy, philosophy refuses this situation and claims to make the One fall under the antinomy, concluding that it is either thinkable, unthinkable or an amalgam of the two. It is this primary refusal opposed to the Real by philosophy, the refusal of its most original powerlessness to think the One, that is the secondary foreclosure. When philosophy declares the One-in-One unthought or unthinkable, or when it is forced to regulate this problem through a negative henology, it radically rejects it without even trying to repress it. Such a foreclosure is at the origin of a radical transcendental appearance that affects philosophy.

It consists in a transcendental rejection of another being-foreclosed, specifically that of vision-in-One. The primary foreclosure is more universal – it concerns both philosophy and non-philosophy, and above all it is the cause and the object of the secondary foreclosure. This is the real essence of vision-in-One's indifference with regard to any thought, whatever it might be, or any immanent given in regard to any givenness: of itself, without subtracting itself from thought, without retracting from it, no doubt also giving itself over to the solicitation of the latter but without denying its indifference, without having any need of it, i.e. of a givenness. Real indifference is not an absolute indifference, i.e. an indifference through transcendence, autoposition or metaphysical abstraction. It is a radical indifference through flawless-inherence-(to)-self or immanence. Rather than a retreat outside thought or a repulsion from it, the One is positively given-(to)-self in the sense that it is constituted by this given or this identity without any need of a givenness by thought or being so as to confirm it, just to request it or to motivate the acting of the Real. Such an indifference, real rather than transcendental, neutral rather than affirmative and positing or negative and denying, takes place before any reciprocal relation with thought. But it is on the one hand a 'negative' (and not 'negating') condition for every thought, in virtue of its radical inherence – vision-in-One is imposed non-violently upon indifference, and the latter is necessarily condemned to 'pass' through the former, not to affect it but to let itself be affected by the One and its being-foreclosed. And on the other hand, it cannot alienate itself like an absolute being, given its radicality, but can always be the cloned of thought, which means that unilaterality is not the absence of any relation but a certain type of complementarity of the One and philosophy.

Thus the secondary being-foreclosed of the One is a rejection or a transcendental foreclosure rather than a repression; it takes on the form of a specifically meta-physical attempt not to repress or forget it but to pro-duce its anamnesis, to think it 'at last'. But its primary being-foreclosed is no longer symmetrically a rejection of thought by the One itself, but instead immanence as radical inherence of the given-without-givenness, a being-foreclosed that necessarily affects thought. This immanent One has its own way of being given to thought without losing itself in it, like a cause-through-immanence which can only act as a sine qua non universal cause, universal as generic precisely to the extent of its immanence-(to)-self. The thought that registers this radical being-foreclosed rather than rejecting it, and is adequate to it or maintains it and makes it valid in the World or philosophy, is non-philosophy. The latter ultimately refuses (for positive reasons, not through powerlessness like philosophy) to think the One-as-such in-person once again as an object or in a similar mode through its transcendence of that of the object (as Other, for example). Non-philosophy is the solution to the following problem: what is the thought adequate to the One insofar as it (is) One rather than insofar as it is, i.e. insofar as it is taken in its identity radically on this side of Being and non-Being, the Other and the Multiple, and generally insofar as it no longer falls under Parmenides' hypotheses? The identity of immanence has been labelled unthinkable by philosophy, which has discovered the expedient of its convertibility with Being and then the Other so as to think it. But non-philosophy is the thought that recognises for positive reasons, without auto-critique, auto-negation or 'tribunal', that the One or the Real does not require philosophy except as a material, occasion or aid – in short, as a means.

The problem symmetrical to the preceding one is then posited: does the One such as it is in-One, Identity outside-Being, suffice by itself to determine a thought? The solution is that it suffices to determine – but only in-the-last-instance, thus with the aid of philosophy and science, of the worldly forms of thought as occasional cause – thought as 'force-(of)-thought' and in general as thought whose objects and means are taken from science and philosophy but treated as mere material. In order to resolve this problem that philosophy has always deemed aporetic, it is necessary to discover the 'key' to non-philosophy in cloning and determination-in-the-last-instance, which dictate that the real One no longer be posited as object-to-be-thought and instead be posited as immanent cause for a thought-according-to-the-One. But the thought adequate to the One, as to its cause rather than to its object, must also be a non-philosophy, i.e. inseparable from philosophy taken in its phenomenal sense, though obviously not in its sufficiency. Absent any recognition of philosophy as a complementary occasional cause of determination-in-the-last-instance, even non-philosophy itself will give birth to a new metaphysics; it will be born from the refusal to recognise this resistance of philosophy and this incapacity to limit the hubris of metaphysical transcendence. Thought-according-to-the-One is the phenomenal content, real-in-the-last-instance, and thus the critical content, of the old Greek project of a 'science of the One'. It is the radical residue, the real kernel that it exhibits when the reduction of philosophical sufficiency is carried out by the transcendental subject now as clone of the Real.

RADICALITY, UNILATERALITY, COMPLEMENTARITY

If categories are the concepts of the apophantic structure of ontology, the transcendentals still more universal concepts of all philosophical discourse qua onto-theo-logical or metaphysical system, philosophy has at its disposal yet another distinct type of operative concepts, which are like its own 'predicables': 'identity' and 'difference', 'absolute' and 'relative', 'totality' and 'system', 'convertibility' and 'reciprocity'. From this point of view, the main 'predicables' of non-philosophy, which distinguish its general style from the philosophical, are the radicality of the immanent phenomenon and the unilaterality of relations. The first is the major concept of the experience of the Real that is at the core of non-philosophy, the second the concept of the strange syntax which assembles the terms or rather the identity of the terms or relations, i.e. 'mixtures' (another predicable). It is another organisation in the form of 'unilateral dualities' that assemble phenomenal identities (the real nucleus of terms and relations) and their mixed philosophical forms, specifically the form of the terms and relations. In reality, mélanges or amphibolies form the only complete and concrete fabric of philosophy, a fabric from which are cut out the old antinomies of the terms and relations, of external and internal relations, by an entire system of operations and distributions which are analytic, synthetic, dialectical, differential, atomistico-logical, etc. For these two reasons, non-philosophy is not a thought of terms rather than relations, of the parts rather than the whole, of the local rather than the global, etc.; but of unilateral identities (individu-alities or undivided-dualities) which 'invalidate' philosophical antinomies.

'Radical' is neither 'absolute' nor 'principial [*principiel*]', but is said of the One as vision-in-One, i.e. as lived identity and lived experience-(of)-identity or immanence through and through. Identity as such, that of which philosophy knows nothing or whose 'existence' it refuses (and precisely because of this wants to make it be or exist when it is without-being or worldless) is neither a new absolute – for the absolute is always both relative and absolute, a mixed entity with neither the simplicity nor the radicality of the One – nor a new principle or a first cause – for a principle is a mixture of primacy (the real) and priority (thought) and does not simply enjoy primacy like the real One. Only the transcendental clone, the subject, can be the first cause, or indeed itself *is* it – but only qua clone. Radical is said of identity as an autonomous sphere or instance, precisely autonomous in a radical and not 'absolute' way; or of immanence insofar as it does not contain within it the least bit of transcendence (world or philosophy) and such that the radical 'precedes' radicalisation or determines it in-the-last-instance rather than being the product of its operation. Precisely because of its universality, radicality understood as that of the Real prohibits a new systematic thought and inaugurates a generic theory of philosophical systems (rather than a 'theoretical system', which is an abstract formula), a theoretical practice open to philosophical and scientific givens. In other words, vision-in-One announces the suspension of the validity of thought by 'principles', or acts as a 'radical' reduction of the philosophical or worldly stance, which are henceforth the same thing. The 'radical' style takes the 'principial' as its object, just as its axiomatic – cloned from the mathematical and purely transcendental – can take the mixed ontologico-mathematical axiomatic of philosophy as its object.

'Unilateral' no longer has any philosophical meaning, although philosophy has incessantly required it, but specifically as a foil, so as to identify it with the 'abstract', the 'dependent' and the 'incomplete'. If the philosophical concrete is always bi-lateral and perhaps even tri-lateral, thus adequately corresponding with the system as relative-absolute, the non-philosophical radical adequately expresses itself through unilateral dualities or, more rigorously, 'mixtures' (but not mélanges) of immanence and transcendence, which are both a priori and valid in-the-last-instance for philosophy. But don't dualities contradict the radicality of unilaterality? Its potential absoluteness, but not its radicality. In short, schematically, *the radical is the Real which (1) sometimes is lived as One without forming an all or a unity; (2) sometimes presents itself as a duality which (3) while fulfilling itself practically as unifacial or one-sided, is immediately interpretable, at least by philosophy, as one of these dualities of opposites which are the life and movement of the latter.* These dualities are unilateral due to their relative autonomy, due to the non-intervention of vision-in-One which determines them without amalgamating with them, and due to its indifference which has its 'negative' specific 'action' of indifference. 'Unilateral' has a double meaning that is not completely circular, because it can precisely only make a one-sided circle. It is said of the term of empirical origin 'against' the real One, against philosophy, and above all against the transcendental One or the subject with which it establishes a circle of objective appearance. It is also said as 'unilateralisation' which indifference, exercised by this transcendental One of the subject upon the empirical term, produces by combining itself with the autonomy of the latter.

Unilaterality is said not so much of the Real, which is but its negative condition, as of the dualities aroused by the occasional cause which is the philosophy-world. It is the minimum of relation or syntax tolerated by the transcendental One, signifying the suspension, if not the dismemberment, of philosophical syntaxes. It constitutes a new 'form of order' which no longer amalgamates priority (now assigned to the empirical term and its occasional intervention) with prior-to-priority (now assigned only to the Real, to the phenomenon which is always in-the-last-instance), and which therefore 'radically' dismantles philosophical hierarchies. For example, it is neither an internal, substantial and idealist relation, nor an external, logical and atomistic relation, but permits the elaboration of a 'unified theory' of external and internal relations, and thus (to jump forward a little) of 'Continental' philosophy and so-called 'Analytic' philosophy (of the predicative-transcendental style and the logical-propositional style, etc.). Here as elsewhere, however, it is possible to make a philosophical misuse of radicality, where the latter is no longer anything but an attribute of immanence instead of being its real essence; and of unilaterality, where this transcendental property cloned by the Real is confused with transcendence, which is of philosophical origin, and doubled.

As always, non-philosophy has no quarrel with any philosophical habitus as simple objective property of the 'phenomena', but for the remainder, i.e. the essentials of its stance, it is more than an ascesis, it is, if you will, the 'spirit of ascesis' that moves in the already-reduced before any reduction. It begins when it is forced to renounce certain facilities which all philosophers (not only contemporary philosophers) agree to define philosophically, and through an auto-cutting-out of that which critique or deconstruction should suspend or eliminate. It is therefore no longer dogmatism (Kant), representation (Hegel, Nietzsche, Heidegger), logocentrism (Derrida), i.e. the inferior and limited, inferior or metaphysical forms of philosophy, that it 'critiques', but instead what is most 'superior' in philosophy and is of a piece with its most representative forms. No matter what object or theme, from the most empirical to the most transcendental, it is indifferently valid for both object and material and that which deserves an a priori explanation, provided that it relies on philosophical-type thought or that it be philosophisable. To that end, it invents its own theoretical instruments in view of its main practice, which is precisely dualysis, the manifestation of the unilateral dualities that conceal themselves in every unitary concept of philosophy. Hence the organon of the force-(of)-thought acting upon these philosophical givens and inferring, identically through transcendental induction and deduction in accordance with the subject, these dualities which are new a prioris of generic origin. The substitution of generic theory for the philosophical system is decisive here, namely because it is a question of a transcendental theory, and thus of one that conserves an essential philosophical ingredient, but in reduced form.

The general form of its a priori explanation is this relation of unilateral duality which is the identity, a radical identity, (of) the reciprocal or bilateral relation of philosophy and the functional relation of science. From this point of view, non-philosophy first realises itself and exerts itself as what we call a unified theory of science and philosophy. It introduces (but under the reason-of-the-last-instance of vision-in-One) the scientific relation to objects into philosophy and the philosophical relation into science. More precisely, the transcendental One as clone of the Last Instance brings about the unification-without-synthesis of the transcendental relation to the phenomena proper to philosophy, and of the heterogeneous explanation to the supposedly 'in-itself' properties that belong to science, because *it conceives the Real in itself postulated by science as being in-the-last-instance phenomenon through and through, and because it conceives the phenomenon as in itself or real.*

A MYSTICAL KNOWLEDGE-(OF)-WORLD

To the widespread question: what is it to think?, non-philosophy responds that thinking is not 'thought', but performing, and that to perform is to clone the world 'in-Real'. Above all, it does not think the Real (that would be yet another philosophy) but is the minimal and the radical that ultimately oblige thinking and inventing, the most One-adequate thinking, adequate to the One's principal inadequation to the Real. Thinking the world according to the last or before-first One rather than according to the couplet of the One and Being, of the One and the Other; of the One insofar as its solitude is before any abstraction, outside these mélanges. In other words, a mystical knowledge of the world is here not a clinging to, but on the contrary a detachment from, the world.

The being-foreclosed of the real-One seems to render any thought impossible, but it only renders the claims of philosophy impossible. This is not because the real-One is open to every thought that presents itself to it, open rather than closed; it is because it has its own way of necessarily affecting thought by virtue of its very indifference. Yet this indifference no longer affects it through a direct operation and an objectifying activity that it merely receives passively. If identity truly remains in itself, in its radical inherence-(to)-self, without consequently passing through the double transcendence of philosophy, it cannot but 'affect' every thought insofar as it is its negative universal condition; or, any thought can only exist by being forced toward it or having to 'pass' in one way or another through its immanence, which it 'gathers up', if you will, through vision-in-One. Ordinarily, either the 'first principle' actively affects thought, or is actively affected by it or by the World, of which philosophy is the universal figure. But the One, not as a possibility but as reality, affects every active or passive possibility of thought. The being-foreclosed of the Real is paradoxically what 'opens' it to the World, or instead opens the World to it. Radically autonomous, or indifferent rather, in regard to the World; but precisely no more exclusive than inclusive of the World, no more turned toward it than turned away from it, simply because it is neither negation nor annihilation of the World and its predicates (Being, Thought) but foreclosed to the world, its 'negative' universal condition. It is paradoxical that a 'vision-in-One', so mystical in its essence but not in its objects, settles neither for any withdrawal outside the World nor for any exclusive contemplation of the One as divine. Here there is no longer an active, always transcendent, contemplation of the One. And if vision-in-One does indeed determine a mystical stance, it is a mysticism-(of)-World – and no less so, moreover, than a passive and lazy acceptance, like that of which philosophy can always be suspected due to its idealism.

Non-philosophical knowledge properly speaking – once the essential first terms are posited quasi-axiomatically – is of the order of an inference of the most universal theoretical structures, a priori structures that are valid for and that speak of, no longer a primary experience, but this new experience constituted by philosophy and science in their unitary separation, their unitary exclusion and synthesis ('epistemo-logical Difference'). Such an inference proceeds via induction and deduction, but transcendental induction and deduction. Therefore this is a radical phenomenalisation in-the-last-instance of philosophy in its a priori structures as well as a process involving scientific-type reasoning. Non-philosophy is nothing but the continuation of the vision-in-One at the core of philosophy and science through procedures that are identically scientific and philosophical. Ultimately, if non-philosophy complies with a theoretical and pragmatic interest, it is paradoxically a question of an interest in the World, i.e. philosophy, which gives it every possible form and which it transforms through its explanation.

Philosophy is interested in the World only via some withdrawal or difference, thus in a divided and deferred thought favourable to bad conscience and ressentiment. Instead, vision-in-One throws thought once every time, without deferral, to the World. There is no higher function than to explain, a priori, the World, i.e. the unity of the primary experience, of science and of philosophy. But the renunciation – for the positive reason of vision-in-One – of the culture of the metaphysical One, of the transcendental as supposedly real and first, is the condition for the emergence of a unilateral or 'unidirectional' thought attributed unreservedly to the World in this new sense. This renunciation of meta-physical hubris, of a divided or double thought, is thought according to the One. One of non-philosophy's implications is that man as vision-in-One is a generic subject rather than a metaphysical animal, consigned to philosophy for reasons of which he knows nothing.

THE FUNCTION AND RESISTANCE OF PHILOSOPHY

Let us broach the most unpleasant aspect of the relations between philosophy and non-philosophy: its reception through its resistance. There is nothing glorious in this, but it all merits an analysis. The place and function of philosophy are deduced exactly from the radicality of vision-in-One and the duality of the two causalities it requires: that of the real One as determination-in-the-last-instance and that of philosophy as occasional cause. Both are necessary, for heterogeneous reasons, for the production of non-philosophy. In particular, philosophy is simultaneously an object of experience or a field of objective properties and, owing to its basic sufficiency, a new 'expanded' concept of the world. The impression that philosophy plays an excessive role in non-philosophy stems from the fact that the functions of the former are now clearly defined and specified. Under the regime of the Principle of Sufficient Philosophy, philosophy incessantly refers to itself, but this interest in or concern for itself goes unnoticed or passes for natural, since it is not truly elucidated but merely practised naively or unconsciously. This simple difference, however, is still insufficient: it is clear that philosophy is far more decisive and important for itself under the regime of sufficiency, than it is for non-philosophy once the Principle is suspended. The objection according to which non-philosophy overvalues philosophy or has not invented its 'own' language would be laughable were it not the direct expression of philosophy's resistance. And this is the case in all possible instances.

Indeed, when this objection comes from militant philosophers, it sometimes means that they no longer want philosophy at all, or that they imagine that the project of non-philosophy is a putting to death and a radical overcoming of philosophy; sometimes it demonstrates that they regard non-philosophy as 'still' (despite their own objection) and 'basically' philosophy, and as crudely self-contradictory. These two forms of the objection comprise a system and echo one another in the circular service of resistance; they form a philosophical antinomy because resistance can only operate under the antinomian form on the grounds of a global refusal or foreclosure of the identity-(of)-philosophy. The debility of these objections, in all its unfathomable depth, is ascertained quite precisely whenever they are concentrated in the accusation of 'philosophical parasitism' – as if the physicist, for example, were the parasite of the object she studies, the parasite of 'particles'. Here too, the sufficient philosopher, who is content with consummating philosophy by producing its minimum – remaining especially preoccupied with reproducing its consummation even when she produces works, being effectively parasitical upon tradition, living on and from Plato or Hegel or Nietzsche – projects onto non-philosophy her bad conscience and ressentiment. If there is an ultimate residue of 'parasitism' in non-philosophy, then it stems from this basic philosophical parasitism, but with the benefit of its transformation, such that the non-philosopher is kept from practising a simple retaliation. But the argument from resistance possesses an even more comical form: non-philosophy does not invent

its own concepts, its own language? Either there is a reading error, a dyslexia before the non-philosophical text,
whose labour of syntax, conceptualisation and above all
formation of a new vocabulary is not perceived; or there is
a fetishisation of the word, that is held to be either ancient
or new – a logocentric illusion, if ever one existed, of the
ex nihilo creation of the words of philosophy. When it is
known that philosophical language at every level is but
natural and common language reworked, functioning
under a regime of 'superior' meaning, it must again be
proclaimed that philosophy is in a far less favourable
stance for what is called inventing a new language than
is non-philosophy. Even what, to all appearances, owes to
the idiosyncrasy of its author – a conceptual concentra-
tion and over-determination felt to be excessive – also
finds in the non-philosophical style of thought and its
usage of the concept a reason and a justification, neither
of which is absolute.

Now, when the objection comes from the side of the
direct neighbours of non-philosophy – certain users of
radical immanence – it bears witness to a misunderstanding of the precise meaning of the endeavour, a misunderstanding that grafts itself onto philosophical resistance,
which finds therein one last trick. The main axiom of non-
philosophy can be formulated in entirely quasi-Kantian
terms (nevertheless remaining not anti-Kantian but simply
non-Kantian): if immanence is truly radical, if it is truly an

identity, then it must be, as much as the 'thing in itself', but not in the same way (through immanence rather than through transcendence) absolutely devoid of any determinations or predicates other than its identity, which is not a simple predicate in its essence or its content alone, but identity through and through. Consequently, immanence is not inner sense, neither internal transcendental experience nor any other depth that would be attributed to the One. In order to describe immanence, on the other hand, one cannot avoid using philosophical models such as that of the internal, and eventually scientific ones; but they must be used precisely as mere models of an axiomatic, and no longer as predicates. These models are no longer 'anthropologies' (Leibniz) or 'metaphors', but ought to be called 'philosophies' in which the concept is required only insofar as it is material to be reworked according to exact rules, and as a support for non-philosophical a prioris. By ignoring the duality of the Real, or more exactly that of its clone and its positing/givenness – a duality in which the former determines-in-the-last-instance the latter – one slips imperceptibly into philosophy and its prejudices, and again into amphiboly, mixture and every philosophical teleology. It is inevitable that such a transcendental appearance (re)constitutes itself and that non-philosophy is put back into circulation alongside philosophy, re-established on the philosophical scene, upon which it must then cut a sad figure.

To summarise these considerations touching upon the situation of non-philosophy within an intense philosophical milieu:

1. In the eyes of philosophy, non-philosophy has only a single fault, which is not 'theoretical': the fault of existing. There are neither objections nor responses to objections; there is a resistance, and there is an a priori defence against non-philosophy.

2. In the eyes of non-philosophy, philosophy possesses the merit of existing but the fault of concluding from existence to the Real.

THE PHILOSOPHICAL PROHIBITION OF IDENTITY AND CLONING

Thinking is the clone of the Real, but precisely not *as* the Real or any part of it. Cloning is no longer the active operation of a duality or binary fission, a division, but is instead vision-in-One, as One itself, (of) thought or of an Other, extracting a clone from it: not a double of thought or the One itself, but a (transcendental) identity that is said of thought or is related to it as its occasional cause. Here cloning is itself differentiated: if the One clones thought in the form of the transcendental One, then philosophy is also cloned by it in the form of unilateral dualities, the essence of which is identity. In this sense, philosophy is cloned in the form of a unilateral identity, insofar as it is reproduced under conditions of philosophical repetition, i.e. under conditions that exclude Difference. The transcendental One is the originary clone, the essence of empirical clones that are of regional or fundamental origin. Cloning is a biotechnological procedure that seems to threaten human identity but really threatens only the difference – particularly (but not only) sexual difference – that is supposed to define the essence of man. It could be that non-philosophical cloning, although extremely different, is also entirely 'prohibited' by philosophy, i.e. by the supposed 'difference' of the essence of man. Either non-philosophy will sink with all hands into the philosophical indifference to which resistance will turn; or it will have circumvented a covert barrier, namely the prohibition of identity, which is as essential to philosophy as the prohibition of incest and cloning is to societies. This is what lends a profundity and a seriousness to philosophical resistance – to resistance and misunderstanding. For clearly, from non-philosophy's point of view, incest and the bad identity of difference, the lack of true heterogeneous duality, are, on philosophy's side, powerless to think identity and duality in their radicality. Cloning is the surest destruction of the image of thought, of the procedures of projection and reflection at the heart of 'representation', processes from which philosophy has never been able release itself, captivated

as it is by the transcendental imagination even once it has
escaped from the empirical image.

THE INCREDIBLE CLAIMS OF NON-PHILOSOPHY

Philosophers, who love rashness, i.e. sufficient reason, also
love to have the last word; non-philosophy would refuse
'discussion' or 'dialogue' and shatter the consensus that
founds the community of thinkers and even the essence
of thought itself.

1. What thinker, whoever it may be, would not want
to shatter the consensus that is always that of ancient
thought, that of the old normalising alliance? Who does
not thank Freud for having shattered the consensus of
the psychologists and philosophers?

2. What concept is more oppressive or suffocating than
that of consensus? Consensus is the lazy and hackneyed
argument of contemporaries (even the notions of 'demo-
cratic discussion' and 'communication'), the de facto sanc-
tification of the state, as well as that of the institutional
normalisation and fetishisation of thought. Philosophers
who invoke such arguments clearly do so out of weariness
at the struggle, renouncing their single-handed maintenance of the sullied honour of philosophy. They do nothing but reveal the sophistical and opportunistic resources
of philosophy, its cultural and institutional bases.

3. Contemporary philosophy, which begins with the 'linguistic turn' and its different modes, has added a fifth question to the four Kantian ones, because it has not responded satisfactorily to man's question: *about what can I speak* (and not simply *what can I think*)? Clearly, it has thereby only revealed an originary possibility of philosophy. But discussion and communication, ordered up to this point by the will to science, have unleashed themselves as the will to speak and have given rise to a micropolitics of speech which is the low point of thought, the point at which philosophy dissolves itself into its own doxic and linguistic nature and cannot resist the temptations of its essence. Against this congenital decline of philosophy – a decline which is neither its 'death' nor its 'end' – non-philosophy opposes not the beginning of a new philosophical position, but the undertaking of a unified theory of science and philosophy, unified under minimal conditions.

Philosophy and Non-Philosophy

(1991)

Translated by Anthony Paul Smith and Nicola Rubczak

The expression 'non-philosophy' can take on two complementary meanings.[14]

In its widest conception, it is a new distribution of the relations between science, philosophy and thought, a distribution established on the basis of distinctions and definitions that are no longer of philosophical origin but which, strictly speaking, we must call scientific. We will explain why. In its narrowest conception, it is a new practice – precisely, a scientific practice – of philosophy, which is thereby relieved of its own authority.

---

14 On the foundation of non-philosophy and its practice, the reader is referred to the preceding 'Letters' [in *En tant qu'Un* (Paris: Aubier, 1991)] and above all to my *Philosophie et non-philosophie* (Liège/Brussels, Mardaga: 1989).

Broadly speaking, non-philosophy registers a twofold discovery regarding the traditional claims of philosophy: 1. *Thought* – as distinct from understanding – is not the privilege of philosophy; there is an authentic and specific thought *in* science, a thought whose form is in fact completely different from consciousness, reflection, meditation, a form that is, in particular (but not only), 'axiomatic' (meaning: anapodictic, irreversible and proceeding via invariant identities); 2. Access to the *real*, to the ultimate and absolute essence, is no longer the privilege of philosophy. In and through science, there is an experience of the *last* instance of the real or absolute, qua *intrinsically finite or immanent*, precisely in so far as science also comprises a *thinking* and not only a stock of knowledge. This specific real of science is characterised by its radical immanence, without relation or transcendence (...of transcendence). It may be called the One, and is completely distinct from the Being that is the principal object of philosophy. In its essence, science offers the experience of thought outside of the limitations of Being. This thought-correlate of the One takes the form of a mathesis distinct from every ontology or metaphysics. And since it is a real or transcendental discipline, it is also distinct from logical axiomatics and not just from the transcendental logics that constitute so many philosophies. In any case, it demands a thoroughgoing correction of the Greek and ontological concept of the One: this is what we call the 'vision-in-One', for which transcendence (Perception, Reason, Language, Representation, World, Being, etc.) is no longer constitutive, but functions merely as *occasional cause*.

This is the 'minimal' and positively 'minoritarian' form of thought. Concealed by philosophy – by the thesis that transcendence is co-constitutive of the real – it must be exposed and systematically described in its effects: for example, in the refusal of the *philosophical* distinctions between philosophy and science, sense and nonsense, reflection and operatory technoscience, etc. It has become possible to overturn that traditional distribution, made by philosophy for its own profit, by making thought, in its new conception, slide from philosophy toward science. Although the bringing to light of this thinking grounded in the One – and thus by its nature at once experimental and axiomatic, but in a transcendental and no longer a logical mode – is not undertaken against philosophy, but against its claim to the absolute real, a claim now consigned to the sphere of transcendental illusion.

In a stricter sense, 'non-philosophy' designates the new response, thus rendered possible and grounded, to that which must be called the 'labyrinth of philosophy'. If reason, as Leibniz remarked, is put to the test by the labyrinth of the continuum and that of predestination, thought is put to the test by the labyrinth par excellence that is philosophy. Regardless of the attempts at a 'rationalist' solution, involving the closure or the suture of Philosophical Decision onto some constituted field of knowledge, philosophy has ceaselessly (and now more than ever) tested itself, like a thought in a state of unease, circular and aporetic, vicious and amphibological, amalgamating impossible contraries, affirming its incoherence as a new coherence, refusing the self-dislocation toward which it nevertheless tends. For two-and-a-half-thousand years, this thought has ceaselessly fired off its vain pyrotechnics, paralysed itself in the 'grammar' of its Greek decision; it has obfuscated every search for a thought more rigorous and free. So do we need some new critique or therapeutics? Not at all: philosophy has no need for this injunction to take care of itself – it is already this care of the self. Only a thought whose origin is other than ontological constitutes the appropriate treatment for this aporia in action. Non-philosophy is the 'scientific' treatment, through rigour and reality, of the labyrinth of philosophy – the solution brought to bear on this infinite (and no doubt indestructible) predicament of thought, but the only treatment that respects this difficulty completely while preserving the possibility of a 'thought' that otherwise risks disappearance, between understanding and reflection. The science of philosophy, its thought-in-One, a real rather than a logical operation, is the means by which thought leaves the labyrinth, which is to say the means by which it recognises that it never entered into it.

We shall lay out a brief parallel between philosophy and non-philosophy, of that which we call, on the one hand, *Philosophical Decision* and, on the other, *vision-in-One*.

1. *Injunction or drive*? Philosophy is the unitary and authoritarian style in thought, a style of the injunction or of the question posed by the Other. A Greek injunction ('take into care beings as a whole') or a Jewish one ('keep care for the other as for a brother'). Thinking by way of a motto: that which we *must* think, do, hope. That supercategorical injunction defines a duty to philosophise, and a tradition; it is an authoritarian thought that does not know the real as given, but only the *supposedly given*, and demands that we believe in it: a philosophical faith and a residue of mythology.

Non-philosophy is the style of the inner drive of thinking in thought. Rather than duty and calling, it is immanence as sole internal rule, it is the force-(of)-thought that remains in itself even in its efficacy. Far from responding to an injunction or corresponding to a call from the Other, it is a stance [*postural*]. It grounds itself in the given (immanence) rather than the supposedly given (the transcendence and mythology of rational facts and language); within the finitude of the real-One, that without which thought would be irreal and evacuated, would be mythology.

2. *Linguistic bondage or freedom?* Philosophy is the idea that language is not merely an object, but is co-constitutive of

the real – and thus of philosophy. Philosophy amalgamates language with the real-One and attributes to it an a priori and transcendental pertinence – it is the Logos as the original linguistic turn of thought. There is no philosophy that does not organise itself according to a double articulation that reproduces in 'superior' form the linguistic form of the latter. One half of philosophy doubtless consists in a transcendental topology, but its other half is a transcendental linguistics, even when it ignores the problem of language.

Non-philosophy suspends that constitutive claim of language, and recognises language only as conditional condition, as an element that is necessary only *if* a description of the real is attempted, but which does not amalgamate with it; an element that represents the real in a non-speculative and non-constitutive manner. It frees itself from contemporary textualism and, in general, from philosophical prestige, through an occasionalist conception of language (of syntax, textuality, etc.). For, when taken in hand by philosophy, language becomes the element of all injunctions and the heaven of all mythologies. Whence the complaint of philosophy: we lack words (Heidegger), syntax (Russell, Heidegger), grammar (Wittgenstein), writing (Derrida). The call-to-language turns back on itself, as a call-from-language. For non-philosophy, on the contrary, language is in excess, something more, but not as an Other; it is not constitutive of the real, but is the occasion of a mere representation; flung back from the real toward the knowledge that represents it without constituting it.

3. *Thinking = amalgamating or identifying?* Philosophy, although it is more than this, is thus always an exterior image, specular and then speculative, of the relation between thought and the real. To think is to alloy and temper contraries, one by the other (the universal and the singular, for example). It annihilates them as terms by dividing or crossing them out, then by doubling or repeating the one with the other. Philosophy inhibits or paralyses terms or individuals, it cuts out what it can from force-(of)-thought by dissolving it in alloys, mixtures and doublets.

Non-philosophy is the exercise of purely internal or real-identical force-(of)-thought, with no transcendence or image, except an occasional one. It goes from the real to that which it is not (representation); from the given to the supposedly given, by transforming it in turn into an adequate representation of the given. So one term is thought through another? Doubtless – on condition of conserving the asymmetry in the causality, not transforming the 'through' into 'each through the other' or 'reciprocal determination'. To think is no longer to amalgamate the universal and the singular, but to assemble universal representations as functions of the 'individual' real or so as to represent it *in the last instance alone*. The rules of that assembly are the rules of non-philosophical practice.

4. *Appropriation or liberation of the sciences?* Philosophy carries out a threefold operation with regard to the sciences: (*i*) *appropriation of constituted knowledge*, produced by the sciences, which philosophy needs and from which it draws a surplus-value of authority and reality; (*ii*) *resistance to all properly scientific thought*, for which it substitutes itself; (*iii*) *unitary- or hierarchical-type unification* of science – which it exploits as knowledge and represses as thought – and of the philosophy which dominates it.

Non-philosophy, as a specific thought of/in science, is characterised by a wholly other approach: (*i*) it *lets be* knowledge and its object without appropriating them to itself through philosophical-type objectification. It places between itself and knowledge a duality that is open and free, never reappropriative or teleologically closed by a mode of objectivation or by transcendence in general; (*iii*) it *suspends* philosophy's claim over the real *without claiming to intervene* in philosophy and dismember it, as philosophy does with science; (*iii*) it is a *unified, not unitary, theory* of the fields of thought: it proceeds via a duality-in-contingency rather than via appropriation, integration, or hierarchisation. The placement of knowledges within the universal space of theory suspends only the hierarchy-form, and lets them be as knowledges without ordering them according to philosophical finalities. A unified theory of philosophy and science proceeds by letting-be their *identity*, by avoiding hybridisation and confusion. Science is a thinking thought that remains within the immanence of its exercise and recognises the *identity* of knowledge *as such*. For example, we shall oppose *axiomatic freedom* to the givenness of philosophical meaning and to violent operations of the same type (reflection, subsumption, supersumption, differentiation, mediation, etc.).

5. *Unitary generalisation or axiomatic generalisation?* Philosophy is universal (*i*) through its *addition* of the principles of experience, through the supplement of alterity and universality: the General and the Total, Being, the World, Reason, Language, Desire; (*ii*) in its *passing* from the empirical to that ideal generality: idealisation or even abstraction, the conquest of ideal neighbourhoods, the passage from a mode to the universal attribute and to the essence; (*iii*) through its *division* of the singular or of the determined by means of that plane or that universal instance; (*iv*) through its integration, subsumption, etc. of this determined to that instance; (*v*) through its idealisation and conservation (regardless of various continuous transformations) of empirical, perceptual and linguistic intuitivity.

Non-philosophy universalises in a completely other way: (*i*) The universal precedes universalisation and can not be added to experience as a supplement. It is contingent experience, universal in a 'gregarious' mode, which adds itself to that which is from the start, by its One-essence, the true 'individu-el' (-al) instance;[15] (*ii*) it neither idealises nor transcends experience; instead, inversely, it *reduces* every essence or ideality to the state, if not of a 'mode', at least of an 'occasion', every attribute to the state of a mere given or philosophically inert material; (*iii*) it manifests the very *identity* of the singular *as such* without dividing it – or rather, it does not begin by dividing it in order to manifest it; (*iv*) it determines or singularises universal representations and orders them according to the invidue(/a)l real rather than the inverse; (*v*) as axiomatic, it frees itself from empirical, perceptual and linguistic intuitivity, and transforms it in a heteronomous or discontinuous manner by putting it in the service of the representation of the real-One. Axiomatic or non-philosophical universalisation runs contrary to the despotic or unitary universalisation of philosophy.

6. *Complexity: through splitting or through simplicity?* Philosophy proceeds via (*i*) division/doubling, scission/ redoubling; the interminable proliferation of vicious circularities, of mixtures, doublets or alloys; a pullulation of linguistico-philosophical artefacts; (*ii*) a complexification

---

15 [Laruelle is here playing on the two different meanings of 'duality' that are available to him in French and inserted into 'individuel/al'. The two forms of duality are markers of standard philosophy, where there is a 'duel' or opposition of one term with another, and non-philosophy, where there is a strict duality of identity between constitutive and accidental conflicts indicative of philosophy and the One as individual. Cf. Rocco Gangle's translator's introduction to François Laruelle, *Philosophies of Difference: A Critical Introduction to Non-Philosophy* (New York/London: Continuum, 2010), xi-xii – trans.]

of the already complex (where the simple is a metaphysical optical illusion); (*iii*) re-division of the amalgam of the universal (-singular); (*iv*) extension (at worst), intensification (at best); (*v*) continued fabrication of mythologies (Being, Reason, Language, Duty, Desire, etc.).

Non-philosophy proceeds via (*i*) manifestation of the simple or the (One) Identity as such before every doublet; criticism of every philosophical complexity in the name of the simple that is really simple (without transcendence) and is no longer metaphysical; (*ii*) an irreversible causality of simple identity over the philosophical complex, real identity over the artefacts; (*iii*) universalisation grounded on the 'individual' who is the true universal; (*iv*) given-manifestation in a really infinite space of understanding, devoid of the teleological closures that accompany extension and intensification; (*v*) production of free axiomatic enunciations, of rigorous fictions that know themselves to be real and freed from all philosophical mythology.

If philosophy is the culture of the Same and of difference as the Same, non-philosophy is the thought of Identity that precedes the Same and Difference.

Non-Philosophy as Heresy

(1998)

Translated by Taylor Adkins

De deux opinions et de leur différence
Trois mots feront par tout le vrai département
Des contraires raisons: seul, seule et seulement[16]
AGRIPPA D'AUBIGNÉ, *LES TRAGIQUES*, CHANT V

Presenting non-philosophy in a somewhat external way, through its effects, we shall say that it is the solution to two problems that the practice of philosophy poses but to which it has never responded without attempting to bias the outcome. The first problem is the programme of a critique that is 'complete', i.e. leaves no presupposition uncritiqued or theoretically undefined. Distributed amongst conflicting systems, parcelled out to the exact extent that it is left to the attentions of 'professional' philosophers, divided internally to the point of being

---

16   [Of two opinions and their difference
    Three words will give the true deviation
    Of contrary reasons: sole, alone, only.]

implicated or compromised in its own critique, it is inevitable that its reproduction prevails over its production, its repetition over its renovation. Its auto-critique leaves it intact in what is essential, i.e. in itself, soliciting nothing but external objects. The duration of a philosophy's active life is extraordinarily short, ephemeral; a philosophy is barely born before it is old enough to die. Consequently, it ensures its survival through its tradition and its institutionalisation, through the heroism of the will and ongoing magic tricks, by means of which it ceaselessly reinforces, more systematically through its perpetual redoubling, the production of the doublets that only signify its weakness and its precariousness, compensated for by sufficiency. It exhausts itself in the research and culture of its own possibilities, from the most elevated or most auto-critical to the basest and most nihilistic, from auto-affirmation to auto-negation (the post-metaphysical, the post-philosophical, etc.). Its most secret mechanism is repetition in the origin, albeit dissimulated in the name of difference, that repetition which is the auto-potentialisation and affirmation of (the will to) power and force. Only the formulation here is Nietzschean; the concept is universally philosophical. Non-philosophy is the motivated, positive and founded refusal, as far as possible, to enter into this revolving door. But only on the dual condition of expanding and identifying philosophy as 'thought-world', the only thought that 'makes' world, and of being given the

conditions of going to the end of philosophy's constitutive repetition, without denying its concept, thus *forcing
it into simplicity*. So we see that non-philosophy will not
define itself by new themes or objects but by a new style
of thought for 'any' philosophical object 'whatsoever'.
In order to make it pass from the doublet to the state
of simple thought, it is no longer possible to leave it to
itself; it is necessary to determine it and transform it into
the object of a thought according-to-the-real, which we
wager is simple or without doublet, is 'One', i.e. non-
exchangeable with philosophy. But the real as One, what
can this mean?

The second problem: that of a human subject *for*
philosophy but one which is not implicated in it, a
subject capable of setting conditions for it rather than
the other way around, and thus limiting its sufficiency.
The two problems merge in this question: what is the
subject of 'Philosophy', i.e. of its identity rather than of its
separate pieces in the form of systems at once individual
and sedimented in a tradition? How to place it under a
determining condition? Non-philosophy is a theory of the
real subject for philosophy, but a theory that represents
in itself a certain rigorous practice of its object. Without
at all neglecting the traditions that serve as its materials,
it is thoroughly non-traditionalist – this goes without
saying – and even 'non-traditional' in the sense that we
understand this 'non-', namely as cumulating the forces of

what we call heresy rather than the false, the non-power of *hairesis* rather than the powers of *pseudos*.

Until now, the critique of philosophy has never been universal, has never been applied to the subject that receives and thinks it, but only to a subject implicated in it. It has always been split between auto-critique and hetero-critique, between metaphysics and philosophy, between a subject who produces it and a subject who consumes it, between scientific rigour and a vision of the world, logical positivity and thinking thought, etc., and more recently between the Greek logos and a 'Judaic affect' which has been as decisive for the twentieth century as the 'linguistic turn'. Divided between 'end' and 'return to …', between post-(metaphysics) and neo-(Aristotelianism, Platonism, Kantianism, etc.), it is not content with arranging here and there the military and commercial frontiers, the demarcations that territorialise thought and bring about veritable transferences of conceptual technology. It is a system of appropriations and delimitations, but in principle always divided from itself. This particular philosophical division of labour is fundamental, but can be overdetermined by more localised oppositions and divisions. In its spontaneous practice, it produces images of itself, sometimes naive in their sufficiency and loftiness ('strong philosophy'), sometimes desolate with superficiality ('pop-philosophy').

A universal critique of philosophy valid for all its divisions and decisions first implies, in a preparatory way, that its problem be posed in all its generality, in the universality of its practices and forms, and consequently lifted above the particular interests of professional philosophers or 'systems'. What concept could thus envelop and structurally span Philosophical Decision on this side of the inter-systemic wars? We posit the following hypothesis to be developed, nuanced and tested, which formulates the structure of Philosophical Decision (the triangle Dyad-Unity) in a new way: philosophy is the capital-form in thought. We do not say that the Marxist account is necessarily pertinent to capitalism, but that it 'fits' and is effective for philosophy. The capital-form here is connected with the commodity-form, and constitutes the other face of the division-form of thought. Thus defined, it is universally valid for all particular philosophical decisions. It is articulated according to a duality of phenomena which combine – this is its identity of division – into a single structure. The first of these levels is in some sense its base: this is the duality or dyad of the opposed concepts through which it commences, the site of its reciprocity or convertibility (according to the type of philosophy concerned), i.e. the exchange-form or marketplace of concepts. The second level is that of the One of the dyad or Identity, which itself has two faces: (1) What might be called the philosophical division of labour, not between the dyad, site of exchange or market of concepts and the superior instance that regulates this exchange, but inside the latter, divided between the production or the market of concepts in which it participates and the appropriation of this conceptual production. (2) This instance presents itself as unique (even if it only functions through the division that it is) and precisely as an appropriation of a share of the conceptual production. Beyond particular systems and their reciprocal critiques, which are merely symptoms of this malaise, the true dimension of philosophy and its 'malaise' is that, obviously without being a simple capitalist phenomenon in the historical and social sense of this word, it is at least homologous with it and represents capitalism and the consumption of surplus value within the organisation of thought.

In turn, the philosophical market has at least a triple form: (1) The internal market of philosophy, the exchanges of concepts, critiques, arguments and techniques among professional philosophers, the whole ideal life of philosophy, with its advances and regressions, its 'new philosophies' and its 'reactivating returns' to ... (2) A second, relatively closed market, but which indirectly underwrites the first: the academic and institutional market of philosophy and its teaching and transmission, a market that has been around since Plato and Pythagoras and whose main function is to normalise, through the experts of 'thought' who control it, a median (albeit very erudite) and transmissible philosophy, later to be purchased by the State and distributed as 'thought-providence' or providence of thought. (3) Finally, more and more active and solvent, the mediatised market of philosophy, which seems opposed to the second but in fact is of a piece with it. Its span reaches from the small-scale commerce of 'ideas' (philosophy cafés, debates) to the exchange-network (Internet), which is drawn on equally by institutional and mediatised users of philosophy by way of the vague approximations of a personal and capricious 'professional critique'. The univocity of the structure of Philosophical Decision as market and division of labour allows it no longer to be abused by these three markets' specific claims of 'originality', of 'seriousness' and of 'popularity'. It gives a universal concept of the field of philosophy that implies its identity as divided. It is all the less divided in a simply external way because it includes or 'programmes' the division of philosophy as constitutive of the latter. It is thus as a philosophical concept that it considers itself 'universal'.

This hypothesis, evidently rather schematic, nevertheless allows a new formulation of philosophy and perhaps at the same time an indication toward the attempt to resolve one of the classical aporias of Marxism. On the one hand, philosophy is the heterogeneous duality of the Dyad (the market) and the One-(of)-division, of capital as division of labour; and on the other hand, their unity in capital, in the use it makes of the market with which it should not be conflated, but with which it is involved, being connected with it: distinct but inseparable. According to Marxist interpretation, capital is inseparable from the division of labour without which it does not exist, but it is furthermore said of the totality that this division re-forms with 'commodity' production when it is appropriated. A nuance is thus introduced which leads us toward the sense of universality we seek: we shall say that philosophy is on the one hand the necessary market of concepts, of their more or less reversible exchanges; that it is on the other hand 'capital' or division of labour of thought; and finally that it is the appropriation of this labour of conceptual exchange and production, to the profit of its identity – its capital – as philosophy. *This capture of its own identity through philosophy itself, we shall call capitalism; but also 'thought-world', so as to give it – since it is precisely a question of philosophy, not of history and society – its full extent.* The structure of Philosophical Decision gives the broadest extent and the real meaning, which develops its cosmopolitical dimension, of philosophy as 'thought-world'.

We all know that philosophy is not any thought whatsoever, that it is partially contingent, no doubt – but that it has found out how to acquire a necessity and a universality that completely surpasses its practical, institutional or geo-philosophical ('occidental') limitations. But why this universality and this necessity? We do not know, any more than we can really explain the universality and necessity of capitalism. An important theoretical step along the path of this explanation is taken when Marx discovers the correlation of the universal commodity structure and the division of labour that spans history. Perhaps it is possible to take a similar step in philosophy, when we note that it has essentially the same internal macro-structure as capitalism, and that 'Philosophical Decision', under which we formalise the philosophical gesture, is the correlation of a universal structure of exchange between notions and a divided unity that participates in this exchange, yet exceeds and appropriates it. It matters little (this is another, more empirical problem) which generated which, or which is traced from the other.

This is the object of a new practice of critique: the thought-world with its philosophical and theological avatars. Any position internal to philosophy, and above all to the doublet that philosophy is, cannot explain thought expanded in this way and understood as world, but in general can be understood through it. The task is then no longer to seek a first or last possibility of philosophy that it has not yet developed. It is even less to participate in its mediatised nadir, its becoming-opinion. A completely different type of decision is necessary 'against' the thought-world, a decision as unknown to the philosophical discourse of the Ancients as it is to the Moderns and

Postmoderns, and which does not rely upon the dominant twentieth-century opposition between Greek and Jew. However, this type of 'decision', which is no longer the classical line of demarcation of the frontier, discovers its choicest employment in religion. This possibility, neither first nor last nor even simply other, has received the Greek name of 'heresy'.

Heresy is formally distinct from the various types of decision with which it tends to be confused. But it is capable of making possible their genealogy without being by definition commutable with them. Our project is now clearer and we shall gladly call it 'generic' rather than 'philosophical'. The generic style of thought operates with two variables, the strictly philosophical and another variable, scientific in the best case, religious in others – religious in the form of this precise 'limit' notion of religious all-encompassingness, heresy. But far from juxtaposing these variables, it multiplies their reciprocal relations through one of them as a factor, and precisely here through heresy. Hence the most precise definition of the generic such as we understand it is the fusion or unity of philosophy and religious heresy under heresy or determined by a heretical regime. It will therefore be necessary to distinguish meticulously the philosophical doublet from the apparent repetition of heresy as variable and as factor.

What relation can there be between non-philosophy and heresy? The preceding 'critical' motivation of non-philosophy is still partially driven by the spirit of philosophy. If non-philosophy takes its material from philosophy, it takes its principle – its cause rather, and its general style – from a stance we shall call purely heretical or heretical *as such* so as to distinguish it from the specified historical forms of heresy. Non-philosophy has 'occasional' philosophical causes or origins, but in principle it is not any kind of philosophical position whatsoever. It is the response to the following question (itself not especially philosophical): what are the conditions of heresy? Not of religious, scientific or artistic heresy, but pure heresy and its emergence? And is it a question of introducing the spirit of heresy into philosophy – into philosophy where there are torsions, reflections, deformations and deviations, but no heresy? It is not a question of replaying the 'philodrama' of the moderns and the postmoderns, of leading philosophy back to its limits, its limitrophic alterity, margins and decentrings, to its death or its 'end', etc., of restaging the spectacle of the Greco-Judaic conflict – but of introducing a heretical variable into the generic relation to philosophy.

It is impossible to resolve these problems without recourse to this thought, this most incisive thought, when confronted with philosophy, the most enveloping philosophy; nor without defining pure heresy as non-philosophy rather than specifically non-phenomenology, non-Marxism, etc. How do we give heresy its concept and the form of a rigorous thought? In the first place, it must no longer designate the deviant quality of a scientific theory or a religious interpretation, the errancy and unorthodoxy of a doctrine – it must no longer be a critical or insulting attribute, instead being elaborated and treated as a consistent, autonomous manner of thinking possessing an internal essence that can be ascribed to nothing else. It is not even a question of introducing the concept of heresy into philosophy, but of directly constituting it through non-philosophy. One can be 'heretical' in art, in religion, in science; this is a formula of doxa, but what is the identity of heresy as such? This problem is barely philosophical save through the objective appearance of language, because it is the answer that contains the question, rather than the other way around: *the identity of heresy is that identity is heresy itself or 'in-person'*. This is a tautology – is it some kind of joke? Precisely not: this formulation is still incomplete, and the doubling or vicious circle that it seems to manifest is precisely a philosophical type of response, this tautology tolerating several nuances and differences in identity. To be called non-philosophical, the formulation must be completed: *identity is the cause-in-the-last-instance of heresy; heresy is the thought and practice according to the cause-in-the-last-instance*. In this way, the answer contains the question or determines it –

but only in the last-instance. The discovery that founds both non-philosophy and pure heresy, the former as the latter and reciprocally, is that identity is not simply the object of heresy, but that real identity is its cause – that heresy is thought in-identity and according-to-identity. It suffices to think strictly in accordance with the most naked identity, the identity most deprived of being, meaning and transcendence, the least convertible, to 'make' heresy, secession and dissidence – the only dissidence whose cessation can be nothing but a vain hope, illusion or faith ... all of which would be philosophical. If, for example, heresy is understood as a radical form of alterity, it is immediately necessary to specify that the heretical Other, unlike the Judaic Other, is all the 'more other' in that it is itself determined by a special, philosophically 'impossible' cause, what we call the Real as *vision-of-the-One-in-One*, a concept whose elaboration requires much more attention because of its very simplicity.

As abuse, accusation and condemnation, heresy is an eminently indeterminate and vague term. As a 'philosophical' or 'Greek' concept, it already tends to exceed philosophical authority, signifying separation with unity itself, dissidence-without-return. But even more radically, no longer being a relation to philosophy except 'in-the-last-reference', heresy complicates itself; it breaks the symmetry of the doublet separated-separation, for it is less separation for separation than the Separated without the act of separation that would generate a duality, a multiplicity even. The real kernel of heresy is the One separated *with* the One-All itself, without thereby constituting a mode more or less distant from this All or from Unity. But, furthermore, the act of separation is not denied – or is only denied in the doublet that it forms, for its part, with the Separated. Overall, the Separated acquires its autonomy, frees itself from separation, which also frees itself from itself or from its doublet; and the former determines or under-determines the latter. Heresy is sterile, but in what sense? It is not the 'first' or once again philosophical separation, but the 'before-first', which generates nothing, but which is itself generated without separation by the Separated. Since separation is generated by being-Separated-without-separation, it is as such or in turn consists in its separation-identity. On the other hand, albeit first, it is 'second' in relation to the absolutely first All from which it separates. The Separated is radically first, the All self-implied by philosophy is absolutely first, and finally separation is relative either to the Separated or to the All according to the angle from which it is seen. The philosophically unintelligible character of separation stems from the fact that it does not double itself, that it has no need of an anterior separation – but of a being-Separated-without-separation – and that it does not divide the All.

Given the axioms of pure heresy (the principle of heresy):

• The Separated-without-separation has the primacy of-the-last-instance over separation.

• Separation, determined-in-the-last-instance by the Separated, has primacy over the decision implied in the All (World).

• The Separated-without-separation is not as such because it is self-Inseparate.

• The self-Inseparate or the Separated-without-separation is uni-versal in an immanent (generic) way, not universal in and through transcendence.

• The doublet of the separated and separation is transformed. No longer being a division of the One but the One-(of)-separation, it becomes a unilateral, unequal, non-reciprocal duality.

• We call vision-in-One the determination-in-the-last-instance of the World (All) by the Separated or the heretical.

Consequences: (1) The One is not inseparate from the World. On the contrary, being self-Inseparate, it is, *for its part*, separated from the World which can do neither anything for nor against it. But it is at the same time inseparate from the World – if there is World – in the immanence of its being-Inseparate. It is separated from the World within the inseparability of the World with it, thus for the World's part. This is what we call 'unilateral duality' or the heretical form of thought or even uni-versal ('generic') vision-in-One as pure heresy. Pure heresy is not the direct givenness of the World but being-given-without-givenness which nevertheless gives or brings the World.

(2) Pure heresy is neither the weak nor the extreme 'Alterity' that contemporary philosophy traces cheaply either from the worldly experience of the Stranger or from the religious All-Other, and which has taken twenty-five centuries to discover and explore. It is Identity as self-Inseparate without an act of separation, presenting itself to the World as inseparate separation, i.e. uniface. Radical Identity is alogical and presents itself as unifacial or as Stranger. What distinguishes this postmodern style and the style of non-philosophy is simple. The universality of the thought-world envelops the contemporary attempts at the critique, differentiation and deconstruction of philosophy by recourse to various modes of alterity; it understands the Real as Other and the Other as simultane-ously internal and external to metaphysical representation according to the various propositions. Non-philosophy understands the Real as One-in-One immanent-(to)-itself rather than to the philosophy-world; it presents itself as Other or uniface, but as One-(of)-the-Other in-the-last-reference to the World, thus distinguishing itself from an Other that would retain a direct reference to philoso-phy. Neither the terms nor their combinations are the same. This is why the most invariant double operation of

philosophy, the inversion (in syntax) of old hierarchies and the displacement (in the experience of the Real) toward objects always supposedly more real, or toward supposedly more originary and fundamental grounds, is transformed from the ground up. This schema is detached from philosophy (Platonism) and psychoanalysis. Under the condition of vision-in-One, (1) Inversion or reversal gives way to unilateral duality and a generic universalisation; (2) The displacement of ground by ground, of foundation by foundation, gives way to the utopia or the placeless for the futural Real itself; (3) The thought-world is 'emplaced' in the place determined-in-the-last-instance by the Real-One, an ontological place which phenomenology would call the noema.

The ungraspable force of heresy's rebellion is to be, like immanence, as if it were completely inside the All from which it emerges and from which it separates itself; but also completely external to it, already separated from it, because it does not shatter, deconstruct or break down – without this interior and exterior forming a process at equilibrium, but instead an identity-of-the-last-instance. It is only of the heretic, of the Stranger in the radical sense in which we understand it, that one can say that they did not need to 'exit' philosophy because they never 'entered' it with hands, feet and soul bound, but that they took responsibility for transforming it. This is the paradox: if heresy must have a cause, a heretical cause, it is unalienated in that from which it separates itself through a separation which is in some sense a priori or prior to all alienation, that which can only be an immanent-(to)-self identity. To be first in her own way, the Stranger cannot be an Other person, an Other man; she is the One-(of)-the Other, the being-Separated which is identity. Only identity can be definitively and simply heretical: non-identitarian identity, of course, whose essence is being-Separated-without-separation, forever separated from the Existent, Being, the 'Other', etc. Nevertheless, if it has no need of separation, being-Separated draws out this act in its wake. It must relate itself to the World heteronomously, invalidating it without destroying it since it is related to it in-the-last-instance. It is in this way that the Separated is *also* in a complementary but 'occasional' way an instance of separation-one or One-separation with the All, the unique face the heretical One shows to the world. More precisely, the One separated is the cause of heresy, and the operation of heresy properly speaking can be called Stranger with a certain generality; but more rigorously, the ultimate heretical kernel is not the Stranger but its bearing in the real or in immanence, and the Stranger is separation as operation, but determined by the Real to reveal itself as a unique face, a unifacial Stranger.

This rigorous understanding of the identity-(of)-heresy conforms with the formula that the Roman Catholic Church assigns, with objective irony, to heretical

Protestants: 'our separated brothers'. But we obviously understand it antithetically to the commiseration of the Church, for we certainly are not awaiting the heretic's return. Heresy does not divide, only churches divide – and they do so only so as to unify. The heretic asks for no authorisation but his own, yet he is not just anyone – not a philosopher or a priest, perhaps not a psychoanalyst – but precisely a 'separated brother' in whose place no other – neither State nor Church, nor perhaps a 'community' – can stand, but who can generically be set in place, saying 'we', in the place of every other. This is a substitution that no longer takes place under the sign of the Other, assigning me my responsibility (Levinas), but instead that of the radical immanence of the only non-exchangeable 'belonging', that of the 'human genus'. The rock of non-philosophy as heretical practice is man, who is neither an Ego nor an Other person set against it, but the closest Stranger, the 'brother' in a sphere of humanity we shall call generic, and which puts separation in relation to the thought-world instead of the division in it. In more contemporary terms, man as 'separated brother' is a clone in the sense that every clone is an heretical identity produced not by the division of a One or a Unity, but by identity or the One-(of)-its separation on the basis of the All.

These conditions brought together and correctly understood allow us to identify a universal heretical Idea in the restrained or generic sense; one that is neither a philosophical possibility, nor a rupture within common religious dogma, but which can be valid for all these discourses and treat them as new means at the disposal of generic humanity. No historical heresy is universal – not because qua heresy it would condemn itself to the loss of the supposedly native element from which it is taken, but because in it, the heretical Idea is effectuated under restrictive conditions, either regional and positive or fundamental and philosophical. It is thus possible to endow this formless and polemical concept with positive and precise determinations, to make it function in a non-polemical way. Pure heresy is neither Greek nor Judaic, but it is also neither anti-Greek nor anti-Jewish; on the contrary, through a system of deformations certainly irreducible to any philosophical topology, any 'reversal-and-displacement', it allows the generic depotentiation of philosophy and the Judaic affect of Alterity. This depotentiation is an effect of their identity – identity, the only object of heresy, its 'phantasm'...

We shall strictly distinguish that which philosophical and theological generalities essentially confuse or only distinguish in terms of their objects, historical behaviours or subjective postures: the sect and schism on the one hand, heresy on the other. Sect and schism are quite different but are both separations that reconstitute churches on a partial basis, in a reduced, specific or global form against the universal Church, as rivals of the latter and laying claim to being the authentic church. Heresy is individual rather than partial – indivi-dual even, a formula to be decomposed according to the model of the uni-lateral. Founded on a separation that remains a separation rather than being founded on the partial and its connivance with the all, ultimately it is radically uni-versal, otherwise-than-catholic, because it is universal qua One and not qua All, according-to-the-One rather than according-to-the-All. Heresy is the most profound adversary of churches: sects are limited, watched over and controlled, but heretics are burnt, burnt in the flesh, and moreover, burnt *as* flesh. This difference in treatment cannot be purely historical.

This is certainly not the first time in the history of Occidental thought that rebel spirits have attempted to use philosophy in order to speak of an experience that no longer relies on its competence and authority (Levinas), so as to fold philosophical language to this experience. But we must distinguish between the conceptual or metaphysical abstraction which uses the words of natural language in order to make them signify philosophical meaning, truth and value, and the heretical separation of the same terms of this natural and/or philosophical language, a usage that transforms 'concepts' into 'non-concepts'. Considered in its heretical cause and no longer in its material, non-philosophy is a new language cloned from the ancient, from the philosophical; not exactly a new 'unprecedented' language, then, but a new usage of philosophical discourse. Through its cause, it resembles the language-material from which it is taken; it shares a 'familiar air' with it and 'for good reason'... but this cloning of non-philosophy on the basis of philosophy under conditions of radical identity is not an empirical-type cloning, it is a *transcendental-type* cloning. This is why here the clone is heterogeneous to its 'occasional' parent – cloning produces from the emergent, the Other-than-'cloned'-object-material, the Other-than-philosophical. If cloning is here radically distinct from mimesis, from its specular forms, from differential repetition itself, this is because its principle is simply radical identity, and because identity is not what is produced as a property or attribute of a new being, but is the silently operating cause of cloning itself. Non-philosophical cloning is a philosophically unintelligible operation foreclosed to thought because it produces force-(of)-thought as the clone of existing or given thought and produces it as Other than this given thought-world.

Given its 'real presupposition' (the One), non-philosophy unifies – without synthesis, without Catholic universality – the traditional opposites: theoretical explanation and deconstruction through the undecidable; the non-Euclidean-style universalisation of philosophy and the radical displacement of its terrain; the theoretical and the pragmatic; discovery and invention, etc. Let us take only a few of these non-philosophical unifications. Philosophy is essentially the invention of concepts and logics, terms and syntaxes. Its invention dominates its discovery because it is a tradition and a pre-given structure that favours reorientations, redistributions and new divisions, thus limiting the possibilities of novelty. Even philosophical 'creation' (Nietzsche, Bergson, Deleuze) and 'revolution' follow the thread of invention rather than discovery. More generally, philosophy is of the order of experience and reason at worst, of the (transcendental) imagination at best; it remains a transcendental technology that sometimes believes itself to be a theory but which manages only to produce local and contingent 'systems'. Non-philosophy instead articulates itself through discovery as true novelty, that which is not programmed, distributed and delimited by the pre-given structure of Philosophical Decision and has the power to overturn the theoretical field. Nothing precedes discovery except the Discovered itself, i.e. the Real or the One which determines it in-the-last-instance. But the Real, given or Discovered-without-discovery, is a 'negative' condition that unlocks the possibility of discovery – of separation – and not a positive cause (as the point of view of invention would continue to suppose) that determines such a discovery. If non-philosophy expresses itself through a cause of discovery that gives it its primacy and identity, it nevertheless does not exclude invention, the variable combination of the givens of the

World, or philosophy. On the contrary, it complexifies the invention proper to Philosophical Decision through its depotentiation. However it is important, so as not to confuse non-philosophical invention with philosophy, to orient it in-the-last-instance toward that 'negative utopia' that is vision-in-one and which has no reason in the past-present of thought.

In all fields of knowledge, non-philosophy is an instigator of rebellion, not revolution; an operation of revolt and separation, not direct resistance. It introduces into the relation to philosophy or the world a practice of heresy rather than apocalypse, of transmutation or transvaluation. It does not belong to the philosophical tradition – that of Marx and Freud, as well as Lacan, and of course that of artists, even if only a philosopher can elaborate it. If Marx and Freud have a practice in common, it is certainly not that desolate practice of suspicion, nor that of philosophical heroism (Nietzsche combines both) but that of the discovery that exceeds both philosophy and science and puts them into relations unknown to either. Heresy is closer to a stance of radical fiction, non-fictive fiction, imagination freed of images, discovery and invention of thought for thought. Its resources are not especially those of positive science or those of philosophical and conceptual rationality, but instead are of the order of the 'fictioned' usage of both, as well as art. This rebellion-through-fiction, i.e.

this invention of lived experience or of life, takes, from the object's point of view, the form of a 'unified theory' (of philosophy and a region of thought or knowledge); and from thought's point of view, the form of a theory-practice. Practice and theory are known in philosophy as contradictories: the heterogeneity of the explanation to its object excludes the usage of the latter within the form or essence of thought itself; and this usage excludes the theoretical relation of knowledge. From this perspective, 'pragmatism' is an attempt to unify thought and action, but within the transcendent context of philosophy – an attempt that, consequently, is vicious, proceeding through doubling. Non-philosophy leads pragmatism back to its minimal and radical conditions, in the scientific stance on the one hand (the specificity of theory: the irreducibility of the explanation to the properties of the thing known) and the philosophical stance on the other (the specificity of philosophy: the transcendental relation of thought to the object, thought as the thought of this object). Thus the theory of philosophy is also a certain usage of it, the only possible usage of its identity. And symmetrically, a pragmatics of philosophy or of its identity is the only way to realise its theory: in order to explain philosophy, it is necessary, given the specific character of this object, to make use of it within thought itself and within its means. Non-philosophy makes its own use of philosophy (as material, occasion, symptom) but with a view to explaining it in the most theoretical way possible.

Within the optic of heresy as being-Inseparate-in-itself but separated from philosophy, the latter is considered no longer as 'philosophy' in the narrow sense (the sense that it takes from its belonging to each of the three markets), but more broadly as thought-world. It is therefore only from the explicitly heretical point of view that it becomes material and 'occasional cause'. This is the condition for its making use of philosophy, a usage of theoretical rather than utilitarian means. The thought-world must be explained by statements that are irreducible to it. Explained, because these statements put the properties of philosophy, its 'concepts', into new relations that are simultaneously induced from it as from an object of experience, and deducible. But not explained without being deconstructed or transformed, since these statements are the Other-than-philosophy. The two tasks of theory and critique – of deconstruction through undecidables – are no longer separate.

Pure heresy proceeds with indifference regarding history and philosophy, regarding their common sense which is that of consumerist nihilism, mortifying institutions and worldly and mundane training. But with the indifference that one has for one's unilateral enemy. It is not even that counter-nihilism that Nietzsche called for, which forms a circle (give or take a transvaluation) with nihilism.

True nihilism, namely that of the thought-world, is instead this circle itself which embraces human hopes and malaise in a single flux. Moreover, it does not accelerate history or philosophy as if it were the development of one of their possibilities, a progress, an evolution, a revolution; no more than it breaks them down, if not 'in two' then into a duality in which history or philosophy itself is merely one of the terms. To sum up, the enemy that it faces is Being-as-transcendence and Time-as-history. It is a utopia – real rather than transcendental or imaginary, for the Real is 'without reality', a universal and necessary utopia, but as negative condition. Pure heresy is never actualised, but all the more effectuated in the conditions of existence, the thought-world, with which it cannot be confused even after this effectuation. It conveys neither an ideology of progress nor even that (already more interesting) of the avant-garde. It is a pure verticality as an a priori power of refusal, capable of uncovering the enemy-World, the only enemy proportionate with our identity. Heresy is the eternal and foreclosed protestation of the Stranger who no more has a place in the World than in History. Among other things, it is a protestation against philo-sophical consolation, against philodicy and against not only religious but also philosophical apocalypses, those through which the congenital malaise of philosophy disguises itself as a cure. The philosophical *pharmakon* is not its strength, and the logical therapeutics of thought seems to be a secondary task for it, a consequence or a limited effect. Its problem: to instigate a non-orthodox or non-standard usage of all philosophy but one that is not simply a deviation. The secret of heresy is being-Stranger not as consequence or secondary property, but as before-first, definitive, without recourse. Heresy is being-separated and the jouissance of being-separated; it is hopeless rather than consoled, militant rather than triumphant, urgent... The pure heretic, not the heretic of something, of some institution of knowledge or belief, is therefore the only non-believer, the only Knower, in the sense that only she can say: given that... X, Y, knowing the One-in-One, then... Only heretics have both philosophy and religion, philosophy and science together at their disposal. Only they know how to simultaneously relieve religion of faith, and to bring it permanently into the knowledge and practice of humans...

A Summary of Non-Philosophy

(2004)

Translated by Ray Brassier

THE TWO PROBLEMS OF NON-PHILOSOPHY

1.1.1. Non-philosophy is a discipline born of reflection upon two problems whose solutions finally coincided. On the one hand, the problem of the One's ontological status within philosophy, which associates it, whether explicitly or not, with being and with the other, but refuses to acknowledge its radical autonomy. On the other hand, the problem of the theoretical status of philosophy, insofar as the latter constitutes a kind of practice, affect, or existence, but one lacking in a rigorous knowledge of itself: philosophy remains a field of objective phenomena that have not yet been subjected to theoretical overview.

1.2.1. Concerning the first point, there follow an observation and a proposal. First the observation: the One
is an object at the margins of philosophy, an object of
transcendence stated in terms of the *epekeina* rather than
of the *meta*. Accordingly, it is as much other as One, as
divisible as it is indivisible; an object of desire rather than
of 'science'. It occurs to the thinking that is associated
or convertible with being, without being thought in its
essence and origin ('How does the One necessarily occur
to man-the-philosopher?'). Philosophy establishes itself
within being and within a certain 'forgetting of the One'
which it continually exploits in the name of being while
supposing it as given from the start.

1.2.2. Now the proposal: finally to think the One 'itself',
independently of being and the other, as that which
is incommensurable with them and non-determinable
by thought and language ('foreclosed' to thought); to
think *according* to the One rather than trying to think the
One. But to think this non-relation to thought using the
traditional means of thought; to think this displacement
relative to philosophy with the help of philosophy; to
think by means of philosophy that which is no longer
commensurate with the compass of philosophy and
escapes both its authority and its sufficiency. These are
the terms of the new problem.

1.3.1. Concerning the second point, there follow an observation and a proposal. First the observation: philosophy is regulated in accordance with a principle higher than that of reason: the *Principle of Sufficient Philosophy*. The latter expresses philosophy's absolute autonomy, its essence as *self*-positing/donating/naming/deciding/grounding, etc. It ensures philosophy's domination of all regional disciplines and sciences. Ultimately, it articulates philosophy's idealist pretension as that which is able to at least co-determine the most radical real. The obverse of this pretension, the price of this sufficiency, is philosophy's congenital inability to think itself in a manner that would be rigorous, non-circular, and non-question-begging; in other words, that of *theory*. Philosophy is self-reflection, self-consciousness; it thinks, or in the best of cases, feels itself thinking when it thinks; this is its cogito. Philosophy never proceeds beyond the scope of an enlarged cogito; an immanence limited to self-reflection or self-affection. It is a practice of thought, or a feeling and an affect. As such, philosophy manifests no more than its own *existence* and fails to demonstrate that it is the real to which it lays claim, or that it knows itself as this *pretension*. Implicit in philosophy's existence is a transcendental hallucination of the real, and implicit in philosophical 'self-knowledge' is a transcendental illusion.

1.3.2. Now the proposal: how to go about elaborating, with the help of philosophy and science but independently of the authority of the Principle of Sufficient Philosophy, a rigorous theoretical knowledge, but one that would prove adequate or attuned to philosophical existence, to the philosophical manner of thinking? These are the terms of the new problem.

THE IDENTITY OF THE PROBLEM OF NON-PHILOSOPHY OR THE SOLUTION

2.1.1. The principle of the solution: this is the same thing as positing the One as a radically autonomous real with regard to philosophy, but a real thought according to a novel use of philosophy's now reformed means. It is the same thing as making of the One the real condition or cause for a theoretical knowledge of philosophy. The solution constitutes a new problem: How can we, using the ordinary means of thought, conceive of the One as no longer philosophisable or convertible with being, and at the same time as capable of determining an adequate theory of philosophy?

2.1.2. Non-philosophy typically operates in the following way: everything is processed through a duality (of problems) that does not constitute a two or a pair, and through an identity (of problems, and hence of solution) that does not constitute a unity or synthesis. This way is known as that of the 'unilateral duality' which is just as much an 'identity'.

2.1.3. The resolution of the problem requires two transformations which form an identity of transformation. First, the transformation of the philosophical one-other into a radically autonomous One-in-One; the transformation of the One as object of philosophy into vision-in-One and into a phenomenality capable of determining knowledge.

2.1.4. Second, the transformation of the self-referential usage of philosophical language that regulates the statements of philosophy, into a new usage (both real and transcendental, of identity and of unilateral duality) that furnishes those statements with a double yet identical aspect: at once axiomatic and theorematic. The statements of the One and of its causality as vision-in-One, rather than as object or instance of philosophy, are generated by gradually introducing terms and problems of philosophical extraction, but terms and problems that are now subjected to a usage that is other than philosophical; a usage with a double aspect: axiomatic on one hand, theorematic and thus transcendental on the other; or relating to the real on one hand, and to its effects on philosophical existence on the other.

2.1.5. The One is not an object or entity 'in itself', in opposition to a language subsisting 'in-itself', such as to compose a philosophical or dialectical pairing of opposites. Vision-in-One as matrix of thought is a 'speaking/thinking *according to* the One'. Nor is it a relation of synthesis between the One (i.e. the real) and language. It is a non-relation, a 'unilateral duality'.

2.1.6. All the statements of non-philosophy appear as axiomatic insofar as they constitute the identity (in-the-last-instance) of the unilateral duality, and as transcendental theorems insofar as they constitute the unilateral duality that accompanies this identity. The theorems may serve as axioms on condition of determining-in-the-last-instance other theorems; the axioms may serve as theorems on condition of being determined-in-the-last-instance by other axioms. Axioms and theorems do not constitute two distinct classes of expressions, as they do in science. But nor do they constitute a reciprocal duality of propositions whose donation and demonstration are, certain exceptions aside, ultimately convertible, as they do in philosophy.

FROM THE ONE TO VISION-IN-ONE

3.1.1. *Immanence.* The One is immanence and is not thinkable on the terrain of transcendence (*ekstasis*, scission, nothingness, objectivation, alterity, alienation, *meta* or *epekeina*). Corollary: the philosophies of immanence (Spinoza, Deleuze) posit immanence in a transcendent fashion. Even Henry posits in a quasi-transcendent fashion the non-ekstatic immanence he objectifies.

3.1.2. *Radical immanence or self-immanence, the One-in-One.* The One is self-immanence without constituting a point or a plane; without withdrawing or folding back upon itself. It is One-in-One and hence that which can only be found in the One, not with being or the other. It is a *radical* rather than an *absolute* immanence. The 'more' immanence is radical, the 'more' it is universal or gives-in-immanence philosophy itself (the world, etc.).

3.1.3. *Identity, the real and the ego.* The other possible first names for the One are identity, the real or the ego. The One is identity 'in flesh and blood'; the identity that is no longer attribute or even subject. It is the ego rather than the subject, the latter being determined-in-the-last-instance by the ego. The One is the radical real which 'is' not, not because it could have 'been', but because it is 'without-being'; the One or the real does not 'exist' but (is) in-One.

3.1.4. *Non-intuitive phenomenality.* The One is vision-in-One. The latter manifests the One alone and manifests it according to the mode of the One. Consequently, it is not a mode of perception; its phenomenal-being falls neither within the purview of perception nor that of the phenomenological phenomenon. It is devoid of intuitiveness in general, neither an objective nor an intellectual intuition and devoid of thought or concept; it does not think yet it 'gives' ... without-givenness. Its radical non-intuitiveness allows philosophical terms to be used according to a mode of axiomatic abstraction, but one that is transcendental.

3.1.5. *The given-without-givenness.* Vision-in-One is a mode of being-given that is without-givenness (devoid of any mixture of given and givenness, devoid of any 'backstage' or 'background' givenness, and devoid of any self-giving). It does not give, it is the given, but it is able to give an instance of givenness according to its own mode of being-given, which is neither that of cognition nor of representation: this is its universality.

3.1.6. *Non-consistency.* Since the One is not beyond (*epekeina*) essence or being but only in-One, it is devoid of ontological, linguistic, and worldly consistency. It is without-being and without-essence, without-language and without-thought, even though it is said to be thus with the help of being, language, and thought, etc. This non-consistency entails that the One is indifferent to or tolerant of any material, any particular doctrinal position whatsoever. It is able to determine the usage of any material so long as the latter possesses the ultimate form of philosophy. This does not mean that the One subsists in-itself, in transcendent isolation, absolutely unrelated to language, etc., but rather that it is foreclosed to any 'reciprocal' causality exerted through language, thought, or philosophy. Nevertheless, although it has no need of them, it is able to manifest them or bring them forth according to its own particular modality (*if* they present themselves). With philosophy given as a condition, the non-consistency or indifference of the real becomes a transcendental indifference, yet the latter adds nothing to the former.

3.1.7. *Non-sufficiency.* Since the One is nothing but the being-given-without-givenness-(of)-the-One, it in no way produces philosophy or the world (whether through procession, emanation, ontologico-ekstatic manifestation, creation ex nihilo, onto-theo-logical perfection) – there is no real genesis of philosophy. This is the *non-sufficiency* of the One as necessary but non-sufficient condition. The real is a 'negative' condition or condition sine qua non for ... precisely because it is not itself nothingness or negation. Consequently, it is *additionally* necessary that philosophy be given in order for the vision-in-One to be able to give philosophy according to its own mode of being-given.

PHILOSOPHY'S EFFECTUATION OF VISION-IN-ONE

4.1.1. *The existence of philosophy or the affect of the world, and its real contingency.* Vision-in-One gives philosophy *if* a philosophy presents itself. But philosophy gives itself according to the mode of its own self- positing/givenness/ reflection/naming, or according to that of an enlarged self-consciousness or universal cogito. It is, at best, existence and gives itself with the feeling or affect of its own existence ('I know, I feel that I philosophise'), taking the latter to be the real as such rather than merely its own reality. But existence cannot engender knowledge of existence; knowledge that would not be viciously circular. The existence of philosophy amounts to an automatism of repetition that believes itself to be the real because of a well-founded hallucination; a hallucination that only the vision-in-One can expose.

4.1.2. *The effectuation of vision-in-One by the givenness of philosophy.* Because of its non-sufficiency, vision-in-One requires that philosophy (which provides a usage of language and of thought) be given in order to be *effectuated*. The effectuation of vision-in-One does not cancel its status as negative condition, or render it 'sufficient'. Thus, it is neither the actualisation of a virtual nor the realisation of a possible. It is a sign and witness of philosophy's relative autonomy (one that is not absolute or in-itself) once the

latter is given according to the mode of being-given-in-
One. It is the taking into account, not of philosophy in
general, or as something supposedly in-itself, but of the
autonomy of philosophy, once the latter has been released
from the grip of its own hallucinatory absolute form, such
that this autonomy indexes philosophy's specific reality
and structural consistency as 'Philosophical Decision'.

4.1.3. *Non-philosophy as unilateral duality*. Non-philosophy is not a unitary system but a theoretical apparatus
endowed with a twofold means of access, or a twofold
key, but one that is radically heterogeneous because one
of these keys is identity. This is the 'unilateral duality'.
Because of its radical immanence, which refuses all positing or consistency for itself, vision-in-One is never present
or positive, it is never given within representation or
transcendence or manipulable in the manner of a 'key'.
This duality does not have two sides: the real does not
constitute a side, only non-philosophy or philosophy's
relative autonomy does so. This is no longer a bifacial
or bilateral apparatus like that of philosophy, but rather
one that is *unifacial* or *unilateral*. A duality which is an
identity but an identity which is not a synthesis: this is the
very structure of determination-in-the-last-instance. Non-
philosophy thinks without constituting a system, without
being unitary. For example, the subject in accordance with
which it is produced ('the stranger') is not something

facing me, it is as a uniface and is for this reason a stranger to the world, a stranger to the law of bilaterality which is proper to philosophy and to the world, yet it is not a stranger to the real.

4.1.4. *Contingency and necessity of the non-philosophical effectuation.* Because of the philosophical origin of the material from which its axioms and theorems are drawn, and thus as instance of thought in general, non-philosophy is, from the viewpoint of the One, globally contingent relative to the real which remains foreclosed to it. But as thought determined by the real, it acquires the real necessity of vision-in-One that is also the transcendental necessity of this real contingency. The One does not legitimate philosophy as it is or as it gives itself, but only insofar as philosophy becomes transformed in its 'being-given'. From the viewpoint of philosophy, non-philosophy is necessary but partly tautological. To think according-to-the-One (to think philosophy according to this mode) is, on account of this aspect, a philosophical objective, one that utilises philosophical means.

4.1.5. *The being-foreclosed of the real One.* Non-consistency implies or presupposes (these are equivalent here) the being-foreclosed of the real to thought, whether the latter be philosophical or non-philosophical – a thought which, nevertheless, the real is able to give according to its own mode of being-in-One. Consequently, thought does not affect it, the real does not *receive* it but *gives* it and does nothing but give it. That which is given-in-One is without a prior reception. This is the radical autonomy, the primacy of phenomenality over phenomenology, of the phenomenon over the empirico-philosophical model of donation-reception, passivity, etc. The being-foreclosed of the One is not cancelled once there is an explicit effectuation of the vision-in-One by philosophy; it is maintained through this effectuation. This being-foreclosed suspends philosophy's causality with regard to the real, but it does not suspend the entirety of philosophy's causality relative to thought as such, for which philosophy represents a mere effectuating 'occasion'. In any case, this being-foreclosed does not prevent the One from giving (-receiving) thought, language, and, more generally, the world.

4.1.6. *Philosophy's relative autonomy.* Philosophy gives itself as absolute autonomy. The latter is revealed to be the same real hallucination and 'transcendental' illusion concerning the One as was philosophy's sufficiency or pretension with regard to the real. Absolute autonomy is also effectively given – *according to* – the One as a merely relative autonomy. This preserves the autonomy of its reality as occasion and hence as material for non-philosophy. This autonomy is relative insofar as it is limited with regard to philosophy's spontaneous belief, and relative also in a more positive sense insofar as it is now transcendentally legitimated by the real, which ratifies philosophy's structural consistency, its quasi-materiality.

THE CLONING OF NON-PHILOSOPHY ON THE BASIS OF PHILOSOPHY

5.1.1. Effectuation is the taking into account of philosophy's reality, of its relative autonomy. This reality and autonomy imply that the One no longer gives philosophy just as a mere 'occasion', but that it fulfils a new role with regard to the latter; a role which is now 'decisive' and which constitutes a positive 'intervention' within philosophy. The real as One thereby assumes a transcendental function, while remaining the inalienable real that it is, without changing in nature or 'becoming' a second 'transcendental One' alongside the first. This transcendental cloning of the real on the basis of a philosophical material is possible without contradicting the real's radical autonomy since philosophy is already given in-One and consequently the real does not enter into contradiction with itself by assuming a transcendental role with regard to philosophy. Unlike philosophy, non-philosophy does not proceed from the transcendental to the real (and from the a priori to the transcendental), but from the real to the transcendental (and from the latter to the a priori).

5.1.2. The clone is that which is said of non-philosophy, not of philosophy as material for the latter, and even less of the real which, without being transformed, is rendered agent, *transcendental agent*, of cloning. The non-philosophical clone is in essence or according to its matrix a transcendental instance, which is to say a vision-in-One which is said of this or that material of the philosophical type. It is thus the exact content of all speaking or thinking *according to* the One. The transcendental is a clone because it is said of the inalienable One, but said with regard to the material whose autonomy and reality are now taken into account or introduced. The clone is thus 'transcendental' and not real, but it remains real-in-the-last-instance or, more precisely, the clone is the concentrate of the entire structure of determination-in-the-last-instance as such.

5.1.3. The '*according to*' or clone appears to exceed the One, just as the transcendental appears to exceed the real. In actuality it does not exceed it: it is a mode of the in-One, which does not exceed itself within philosophy by 'becoming' transcendental. It is rather philosophy that exceeds the in-One (duality), but it does not exceed it in exteriority (philosophical dyad) because it is already and in any case given-in-One. It only exceeds the One through its own intrinsic reality 'within' its immanent-being-given or being-given-in-One. Cloning is necessary *if* philosophy presents itself or rather *if* it is taken into account according to its own consistency and autonomy, and it is possible or non-contradictory from the viewpoint of the real.

5.1.4. The clone is not the double of a given identity which is in reality already a double or doublet. It is 'on the contrary' *the real-transcendental but indivisible identity (of) a philosophical double*. The real is not a clone of itself, it is a radically simple identity, neither divided nor even clone (of) itself. But it is thereby able to *determine* non-philosophy (rather than philosophy as such). To clone, to determine-in-the-last-instance, to bring-forth non-philosophy: all these formulations express the same operation and they express it better than would the term 'produce'. The Subject and World-Thought (Essence, Existence, Adsistance)

6.1.1. Non-philosophy is a globally transcendental discipline, that is to say, a discipline that is real-in-the-last-instance (one that makes use of philosophy's transcendental dimension in order to formulate itself). It is at once the determination-in-the-last-instance of a theory (of a knowledge that remains distinct from its object, adopting a model taken from science), and also of a pragmatics (of a *usage* of philosophy 'with a view to' the non-philosophical subject, adopting a model taken from philosophy). It is theoretical by virtue of one of its models: science. But it is neither a philosophical and therefore self-positing theoreticism, nor a philosophical and therefore self-positing pragmatics. It is theoretico-pragmatic only by virtue of its aspect as a non-philosophical operation, but real or practical by virtue of its cause. Thus, it is not a 'negative' theory-pragmatics either, but rather one requiring that the vision-in-One be effectuated by invariant scientific and philosophical models.

6.1.2. The non-philosophical subject distinguishes itself from the subject of the philosophical type. It is a purely transcendental subject, distinct from the real ego, turned toward the world to which it is a stranger and toward which it turns itself as stranger. But it is ego-in-the-last-instance. The unilateral duality of ego and subject marks the end of their unitary confusion. The subject does not use philosophy as if it were already consti-tuted, it *is* that use. It is not only pragmatic, making use of world-thought, but also and equally theoretical. Moreover, it does not 'do' theory, it *is* the theoretical. *Transcendental science*, which is the *clone* of philosophy-science, is thus the subject-as-such-(of)-non-philosophy ('force-(of)-thought'). The subject is theoretical and prag-matic through the scientific and philosophical material in accordance with which it varies, but it is globally transcendental as real-in-the-last-instance, or as ego that clones the real subject transcendentally.

6.1.3. Non-philosophy is the transcendental science that constitutes the essence-of-the-last-instance of the subject – 'force-(of)-thought' – one that may additionally be specified on the basis of the particular material indexed by 'ego-subject-other'. Thus, the subject is *existence* solely on account of the philosophy that it integrates, the *ekstatic* nature of the latter representing its aspect as 'existence'. Accordingly, the complete unilateral duality of the subject cannot be said to 'exist' in general but pertains instead to another structure of thought: it is *adsistance*, according to a theoretical and pragmatic mode, *of* and *for* world-thought.

6.1.4. Non-philosophy demands the identification of that which is philosophical and fundamental, and that which is regional (art, science, ethics, technology, etc.). But it identifies them only in-the-last-instance, rather than through their immediate confusion or by collapsing one into the other in conformity with the law of their philosophical association or 'mixture'. Non-philosophy postulates the identification-in-the-last-instance, through cloning, of philosophy and world in a 'world-thought'. The hypothesis of a world-thought is one that could be legitimated for philosophical reasons (the 'world' as philosophical concept, philosophy as cosmo-logy, cosmo-politics, onto-cosmo-logy, etc.) and in accordance with the authority of philosophy alone, but this concept partakes of the real contingency of the world in general.

Yet it is also amenable to a more profound legitimation through non-philosophy insofar as the latter posits it in a theorem as identity of a clone. It then possesses the 'given' status of an axiom, along with the transcendental status or status as given-in-the-last-instance of a theorem 'for' philosophy.

6.1.5. What does this non-philosophical adsistance mean? It cannot 'transform' (produce, engender, create, etc.) the objects of philosophy or the entities of the world. But it can *transform* (cause to occur according to their being-determined-by-the-One-in-the-last-instance, or according to their relative autonomy, or cause to be *brought-forth* through the vision-in-One as cloning) philosophy as a whole which is a self-presenting hybrid of identity and difference. It does not intervene 'within' the specificity of experience, in the manner in which philosophy often and mistakenly claims to, nor does it even provide that specificity with meaning. It is not, generally speaking, an operation or activity to which the subject would remain external. The subject *is* adsistance in its very essence (essence which is without-essence in-the-last-instance). If adsistance is neither interpretation nor practical intervention, it is the bringing-forth of world-thought, one that is practical only in-the-last-instance – the being-brought-forth or being-given which transforms the latter's type of autonomy and liberates it, and thereby liberates the subject (as transcendental identity (of) world-thought) from its entrapment by the hallucinatory belief in its own sufficiency. This transcendental identity, which is that of *philosophy as such*, remains incommensurable with 'philosophy' in the philosophical sense.

From the First to the Second Non-Philosophy

(2010)

Translated by Anthony Paul Smith and Nicola Rubczak

NON-PHILOSOPHY'S GENERIC TURN AND ITS QUANTUM REALISATION

Non-philosophy was and remains based on two main principles that appear to contradict each other. The first principle is that of the real specified in terms of a radical immanence, symbolised by the One rather than by Being. This *radical* immanence is distinct from the absolute or infinite immanence associated with Spinoza or Deleuze. The second is a principle of method or syntax, based on a duality said to be unilateral, not on a reciprocal or reversible unity. They have functioned together as 'dualysis', a method that is neither analysis nor synthesis. Despite these 'principles', non-philosophy might *appear* to be a crime of *lèse-philosophie*, an assassination of Parmenides that extends to his entire family, i.e. to all we philosophers. But the non-philosopher does not feel himself to be a child of Parmenides alone; he complicates the philosophical filiation, attributing to himself an ancestry that diverges from the twentieth-century norm (a Greek ancestry affected by Judaism). He is the complex descendant of philosophy, of that modern science par excellence, quantum physics, and of a certain religious affect introduced by Christianity. In recent years I have given a more precise, less abstract, content to radical immanence, to the method of dualysis that exploits it, and have also proposed other names for this stance. Non-philosophy has always wanted to place philosophy under a scientific condition that is determining in-the-last-instance, so as to make it a problem, rather than a question for itself, and above all to make it an inventive rather than an historical method. This is what I now call a 'generic science' (GS) of philosophy – utilising quantum positivity and philosophical spontaneity only on condition of their 'generic' suspension – or even a 'non-standard philosophy'.

The two principles of non-philosophy have an affinity with the two main principles of quantum physics: radical immanence with what is called 'superposition', and unilateral duality with what is called 'non-commutativity'. Two wave-phenomena necessarily are superposed when their addition produces a third of the same nature or an idempotent result (1+1=1), a result that is neither analytic nor synthetic. Non-philosophy can make use of quantum mechanics as a model and only as a model – this represents just one possible use of it, which does not claim to exhaust its meaning. Both call into question traditional philosophical categories in a way that is completely novel in relation to the critical method and its extension in deconstruction. A new way is opened up – more rigorous, but also more intuitive – for a second version of non-philosophy. The problem is to find a conceptual or natural language equivalent for the (essentially algebraic) mathematical operator of this physics. An equivalent that makes use of philosophy, allowing it a certain function while at the same being capable of questioning its 'sufficiency'. All the more so given that there are, reciprocally, quasi-quantum phenomena in philosophy (the undulatory flash of the Logos and the Heideggerian sendings of Being, the corpuscular One and Identity as the form of concepts, the spin and rotation of concepts, Deleuze's oscillating and resonance machines) that suggest the possibility of a more explicit, quantum theory of philosophy.

Additionally, another old but global theme of non-philosophy, that of the Determination in-the-last-instance of philosophy by humanity as an ultimatum addressed to it, has received the support of a new thematic that brings together all the oppositions to the classical practice of philosophy: that of the generic, from both a mathematical

(P.J. Cohen, followed by Alain Badiou) and philosophical (Feuerbach and, in part, Marx) background. All the classic objectives of non-philosophy are rediscovered within it: humans as subjects of a generic nature, the non-metaphysical unity of science and philosophy as variables combined in a humanity-function said to be of-the-last-instance, philosophy placed under the under-determining condition of science. The most recent figure of non-philosophy, which is a plastic and open discipline, finds it resembling an unexpected synthesis of quantum mechanics and Marxism.

'Generic' signifies that science and philosophy are no longer anything more than means or predicates that have lost their disciplinary sufficiency and autonomy; bodies of knowledge forced to abandon their specific finality in order to take up another that is generic, a form of universality that traverses their traditional domains of objects as modalities of the philosophical All. So let this be the formula of non-philosophy renewed or renamed as GS or Non-Standard Philosophy: it is *the fusion of science and philosophy under science, a fusion under-determined in-the-last-instance by science, i.e. quantum physics.* This is our guiding formula, that which we call the generic matrix.

To take an image from physics, the generic matrix is an experimental chamber that brings physical and philosophical particles into combat or collision, in order to produce new knowledge. In other words, the generic matrix is a concept collider, more modern than those other colliders, the Parmenidean Same, the Cartesian cogito, the Fichtean transcendental Imagination, and the Nietzschean or Deleuzean eternal return of the same. The collision is assured by the chamber of radical immanence, the acceleration of the conceptual particles assured by unilateral duality. This injection of quantum means into the former non-philosophy imbues it with the air of a physics, but paradoxically, one that is not mathematical or calculative. The science of philosophy is a *quasi*-quantum physics of concepts. But more generally it is a confrontation of two mirrored players or bodies of knowledge, one of which – the quantum and not the philosophical – forces their specularity to evaporate under the form of the Real or in immanence. In other words, our descriptions follow the suggestion of the quantum rather than those of perception.

THE NEW IMAGE OF THOUGHT
1: THE WAVE ASPECT

The deconstruction of 'representation' by contemporary thinkers is an overly general critique, because the signifier, the molecular, alterity, difference, the simulacrum, etc., are in general still discussed in a spirit at once corpuscular and realist – two characteristics that only a quantum approach can detect and call into question. Why? Philosophy is not at all as simple as such philosophers implicitly suppose, and so it remains basically undisturbed by these types of operators which allow the subsistence of an essential presupposition, a background horizon, a sufficiency of philosophy as sole autonomous and ultimate master of knowledge. There is always a specular doublet, a double layer, double stratum or double face, either parallel or arranged in a Moebius strip. One believes oneself to be critiquing the whole of representation whilst in fact one critiques only one stratum. Hence the return of the doublets and of specularity that obliges the critique to begin again, and prevents it from transforming itself into a fully inventive activity.

Non-philosophy sets up another thought-experiment: The real is no longer made of objects, autonomous or in-itself terms; neither is it composed of elementary micro-objects (signifiers, partial objects) – this is the end of specular realism and even of the modern micro-fetishism that believes itself to have put an end to such realism. The new model of the real is of a quantum kind; it is ultimately constituted by asymmetrical or strange dualities, continuous on one side and discontinuous on the other, like uni-lateral quanta. These entities are sometimes apprehended as dualities, sometimes as unifacial phenomena – sometimes bifacial, sometimes unifacial. They are not doublets or modalities of a complete circle, that basic cosmic model that impregnates every philosophy and persists in the modern figure of the Moebius strip. They are the Real in the state of a half-circle, and therefore as a wave with one face configuring a particle that is inseparable from it. The undulatory *morphē* as inseparable correlation ('unilation') of the curve of thought and its content, a curve with which the intended object coincides, at once in excess over it and included in it. Now, the wave is defined by its amplitude or its wavelength, not by the straightforward, objective intention of objects in themselves or of corpuscular representations. Amplitude is the periodic variation of the interval's maximal value. Therefore it is distinct from phenomenological or ecstatic distance. The latter belongs to the complete circle – the depth that extends before the subject is a circle flattened onto itself, the identity of a going/return which can laterally open up, and ends by crossing and reversing itself (Lacan). But amplitude is not ecstatic, just semi-ecstatic, in a single section or a single face without return or closing. The wave is a form that is apparently unfinished, only begun; at best it is completed by its object as being identical to its object (which is not an in-itself). It is no longer phenomenological distance possibly inverted, closing on or making a return to itself. The wave is completed in its objects but without making a return to itself or in itself as a large object. In the same way, if the curve is completed as curve but not closed, its object, the particle that is carried and transported by the wave, is partial as a half-whole, a semi-object with one face which is the completion of the wave. The wave is the beginning of the object and the object the completion of the wave. In the strict sense of the terms, wave and particle are two halves of a half-circle that they share.

First difference with Deleuze: *the undulatory-particulate real is made of machines that are unilateral rather than molecular, oriented rather than disoriented.* Wave-particle or unilateral machines are complexes of non-exchangeable or non-permutable non-separability and separability; the undulatory flux is also – but in a single sense, not reciprocally – the objective morphē of the particle. In reality, Deleuze's break-flux machines presuppose from the start the multiple 'in itself' of partial objects or breaks, and introduce different types of their reversibility, including that of the Body without Organs (BwO). This is to retain a priority of the multiple or of the empirical instance in the ground of the continuity of the One-All that it molecularises, and to accept an inversion between the particulate and the undulatory, an inversion comprised in the BwO. The generic model invested in the quantum approach imposes a shift in relation to the philosophical One-Multiple: the priority is no longer that of the wave over the particle, or the inverse. Instead, there is a priority of the wave alone as a priori over the particle, and a prior-to-priority of the wave-particle as inseparable bloc of unilateral duality over the supposedly in-itself corpuscle (or wave), which are the same duality but seen from the other side, from the side of the particle. Unilateral dualities or machines are only intelligible, only make sense, within the 'complete' generic matrix.

THE NEW IMAGE OF THOUGHT
2: THE VECTORIAL ASPECT

Let us come back to the source of the wave as undulatory-particulate morphē. If the wave is a half-circle, one can still divide and isolate a quarter of the circle or of the turn in which the Real is now concentrated. The quarter represents not an arithmetic number but a complex or imaginary number that quantum theory uses in order to define the quarter and generate the wave. Thought's essence is no longer the still too-intuitive curve, but the vector proper to Hilbert space and which characterises the typical imaginary number of the wave function. The vector is an even more elementary machine than the wave, but it repeats the generic structure; it is like an atom of thought, an inseparable fusion of the arrow and the angle, of the module and the phase. If the wave form was noematically oriented as a priori over the particle, the vectoral form is noetically oriented toward the subject as Last Instance.

In anticipation of what is to follow, and in order to indicate the stakes, we will say that the curve is the a priori form of thought as quantum theory and philosophy mixed, giving rise to an aesthetic that is undulatory rather than corpuscular like Kantian aesthetics; but that the vector is, in first approximation, the real condition of possibility, the Real itself, of quantum experience qua 'transcendental' (to speak provisionally and in the classical manner). But it is evident that our matrix qua generic forbids us from settling for that traditional solution. All the more so since it defines a theoretical strategy of the invention or design of concepts, of philo-fiction, and not only of the struggle against philosophical sufficiency. The matrix stipulates the fusion of quantum theory and philosophy (which is what we have done) but under or in a dominant quantum regime, not under philosophical dominance (which we have just ensured once again). So we must now cut out the excess of philosophy that we no longer want, and *in the same gesture* give to the vector or to the 'quartial' object their proper consistency and genetic force. The fusions and the distinctions that have been asserted are brought about in the quantum regime. This overthrows the primacy of a philosophy of science, but does not lead to a positive science of philosophy, since the overthrowing is achieved by philosophised quantum means, and is the enactment of generic unilateralisation. It is a question of making a transfer that is unilateral or broken by subtraction and addition, of cutting out the excess of transcendence in which the vector is bathed, and thickening its immanence according to a distribution that follows the divisions of the circle, but by way of unilateral duality. Inversely, the 'philosophy of quantum physics' is a counter-transference of generic science.

DUALYSIS AS PRACTICE OF UNILATERAL DUALITIES: FROM THE QUANTUM TO THE GENERIC

As in Platonic division, there is in dualysis a principle of choice for the most real (or 'best') half. Instead of dismembering the All into its terms, or differentiating it into Being-beings or some other difference that is not (quantum-) scientific but philosophical, we have twice geometrically divided the circle that symbolises the All, but each time choosing one of the sides as bearer of the Real (or of immanence), and thus of the One rather than of Being. The Real is a sort of coefficient symbolised by the One. The other side is not denied or abandoned; we shall say that it is determined in-the-last-instance by the real-One without our even knowing yet what is behind this expression 'last instance'. It is now the quarter which is the real-One, and it determines the wave in-the-last-instance. It is the quarter that must be thought generically for itself.

The generic takes the ways and means of quantum theory as far as possible, but only in order to turn them against themselves. For its problem is that of acting on the 'alls' that philosophy proposes, and of extracting what there is in them of the Real, without analysing them and without synthetically producing yet more of them; to extract from the All that which it has in excess or excessively over itself, its pretention or sufficiency over the Real, then; to impoverish the function of the All in the sphere of the Real without absolutely destroying it (a radical, but not absolute, deconstruction of the All). But also, and complementarily, its problem is also that of 'forcing' the terms that fell under the law of the All, not in their singularity but in their indivi-duality, forcing them into uni-laterality rather than totality. Indivi-duality (or uni-laterality) is not the more or less corpuscular individual, it is at once non-separable from self or immanent and at a semi-ecstatic self-distance; it is thus in an indirect self-relationship which is neither phenomenological distance nor its opposite, affective interiority. The generic does not reinforce the mediation of singularity by the All (the singular universal). On the contrary, it raises the terms in the mediation, elevating them to the state of means or mediates in their very existence, which is the Real. The generic is the process of a 'broken transfer', a continuous or discontinuous operation, of consistency, of the power of determination, from philosophy toward indivi-duality, from transcendence toward complex immanence, from the particle toward the wave and finally from the latter toward the quarter-turn. But it is not the same reality that will be passed on or exchanged or which switches from one side to the other. This is not a redistribution of wealth on an equity basis, but a radical redistribution of the means of production. Or even of reality's force toward the Real. On the side of reality one subtracts, on the side of the Real one adds or augments; it is therefore not the same thing. This method is dualysis.

Second difference with Deleuze: *there is no Body without Organs* (BwO) *or Eternal Return of the Same* (ERS), *only a Last Instance*. Rather than finishing the treatment of the All with the half-circle or the wave – which would be to remain within the orbit of the philosophical circle or the All (or the Spinozist One-All) – it is a matter of taking up an extreme, and perhaps 'fictioning' thought-experiment, of introducing into the generic the approach via quantum means, the quarter of the circle or imaginary number, and not as a simple half-circle whose genetic key one does not possess. In another sense Deleuze is very close to a quantum thinking, but as a positive science that he wants to philosophise *about*: he lacks the passage to the generic, and thus also a quantum thinking in so far as it allows that passage – as evidenced by the themes of the One-All, the BwO and the ERS, of the twisting plane of immanence, which fall back on the desiring machines, the constant practice of a doublet (disjunctive synthesis) that is certainly non-metaphysical but nonetheless insistent, the empirico-transcendental style in general. Non-philosophy has always opposed unilateral duality or unilateral complementarity to disjunctive synthesis; the former are no longer doublets for which transcendence is axial, but superpositions for which immanence is axial. *The matrix is precisely not structuralist or mathematical, nor is it philosophical or transcendental; it is uni-lateral, and every doubling is a complementarity, but a unilateral complementarity.*

FROM THE VECTOR TO VECTORALITY, FROM THE IMAGINARY TO INVENTION

The wave, even mathematically rooted in the quarter-turn, is thus not sufficient in itself; it is only an a priori, a certain level that physics reaches. To the two successive unilateral cuts, principally to the second, that isolates the quarter, it is necessary to add an additional operation that will address it, or the imaginary, as generic – something quantum physics does not do since it must make a positive use of it. We transpose to that new object, the quarter, our matrix; it posits the fusion of the imaginary and the philosophical (and so also the geometric and the physical) under or in an imaginary or complex regime. The fusion of the vector and its philosophical interpretation must be determined as the vectorality of the vector, this time generic, neither geometric nor transcendental.

We must now travel the inverse path: Instead of going from wave to quarter-turn, one can only descend from the quarter, but by force of the quarter itself, toward or as wave. Why? Because the generic becoming still forms itself via quantum theory, i.e. via the superposition or the excess proper to immanence. We pass beyond the imaginary by way of the imaginary itself, in a sense; but it is not a reflection of the quarter on and in itself, it is not a reflexive subject, a consciousness, or even a transcendental ego replenishing itself (Henry). It is a superposition of the quarter and the wave, which is possible since the quarter is that which engenders the wave. In this operation, *in being superposed with the wave the quarter is superposed with itself, fills itself.* The quarter is not exhausted by the wave but is only known or thought by and as wave, essence through existence. *It is not delivered to the wave as if to an alienating exteriority, but it only reaches its effectivity, only actualises itself, on condition that it is resumed as immanent or superposed with itself, on condition that it agrees to receive a solicitation or impulse from the wave.* The Last Instance as 'generic subject' is a causality that only awakens given an occasion, but which alone 'decides' that there may be occasions to act. As generic or self-superpositional, the quarter thus achieves a consistency that undoubtedly is no longer absolute or closed upon itself, but concluded each time in the sense that the wave falls (again) into itself only in order to go further, pushed or inclined by the quarter superposed with itself. This ultimate and highest point that non-philosophy can reach, we also call generic messianity.

Third difference with Deleuze: *the plane of generic or transfinite immanence is also the plane of scientific reference.* There is indeed a plane of immanence called a 'generic plane' or plane of messianity. It transcends or 'rises', identical to the transcendence of the wave before falling 'into itself'. But that 'itself' is not an infinite self or the band of a BwO; the wave is cut or arrested before having 'looped' around a turn of the circle. Deleuze conserves the circle as All and molecularises it rather than unilateralises it. Now, the wave can only repeat itself without ever closing itself in a circle, even an infinite one, though divergent. It is transfinite and comes out of its own immanence, that of the quarter. Even closing itself to the infinite is not possible here for a very simple reason: the plane of immanence is at the same time a plane of reference or a scientific, non-absolute plane. On a circle or an all, what can one do? Deduct the all from itself, thus supposing that it remains an all = -1 even if one molecularises disjunctively. Against the doublet of representation, Deleuze correctly simplifies the All to the state of a One-All, but does not pass via quantum theory, which ends by demolishing, without fail, philosophical sufficiency, more than philosophy itself is able to do. Deleuze does not introduce science (here, algebra) into the quarter, and does not achieve a rigorous imaginary, a generic and scientific philo-fiction. As if he disperses or molecularises the human Last Instance in the all-ideology. What he calls 'non-philosophy' is an auto-simplified philosophy, but one that scarcely consents, any more than Michel Henry's, to pass by way of science; it is only absolute-generic and not radical-generic. What consists is always the great macroscopic object, the BwO, and not the broken system of indivi-duality, of the undula-tory quarter as uni-lateral. This Last Instance is vectorality, *generic messianity is 'our' infrastructure*. How and with what can those without philosophy work? We understand the ultimate vectorality of thought as the messianity proper to last-instance humanity, generic humanity. Messianity is the only rectitude capable of adding itself to itself, yet indirectly. It is a transfinite task, neither finite or closed nor infinite.

WHO IS A NON-PHILOSOPHER?

One of the things that motivate non-philosophy is the eternal question 'what is to be done'? In the face of what? In the present situation, in the face of the excess of com-municable knowledge which, potentialised by philosophy become doxa, now harasses rather than alienates us. Plato was surrounded by the doxa of his time, as are we by forms of knowledge, no doubt well-sanctioned, but whose precarious truths, amalgamated with philosophy, produce a toxic and particularly unstable alloy, a new, more complex, high-grade doxa. Humans as individuals possess a universal capital of disciplinary knowledge that grounds them in cosmic inhumanity, like a prodigious life-sapping mythology – the new unconscious of the Moderns, a knowledge that they have but of which they cannot make good use according to their generic humanity. Philosophy is the universal mediator in which forms of knowledge participate, and it allows itself, along with them, to be dragged into a certain corruption, that of communication as universal mediation. But the mediator or the mediate that is without-mediation is still something else: Man-in-person and his messianity. Only this other type of mediator can save us from the corruption of cosmic doxa that is philosophy.

Non-philosophy is a set of technical specifications regarding the means to be used in order to confront that Platonic situation which demands a non-Platonic solution. Opening these specifications to a blank page or a blank computer screen, you have to decide that nothing is written there, that even software is materiality, nothing more. Do not forget that even you yourself are no longer that subject, immediately consistent and self-assured, that you believed yourself to be, but just another machine, almost empty of purpose; and that your only option is to make denser or to superpose the other machines, not just to connect them. You have to make the best use of that which is no longer a blank slate, but a technically-sophisticated experimental chamber containing yet other chambers. It is from this inventive expectation, this indirect action at a distance – which is also that of robots, do not forget – that you will become that which you only virtually are, or that you will fulfil or accomplish yourself as generic subject.

Philosopher, scientist, artist, or theologian, there is no subject, in this well-known sense, that could be non-philosophical from the start, defining itself by a body of knowledge listed in the pages of the encyclopaedia. The non-philosopher holds no place between philosophy and anti-philosophy – she is a mediator of transformation, not transmission, her only mission is to transform (not to transmit) the knowledge that plagues us into simple means – but why? For the invention of her own generic humanity – human in-the-last-instance, not individual humanity. The generic is a strategy of thought that uses means taken from elsewhere or even already exploited (this is not a problem for it), like the imaginary number or quantum immanence, in order to actualise the understanding of the acquired knowledge that one is. Generic humanity is condemned to know itself only indirectly, through interposed *mediatum* and not through the transparency of an interiority. The task for the philosophical subjects that we spontaneously are is to become a generic human that we are only virtually, not actually. This is why we are condemned to an ethics and a practice of means, not of means raised to an undignified dignity of ends, but rather weakened in regard to any possible and imposed purpose. The generic ethic renders destitute both ends and separated subjects in favour of means and their proper immanence; it consists in correctly understanding the specific and original purpose of the means in so far as it no longer exceeds the former but is only the phenomenon of their immanence or their superposition.

Science and philosophy are the extreme means that limit the others and allow humans to forge an adequate and real knowledge-(of)-self that does not stand in contradiction to their generic-being. The understanding of self as generic indivi-duality comes about indirectly through a process and a transformation, mobilising the means rather than believing oneself immediate, direct or even objective. For, exactly, mathematism, just like philosophism, is a will to act too directly, through positivity and spontaneous sufficiency. But humans realise themselves or participate in the real by inventing; invention being the great means of struggle against the claims of received and transmitted knowledge. Now, for the masses to take hold of theory as a means and develop this knowledge-(of)-self, it is necessary that they superpose themselves with it, that the masses 'fuse' with theory, as Marx said; with theory *but this time under theory*. Non-philosophy is the thought of those who have suspended their philosophical faith and found a way to furnish the means of the generic end that is their own. It is appropriate to distinguish the absolute poor –

those who are stripped of all their predicates but full of the bedevilling image of Capital as universal predicate, or of the philosophical All – from the radical poor, who are divested only to the point of making apparent their human root, of being able to use their dispossession and turn their destitution against that image itself; that is to say, to subtract themselves from it.

This situation is not without a certain practical paradox of theory: the non-philosophers who proclaim a certain poverty of knowledge, especially of philosophy, need to acquire more and more knowledge, to master philosophy, in order to subtract themselves from the latter's spontaneous excess if they would produce understanding. Here lies precisely the whole art of invention: the poor are condemned to invent on the basis of bodies of knowledge that exist and that they cannot produce 'firsthand', but must appropriate, not even 'secondhand' but 'lasthand', already-finished. The generic allows the establishment of the form of excess or invention, but also the form of insufficiency or weakness that is appropriate to humans in so far as they must abandon – that is to say transform – the predicate of 'all'. Philosophers must make their way through 'all' acquired forms of knowledge (or at least two), but must do so as if they do not possess them, or as if they were without-philosophy, i.e. without spontaneous faith in transcendence. What will remain for them will be the immanent faith of poverty, inventor of thought.

The Degrowth of Philosophy: Toward a Generic Ecology
(2012)

Translated by Robin Mackay

ECOLOGICAL TIMES

Take a programme entitled 'Struggle and Utopia at the Endtimes of Philosophy'. An anti-Hegelian formula, obviously: all thought is not determined by the philosophy that is supposed to give meaning to history. It speaks of the 'endtimes', not of the end *of* philosophy (a still-philosophical, intra-historical event). 'The endtimes' is an eschatological formula, and the context is that of humanity of-the-last-instance. Such is the new usage – of struggle and of utopia, and of philosophy at last brought within the reach of humans. What function could philosophy still perform in the epoch of ecological distress, an epoch wherein ecological finitude replaces metaphysical finitude?

It is not a question of a 'philosophy of degrowth', such as we sometimes hear of today, but of the degrowth of philosophy itself. The most evident effect of non-philosophy is the reduction of philosophy simultaneously to the state of an object and that of a production material, for a special science called 'generic' which is not a philosophy of positive sciences. Philosophy is but a productive force to place in the service of humans, and I maintain that it is not yet so placed, and never has been, except in a somewhat restricted and perverse sense. I do not claim that philosophy is nothing but ideology; it is a productive force that has been 'turned' to reproduction.

'PHILOSOPHICAL HORROR'

To prepare ourselves, let's begin with a few scandalous statements, under a celebrated heading that no doubt could be further nuanced: 'Man is the most terrible of beings' (Heidegger); 'Man is a wolf to man' (Hobbes); 'Man is a monstrous living being' (a neuro-biologist). Now, 'the philosopher is the man par excellence' (philosophers). And the conclusion is...? We shall call this set of presuppositions the symptom of the non-separability of man and animal. What is this non-separability, which prevents us deciding straight away who is the man in what is usually called man, and who is the animal in the animal? We find ourselves here in a great uncertainty as to the determination of these two entities. Philosophical horror stems from this always possible argument, but also to the ambiguity of philosophy itself.

The primary ideal of overgrowth, above all, that which legitimates if not produces it, is that of philosophy. There is a misunderstanding as to its aims: the increase of virtue or of the good, the diminution of evil – yes, perfcct. But philosophical humanism accomodates itself to that causality called domestication, rearing, breaking-in, which is the content of a realist and determinist ethics. We must ask whether this ethics is truly made for the human genus. Alongside virtues, which are the humanist and median version, there are the transcendentals and their categorical vocation; and higher still, the ideal of the Platonic more-of-philosophy, more enjoyment for the philosopher. And it is true that philosophy is an object of extraordinary enjoyment – now a Foucauldian pleasure, now a Deleuzian desire. There is also the right to philosophy (Derrida, Nietzsche), the duty to philosophise, and ultimately the immanent auto-justification of philosophy. To philosophise is to ultimately justify philosophy, to assure the full employment of the will without having to be measured about it.

PHILOSOPHICAL MODELS OF DEGROWTH

To philosophical inflation, must we oppose (and for what reason) philosophical models of degrowth? Of deflation? Occam's razor? Less philosophy? Its deconstruction, another weaker practice, as the Italians would have it, or more multiple as in Deleuze? Or else its economic marginalisation, its final nihilism? Or, on the contrary, do we need a philosophy that is stronger, always stronger, like Plato and Badiou? These solutions all suffer from a vicious disease: they are continuist, recognising only a *philo-diversity* that is vague, ultimately naturalist, and which, so to speak, lacks any scientific principle. But they do not recognize the complex or dual structure, the specular invariant of philosophy, whose auto-sufficiency and its homogeneity they extend, supposedly transforming it through their own means.

We pose the problem otherwise: How to continue to utilise philosophy, but in conjugating it with a more radical means, one that is truly heterogeneous to it – that is, science within it and outside of it – as opposed to the now vague, now theological alterity of the moderns. Already the science of language shows that *philosophy has the structure of a double articulation*, on two levels, which give it an affinity with language; that it forms a spectrum to be analysed and explained as a doublet structure or a structure in double transcendence; that it is governed, specifically, by the Principle of Sufficient Philosophy, which is the superior strata and the unity of sense that transforms dualities into doublets. In reducing it to a global thought, to one sole stratum with varying degrees, cases or nuances, the solutions evoked above *flatten it onto science as if onto a mirror, without truly making any use of science.* So that, for philosophy, science does not spontaneously think, because to think, one must speak; and moreover, philosophy makes use of science as a looking glass, in which it merely admires itself.

NON-PHILOSOPHY IS NOT A SHORT-SELLING SPECULATION

It is obviously not a matter of simple, continuous and quantitative degrowth – so what would it be to degrow? Such a degrowth of knowledge, of art, of philosophy, of science, of religion would take against philosophical growth, but would in fact be the same auto-philosophical model, understood this time as a conservative reaction and regression. *Generic degrowth, on the contrary, proposes to reduce philosophy to the state of a productive force* – thus, it is only the Principle of Sufficient Philosophy that must be rescinded. And in order for this to happen, we need science.

Philosophy is a speculation that sells short and long at the same time, that floats at once upward and downward.

But this is how it describes itself – as if the wave were being described by the sailor tossed upon it (see Leibniz and Kant). Or, according to another nostalgic trope, agrarian rather than marine, philosophy thinks only to grow like the Cartesian tree, or to root itself in the soil, as in Heidegger. Or again, it projects itself into a great living being. I take seriously all these aquatic, vegetable and vital metaphors of thought, which bear witness to an ecological nostalgia. But non-philosophy is not content to describe fluctuations or oscillations without explaining them, receiving them as affects, contenting itself with undergoing and living them. It is a matter of understanding the undulations, the lulls and surges of philosophy by requisitioning the science of waves (of waves and particles through vectors in a configuration space, or of imaginary numbers). A science for philosophy must respond to specific constraints: not only is it not on the same plane as its object, but this object is very special, since it is philosophy, which never allows itself to be manipulated by a simply positive and brute science. To avoid mere confrontation, and the war that knowledges and thought engage in, it is necessary to invent a device imposing upon them a 'perpetual peace' – a device for the conjugation of the two disciplines which preserves their autonomy, their specificity, while depriving them of their will to domination, rescinding their principles of sufficiency pertaining respectively to philosophical spontaneity and to the positivity of scientific domains.

Thus they are prepared so as to prevent their immediate usage, so as to lead them by force to a negotiation table, to create a common or generic space. This negotiation table is the 'generic matrix'. I do not claim to propose a 'general ecology', only a generic one – this is the contribution I can make, in so far as I live in an originally philosophical milieu, without limiting myself to everyday measures, saving water by shutting off the faucet, for instance. Let us not squander philosophy in tasks of substitution for theology, and above all of specular auto-exaltation.

AN ECOLOGY IN THE QUANTUM SPIRIT

In order for philosophy to become an ecological object or preoccupation, a certain number of conditions must therefore obtain. We must design their implementation, creating, in a word, an adequate theoretical 'installation'. We cannot transfer ecological problems and means of thought directly and continuously into philosophy; we need new definitions of vicinities and risks, new ways of marking out knowledges, and we must set our goals according to them.

1. The Paradox of the Productive Forces of Degrowth

I place quantum physics and philosophy together in a matrix, as non-separable, having a common interest or a common meaning for nature, so as to re-examine each of them in this situation, in terms of human subjects. It is not a question of raising each to the power of the other in an apparently reciprocal manner, seeking a meta-science or a meta-conjugation of knowledges. On the contrary, we wish to deliver ourselves from the stranglehold of knowledges that root us in the world under the authority of philosophy. This is the object of non-philosophy – not just a brute and positivist scientific diminution of philosophy.

The procedure seems to be a ruse, since one multiplies knowledges one by the other as if one was raising their power. But, on one hand, they are no longer disciplinary knowledges posited separately in their transcendence, their spontaneity and under their own principle of sufficiency. *Disciplinary knowledges are now simple states or reduced properties of a human subject=X that they do not determine directly.* And on the other hand, these knowledges deprived, by this device inspired by quantum thought, of their respective principle of sufficiency, are generically ordered according to this subject=X, or indexed to the imaginary number that is the secret of quantum thinking. The multiplication of properties produces the paradoxical effect of a generic degrowth of knowledges oriented by and for a new subject. It is rather a prolonging and an activation, a subjective repetition of the quantum degrowth of determinism and realism, an aggravation of this movement through the putting of these properties at the service of man as subject=X. *The generic matrix resolves the ecological paradox that productive forces with a degrowth or de-productivity effect.* How to produce degrowth rather than always producing overgrowth? Generic science therefore cannot be a general meta-science, but only a 'sub-science'.

2. From Linguistic Doublets to Quantum Dualities

I shall therefore pass from a linguistic or language-based interpretation to a physical and quantum interpretation of philosophy, an interpretation that better respects certain distinctions, and founds a reasoned degrowth. A model of quantum analysis (completed by a generic orientation) replaces the language-based model which favours the logocentric auto-effacement of dualities. The degrowth proposed would be dangerous or irrational, primary and reductive, if it were interpreted within the framework of language-based presuppositions. But the physicist reduction is not physicalist and naturalist – it does not arrive at primary representations, but at dynamic conceptual liveds [*vécus*]. I substitute for the still massively philosophical model of Lacan and Derrida an analysis according to a model that we shall call onto-vector*ial* rather than vecto-ri*ell* – ontological rather than geometrical, even though it uses the underpinnings of geometry. Whereas double articulation and the doublets that underwrite it tend to efface themselves in a language-based practice that stays within auto-philosophy, and which limits deconstruction to being auto-deconstruction, an entirely other duality is possible – a quantum duality, that of the wave and corpuscle, in the form of the vector and the particle. Even if it seems to imitate that of the signifier and the signified, which is the lower layer of double articulation, it is more scientific, mathematical even, and does not risk falling back into logocentrism since in it, vectors are not oppositional, negative and relative (Saussure) but are representable in an imaginary space, what we call a configuration space, determined algebraically by the imaginary number (square root of −1). And moreover the model of the corpuscle and then of the particle allows the subsumption of all forms of signified and of sense. As to the superior layer of the double articulation, that of discourse and units of meaning, it will also be transformed, losing its theological and fetishistic virtues of the enveloping of dualities. Concretely, the double articulation of philosophical discourse will be under-determined – that is to say, in conformity with the quantum model, it will lose its identities as a layer and a hierarchical relation, its identity as sufficient unity, which allows its singularity and philosophical-type universality. It will instead acquire a quantum indetermination and a non-localisation (a signifiant non-opposition, for example) in relation to a subject called 'generic'. The sequencing of philosophical discourse by itself, which continues in spite of everything in Lacan and Derrida, will be prohibited – for this would be a false degrowth of philosophy.

Anyhow, the enterprise does not end there; it also reduces metaphysics in favour of the generic subject. There is a subject of this degrowth, a subject which is no longer the philosophical subject. It undergoes degrowth only in operating it, but in a relation of causality called 'in-the-last-instance'. Degrowth as a theoretical and generic concept (rather than as economico-political doxa) is therefore founded on what we might call, in a remote sense, a 'generic Marxism' – in any case, on a scientific practice. It does not describe a situation in the concrete world, nor a phenomenological anthropology of man in the world. It is a theory of philosophical action in ecology, an action which we must conclude is more probable than certain and dogmatic.

AN ECOLOGY IN A GNOSTIC SPIRIT: THE NATURAL EPISTEMIC MILIEU, FROM WORLD TO UNIVERSE

I propose to change the ultimate reference environment for ecology, and to respond a little differently to the question of nature and environment. The quantum model obliges me to maintain that the correlate of physics (physics as essentially quantum, not the traditional *physis*) is the universe, and not the world. I understand by 'universe' the correlate of modern knowledges, by 'world' the correlate of philosophy. I would add that the universe is not the great mystical All evoked by certain physicists, but an epistemological correlate of physico-mathematical knowledge. The universe, even as object of experimentation and above all if it is an object of experimentation, is an object of knowledge, not a material object. This granted, the reference to knowledges must be distinguished from the reference to the world, and must find the universe as its true correlate – such is the consequence of this gnosis. But aside from these generalities, my objective is very limited in relation to the field of ecology and its Platonic presuppositions (even if gnosticism is in part a product of Platonism). Contemporary humans inhabit a world of proliferating knowledges, rather than a world of sensible objects marked by theology and thus by sin as was formerly the case. Thus we suggest an extension of the ecological domain: man must be prepared to transgress the natural world and to enter into the universe as theoretical object, not only into the world as biological milieu. Ecological or generic finitude cannot exactly replace the old finitude of the subject. Its sensible and cognitive sphere of existence is extended in its materiality, and in its formal possibilities, by renouncing the mirages of totality and the absolute. In terms of this modernised gnostic context, we shall no longer say that man is in general thrown into the world as evil and nothingness, and that his problem is to flee this world-here, but instead (and less religiously) that he is thrown-to-knowledge, that is to say to the universe by way of knowledges. His problem is not to rediscover, like an originary ante-predicative, the universal environment that he would have lost, but to defend himself from the confusion of world and universe by using knowledges against their philosophical capture by the world. The epistemic environment is, doubtless, a carrier of our very own 'disease', no longer absolute but in so far as it still retains its old philosophical form of the 'world'. The ecological problem is then displaced into that of the best usage-without-world, without-the-whole-world, of the natural epistemic environment. Particular attention is required as to the place of philosophy, which is duplicitous, at once one knowledge among others or a productive force, and the world-form par excellence that turns knowledges astray from their usage in view of the universe.

This way of posing the problem does not imply a globalization, but a naturalisation of the episteme. If there is a capital-world, it is that of knowledges; but can one reappropriate these knowledges outside of their world-form? The paradox of the procedure we adopt is to treat philosophy, which gives knowledges their sense and their truth, in its turn as a knowledge, so as to disencumber it of its relation of self-duplication, its closing in upon itself, quantum 'decoherence', in short. Knowledge, including the most ambitious thought, must be treated as a natural ecumenon, an inhabited surface of the terrestrial crust, but more extended, more universal, with dimensions supplementary to those of its ancient relation to physis – *it is universe-oriented rather than world-oriented*. There is an intention of knowledges, and it is the universe, just as the world is the intention of consciousness or of being. It is a matter of naturalising philosophy, in the strong sense of modern physics rather than of physis – not like Quine but more like Marx. The generic extension of humans to the universe is not a continuous, even infinite, extension of the world to the universe in the Husserlian manner. We pass from world to universe, from worldly ecology to the ecology of the universe, by way of what we might call the true 'quantum leap'. Thought is not the intrinsic property of humans that must serve to define their essence, an essence that would then indeed be 'local'; it is a uni-versal milieu. If we tend now to emphasise animality, bringing it within the sphere of culture, then why not emphasise the most elevated humanity, so as to bring it into the universe; and, through a paradoxical example, why not reexamine its links with animality, of which it will then a matter of knowing whether it, also, is universal? Let's suppose an ecology of the relations of thought, of its highest forms of which we can make use – science and philosophy, art and religion, relations with and within the universe which,

I insist once more, is not the mystical great All, but the correlate of knowledges.

THE IMAGINARY NUMBER AND THE RESCINDING OF THE ONE AS MACROSCOPIC SUFFICIENCY

The wellspring of non-philosophy is the One, but this thesis has been poorly understood. Not the One as metaphysics or duplicity of the One-of-the-One, but as radical immanence of the One-in-One which designates nothing other than quantum superposition. This is a new ontology: the representation of variables – that is to say, quantum thought and philosophy, by vectors, as is demanded by the imaginary number used in quantum mechanics – vectors that form a new duality with philosophical representation, but no longer a duplicity. This is a reversal of the One proper to a super-structure in the One-in-One as infrastructure composed of vectors. The imaginary number has a general effect of onto-vectoriel [*onto-vectoriale*] subtraction, or rather under-determination, from knowledges subtracted from philosophical representation but not subtracted from it. In other words, the One as factor of unity or ultimately duplicitous identity is suspended, apparently a little like the one-of-the-count of which Badiou speaks, but the imaginary number suspends only the One of sufficiency, or renders it immanent without suppressing it in a materialist manner.

It weakens the worldly sufficiency of knowledges, that of the encyclopaedia in general, including that of philosophical knowledge in so far as its proper sufficiency is not only the positive naivety of science but is sufficient twice over: once as direct, primary or principal, a second time vectorially or indirectly.

Now philosophy and quantum thought no longer face each other down in their sufficient and macroscopic spontaneity, but are two simple properties or predicates for a subject=X. To refuse to presuppose two, this is precisely the sufficiency of those knowledges that believe themselves to be unique. But our very own rational kernel is not of a dialectical order, but is physical, quantum. Thus what must be rescinded is not the One in general, in its abstraction as unit of the count, but *the-One-as-sufficiency*. I seek in the One-in-One as superposition of vectors the formula of a contemporary gnosis capable of weakening the grip of the world, which is exerted in the form of knowledges in so far as they are overdetermined by philosophy. It is not the sort of imaginary that increases philosophy; on the contrary, the imaginary or complex number is a productive force of the degrowth of metaphysics. It is an amputation of philosophical excess with a directly positive effect, a positivity of retreat-without-retraction or of subtracted-without-subtraction. Onto-vectoriel immanence underdetermines philosophical growth or overdetermination; so degrowth or underdetermination is not an ontology of lack or of the negative, which one might oppose immediately to the full and affirmative ontology of Spinoza, Nietzsche, Bergson and Deleuze. It is a vectoriel affirmation without re-affirmation – but here, the absence of a second affirmation does not destroy every selection. On the contrary. Here, philosophy is 'degrowth-oriented'.

The One-in-One is presently a form of un?conscious or infrastructure – the impossible real, if you like, the real that does not enter into the philosophical order. But it is not a question of eliminating it, as in Badiou, killing it. For it will fuse with the philosophical superstructure and its doublets, but under its own authority, that of the imaginary number or vector indexed to itself as 'last instance'. Standard quantum thought makes for (or helps to make) non-standard philosophy. It is not projected specularly within philosophy, but transforms the latter. The quantum, and then generic, underdetermination by the Last Instance is a general diminution of disciplines to the state of vectoriel properties, and of transcendental principles and absolutes to the state of objective or immanental appearances.

This is to abandon the procedures of Lacanianism and deconstruction (which is a complex Judaic-oriented Lacanianism). Philo-fiction is a parallel genre to science fiction, a diminution of dogmatism and of the philosophical axiomatic to the state of a fiction. Fiction places itself between the real and objective reality, and allows the connection of the two. Philosophical dogmatism strangles truth between macroscopic experience and objectivity. It is a question of slackening this noose that would encircle truth.

THE PRODUCTIVE FORCES OF DEGROWTH (EPISTEMOLOGICAL REDUCTIONS)

We need a new analysis of philosophical duplicity, but also of the semi-conscious (or un?conscious) naturality of positive knowledges, such as they are required in their mutual production and usage. Thus, a new analysis of knowledges that have found their proper form but remain relatively un?conscious in their pragmatic or instrumental purchase. Science and philosophy are theoretical productive forces usable in the circuits of theoretical pragmateia. There is a use of scientific positivity included in any practice of understanding. This is not to say that sciences are nothing but practices; but that we treat them here uniquely as productive forces that do not have their end in themselves, but as both within and without themselves – that is to say, for humans as ecological subjects. Once 'naturalised', science and philosophy are no longer models outside of the order of knowledges, or metaphysical paradigms of thought and life. They are 'only' knowledges used as productive forces in the service of humans in view of a transformed type of knowledge that we might call 'truth'. It is curious, in the context of degrowth, to announce an extension of productive forces. But in reality the naive usage of science and of philosophy under their respective principles is the source of all excessive *dérives*, and their reduction to the state of forces is the best way to put them consciously in the service of humans. It is true that this reduction is implied for and by the construction of the matrix – the matrix already presupposes this reduction, which otherwise would be meaningless. The matrix is the only concrete or real, it is no longer the sciences or philosophy as paradigms which are the concrete.

SUBJECTIVE ECOLOGY OF THE FIRST AND LAST INSTANCE

In what sense are humans ecological subjects? The metaphysical dissociation of man and animal is too simple and macroscopic. As always in the quantum spirit, we work with non-separable dualities. Firstly that of animal and man: their non-separability or non-locality is posited, in various possible versions. And then the primary objective and the prior-to-primary objective, or objective of-the-last-instance, which both apply to this non-separability of man-animal. To preserve the natural environment of existence, to preserve man and his survival qua species even, is the immediate and primary aim of ordinary ecology. Nevertheless we distinguish from this a prior-to-primary aim or an aim of-the-last-instance: again, man-animal, but in his power of under-determination of primary aims. The 'defence' and the maintenance of human environments, spontaneous and naturalist ecology, must be reordered in view of a defence of generic man in (and sometimes against) the environment or milieu of knowledges. This new objective of ecology cannot be called superior or meta-ecological. It is in-the-last-instance a *generic usage* of epistemic milieus, the best appropriation of knowledges (including philosophy itself) in view of the defence of humans against their self-destructive drive, which has its origin in the world. *I distinguish between the philosophical ecology of human animals who live in-the-world, and the ecology of human animals who live generically in-man and thus with a view to the universe; between the protection of the environment and the defence in-the-last-instance of humans.* Whence the subordination of the great classical objectives of philosophy, and even of truth, of the moral conception and the metaphysical elevation of humans, to their ultimate horizon which is the safeguarding of humans in-the-last-instance against violence, including ecological violence.

DEGROWTH: A MERELY PROBABLE IMPERATIVE OF NON-PHILOSOPHICAL ECOLOGY (ECO-FICTION)

All of this allows the diminution or the degrowth of knowledges, in so far as they are governed by philosophy. It is a matter of founding ecology upon a non-Aristotelian, but also non-Newtonian, basis. We refuse philosophical sufficiency and its naturalism (rational animal or creature). We must change terrain at least epistemologically, suspending the metaphysically idealized world or nature – that is to say, the determinism that goes along with realism and which permits anti-animal violence. But after having eliminated causalist determinism through quantum thinking, it is necessary to attain the generic terrain or point of view, a point of view at once quantum or matrixial and indexed on the human as generic subject destined to the practice of eco-fiction, since it is in-the-last-instance an ecology and not a physics.

1. Since it invariably affects that shifting duality that is philosophy, generic degrowth cannot be a quantitative question but must be a qualitative one, and must make use of philosophy itself as its occasion. So it supposes an analysis of philosophical complexity, the quantum device of a probabilist understanding of that special object, philosophy. The degrowth of philosophical sufficiency is founded upon this understanding rather than upon disciplinary practices of rearing and domestication, or of macroscopic transformation.

2. Generic man necessitates an experimental-type understanding, not a mechanically deterministic and substantial deduction. In conformity with the quantum spirit of the two states of the generic object, we should distinguish between its real state named 'generic man', made of

virtual possibilities (non-philosophy as 'prepared philoso-phy') and its state of effective understanding named 'Last Instance' and given as the final measure of humans. The uncertainty of understanding concerns only the experi-mental understanding that leads humans as a generic set, not as philosophers. It is not an immediate understanding, flush with its premises, not a vicious ideological confu-sion. It appears only with the repetition of the experiment or a 'second measurement', as physicists say, rather than immediately with the empirical or a priori givens. If it has a restricted or under-determined 'a priori' aspect, it is not as primary but as 'prior-to-primary' or as prepara-tion of the conditions of knowing. Probable knowing that commands only with uncertainty, with probability, because generic man is not the object of an absolute and axiomatic definition. He is known across his properties, which are variables; he is an observable object before being an observed object. Thus it cannot be a question of a continuous degrowth of transcendence in general – non-philosophical ecology is a 'prepared' ecology.

3. There are negative ecologies in the same sense that there are 'negative theologies'. But the under-determination of transcendence is a positive operation of selection in philosophy, rather than an exclusion of the latter. It is the effect of a pre-emptive operation, or of the sampling of a slice of the most human transcendence, such as it results from unilateral causality, or from what we call the clone

(at once vectorial [*vectorial*] and lived). To preserve the part of transcendence that defines human genericity is the effect of a positive act that no longer aspires, like philosophy, to a sur-transcendence, but to a 'sub-transcendence'. It was incorrect to understand negatively the notions of an a priori defence of man, and of degrowth.

4. For all these reasons, which are the effects of generic man (and not only man as species faced with other species under conjoint genuses, or under the generalities of the animal and of reason, or as dominant, reigning species) we shall refuse the Principle of Sufficient Ecology, and we shall conclude from this to a probabilist ecology founded upon a principle of uncertainty. Ecological sufficiency, or indeed anti-ecological sufficiency, balances up absolute and ideological decisions in one direction or another – for example, the refusal to train or consume animals as supposedly simply natural beings (whether in-man or outside-of-man). This is still to presuppose that man can decide freely, in some all-powerful manner, to safeguard nature or to destroy it. Whereas he does not really have this power to transform it wholesale, since he himself belongs to every decision, is included in it and perturbs it, puts it back into play with every decision or repetition. He has only the power to underdetermine his decisions. What is needed is a reflection upon the non-separability of man and animal, and on the animal as, at once, model for man and clone of man.

APPENDIX I

Experimental Texts

Experimental Texts, Fictions, Hyperspeculation

(1989)

Translated by Robin Mackay

The texts assembled under this rubric cannot be understood outside of the conception of science – of the thinking of the One [...] They belong to a genre that we call 'non-philosophy', which is the operation of science upon philosophical material and, at the same time, its result. These texts are in principle unacceptable to philosophy and its most general codes, but they are produced on its basis. In a word: rather than produce apparently non-philosophical (literary, psychoanalytic, etc.) effects by means of procedures that remain essentially philosophical (deconstructions, for example), it is proposed to use really non-philosophical procedures to produce effects that would have a final semblance, a last 'family resemblance', with philosophy. 'Non-philosophy' is not anti-philosophical, it contains the philosophical genre as a particular case or a limited thought; it is what the philosophical qua genre becomes when it is grasped and transformed by vision-in-One. The statements thus produced only belong to 'philo-fiction' or 'hyperspeculation' from the point of view of the criteria of philosophical thought. In other respects they are 'scientific'. This scientific character is neither founded upon their apparently logical disposition, nor contradicted by their quasi-poetical, quasi-religious, quasi-logical (etc.) effects (poetry-fiction, religion-fiction, logic-fiction, etc.).

Variations on a Theme by Heidegger

(1987)

Translated by Robin Mackay

ORIGINAL THEME

> *Da-sein is a being that is not limited to appearing among*
> *other beings. Rather it has the following ontic distinction:*
> *in its being this being is concerned about its very being.*
> *Thus it is constitutive of the being of Da-sein to have, in*
> *its very being, a relation of being to this being. And this in*
> *turn means that Da-sein understands itself in its being in*
> *one way or another and more or less explicitly. It is proper*
> *to this being that it be disclosed to itself with and through its*
> *being. Understanding of being is itself a determination of*
> *being of Da-sein. The ontic distinction of Da-sein lies in the*
> *fact that it is ontological.*

BEING AND TIME, §4, SZ 12.

I

Dasein – this is retranslated, in the philosophical wherein it is already translated, as Being-as-a-being. It is a being that is not limited to simply being – that is to say (as this is retranslated in the philosophical) to being an object, in the full or phenomenal sense, henceforth, of objectivity. Being-as-a-being is a being, but is not limited to being a-being-as-Being. As a being it has the following, originally ontic distinction, which distinguishes it from every other being: in its objectivity it is concerned about its objectivity. Thus it is constitutive of the constitution-of-objectivity of the Object-as-a-being, to have, in its objectivity, an objective relation to the latter. Being-as-a-being understands itself in its objectivity in one way or another and more or less explicitly. It is proper to this being that its objectivity be disclosed to itself with and through its objectivity. Understanding of objectivity is itself an objective determination of Being-as-a-being. The ontic distinction of Being-as-a-being lies in the fact that, as objective, it understands objectivity.

II

Being-as-a-being is a being that is not limited to simply being a being-as-Being, an object indifferent to its objectivity. It is Difference, the divided point that recrosses – a broken circle of inversion – its twin sides, Being-as-a-being and a being-as-Being. It has the following ontic distinction: that its being is not indifferent to itself, but is concerned by itself; that its objectivity is affected by itself; that its being is not only identical to itself give or take a division through which it is augmented qua Being itself; that it is open to being affected by itself, to inhibiting itself as that being that it is, and of augmenting itself as Being. Ontological Difference is that chiasm of Being and beings, a chiasm with four sides (Being-as-a-being, a being-as-Being) and four forces (two repulsive, two attractive). Being-as-a-being is thus understood as ontico-ontological Difference. Its ontic distinction lies in this circle, broken by an inversion, that returns to it from itself.

III

Being-as-a-being is a being that is not limited to simply being a theme or an object for ontology. It has the following ontic distinction: that of implying ontology in itself and of being this chiasm. It practises it in the mode where it constitutes its own stakes; in every instance it invests all of ontology in the particular ontology that is its own. Its understanding of its being and of Being is, each time, for this being, an ontological game, a decision that implicates all the rules of ontology in the undecidable conflict of two

particular ontologies. The ontological games that it practises are one-player games (Being-beings), that is to say
two-player games (Being-as-a-being, a being-as-Being),
that is to say four-player games (each player 'Being-being'
functioning now as Being for the next being-Being, now
as a being for a neighbouring Being-being). Being-as-a-
being is the friend of those games where good neighbours
take each other on, and upon which it cannot, and does
not wish to, impose the rules of a meta-ontology.

IV

Dasein is resaid, in the philosophical wherein it is already
said, as the 'Saying-as-said'. It is a said that is not limited
to simply being itself said without its saying it again. It
has the following ontological distinction: that of saying
that it does indeed have the ontic distinction of being
able to say that it is not limited to simply appearing as
a said within saying, but that it has the ontic distinction
of having the ontological distinction of saying that in
its saying it is concerned about this very saying, and of
saying that in this saying it is concerned with this auto-
affection of saying, and of having a relationship-of-saying
to the relationship-of-saying that it has with this power of
saying. The Saying-as-said is said as saying itself in one
way or another and more or less explicitly in its power
of saying. It is proper to this said that it is said to itself

with and through its saying of the power of saying. The saying of the power of saying is itself a mode of saying-itself proper to Saying – as said. The ontic distinction of Saying-as-said lies in the fact that it is said as saying itself in its saying. The Saying-as-said is resaid in the saying as the self-saying which, saying its saying, says it each time entirely in every particular saying.

V

Being is not only the Being of the being, it is Being-as-a-being. It is not only ontological, it is ontic. 'Ontological Difference' is the abbreviation – and the idealist reduc-tion – of 'ontico-ontological' or 'ontological' 'Difference'. (Ontico-)Ontological Difference is fundamental, but more fundamental still, in delimiting the latter or meta-physics, is *ontico*(-ontological) Difference. The former is subordinated to the latter, which is the auto-affection of ontology divided, and recombined in itself, by beings or *ontico*(-ontological) Difference. The ontic distinction of this being is that, within its being-ontological, it is the ontic, and no longer ontological, distinction between Being and beings. It distinguishes between the 'ontic' meaning properties of the object-being, or properties grasped within an ontological horizon, and the 'ontic' meaning that which never falls within such an horizon, as withdrawal or differe(/a)nce that renders ontology finite. Unlike other beings, indifferent to their being, and whose infinite ontology gives rise to 'metaphysics', for that being and for the ontology that it announces, the ontic is the necessary reference of the ontological and the site-of-division where infinite ontology must come to pass. The reference in the mode of auto-affection which is that of ontology makes the most undecidable reference still to beings.

VI

Dasein – this is retranslated, in the philosophical wherein it is already translated, as Logos-as-Other, as Presence-as-Other. It is an Other that is not limited to being present. Rather it has the following ontic distinction, as Other: for this Other, and qua Other, its particular mode of presence is such that its presence is divided, is affected *in* itself and is extended as Presence. It is constitutive of this constitution-in-presence of Presence-as-Other to have a relation of presence to presence. Presence-as-Other is grasped again, in its chiasm, as mode of Presence. It is proper to this Other that it be disclosed to itself – that it be divided – in a relation to presence, with and through its guise of presence. But Presence only returns to itself as Other and after the Other. The Other has the yet more fundamental distinction of making the difference between the auto-affection of presence that believes itself the power of Presence upon itself, and the ontic auto-affection through which, as Other, it differs the former without return. Thus Presence-as-Other explains to itself that it must always consider thus the suspension of Presence to the Other and situate Presence in the differe(/a)nce of the Other to Presence.

VII

Actuality-as-subject is a subject that is not limited to being an object of knowledge. Rather, as subject, it has the following distinction: for this subject its actuality is concerned about its very actuality; it is care of self. Thus it is constitutive to its sense of actuality to have a relation of care, itself actual, to its own actuality. And this in turn means that the care of self interprets itself in one way or another and more or less explicitly, in its own sense. It is proper to this subject that this actuality is disclosed, as care of self, to itself and to its actuality, with and through its actuality. The hermeneutics of actuality is itself an auto-interpretation of Actuality-as-subject. The distinction, qua subject, of Actuality-as-subject lies in the fact that it is the actuality of a hermeneutic of actuality.

VIII

Desire-as-lack is a lack that is not limited to being present or absent like a thing. Rather it has, as lack, the following distinction: for this Desire-as-lack, there is Desire for itself, Desire is desire for itself, Desire is desire for self and desires itself as desire for self. It is constitutive of this Desire which disguises this lack or which is its existence, to have a relation of desire to itself in particular and to extend itself as universal Desire. And this in turn means that Desire-as-lack desires itself in its desire in one way or another and more or less explicitly. It is proper to Desire-as-lack qua lack-as-desire that this desire is disclosed to itself as lacking in itself with and through its desire. The distinction, as lack, of Desire-as-lack lies in the fact that it exists and understands itself as desire for desire.

IX

Difference or the mixture of Being-as-One is a One that is not limited to being a mode of Being. Rather it has the following, originally unary, distinction: this One qua One, in its Difference, is concerned with Difference. Thus it is constitutive of the constitution-of-difference of this mixture in so far as it is One to have a relation of difference to Difference, a divided and recombined relation, or a relation of chiasm. And this in turn means that Difference-as-One understands itself or uses itself in so far as it is a mixture. It is proper to this One, to this usage-of-difference of the One, that Difference is more or less disclosed to itself with and through its existence as mixture. The more or less differed autoreference of Difference to itself is a mode of existence of Difference. The originally unary distinction of Difference lies in the fact that it exists actually in the mode of an already-differential thought of Difference.

X

The mixture of mixtures or Difference is philosophical-Decision-as-One. The latter is a One that is not limited to appearing as Difference. Rather it has this specifically unary distinction: it – One in the last instance, in its mode of mixture, Philosophical Decision – is concerned about this mixture itself, which affects itself, reduces itself, or inhibits itself and is resumed as superior mixture. It is constitutive of the mixed-constitution of philosophical-Decision-as-One to have in its mixedness a relation and a non-relation of chiasm. And this in turn means that the mixedness of Philosophical Decision understands itself always more or less explicitly in its form of a mixture or of Decision. It is proper to this philosophical usage of the One that Philosophical Decision is disclosed to itself and understands itself as philosophical with and through its existence as mixed. The philosophy of philosophy is a philosophical possibility of Philosophical Decision. The unary distinction of Philosophical Decision lies in the fact that it exists philosophically in the mode of a philosophy of philosophy.

XI

Dasein – this is retranslated, in the philosophical wherein it is already translated, as *human Reality*. Human Reality is a One that is not limited to appearing as a mode of Being or as object. Rather it has the following unary or real distinction, which is however a distinction of the last instance: its objective existence in the World is affected by itself and tied up in itself. It belongs to this existence of human Reality that it exists in its own mode and that this human Reality should include itself on its own basis. The comprehension of self is a determination of human Reality that is itself ontological. The distinction of human Reality, as unary or real, in the last instance, lies in the fact that it exists in the mode of ontological decision.

XII

Human Reality is not only that by which *Dasein* can be retranslated, and in which *Dasein* can detranslate itself; it is that which describes the real and ultimate phenomenal content that masks *Dasein*. It is the One, but the One that precedes mixture, Being or Difference, and which is not content to be commanded and utilised by the latter. Human Reality has the unary distinction of experiencing itself in itself without having to abandon or alienate itself in existence, being or objectivation. It experiences itself in its reality before any thetic project of self, without passing via Being and *is concerned in its very…* with Being in itself, that is to say via the general form of the World. The comprehension of Being is not a determination of being of the One, which has no such determinations, but a contingent event whose advent in human Reality comes along with the World. The unary distinction of this Reality is to remain in itself and to be able to describe itself rigorously without passing via ontological statements. Man can say the truth of Being without being affected by it; he locates once and for all Philosophical Decision, the chiasm that it makes with itself.

XIII

Being-as-One – that is to say, from now on, human Reality – is a real transcendence that is not limited to appearing among the transcendence of Being nor even to speaking this Being. It does not manifest itself either in a decision and a position, or in this decision and this position. It *is* the trial of a Transcendence that retains itself on this side of disjunction and of the unity of chiasm of decision and position. Rather it has the following unary distinction in the last instance: for this real transcendence, itself no longer concerned with itself, it experiences itself in itself *before* straying into the World and affecting itself, redividing itself, reflecting itself, making a chiasm. It is constitutive of the constitution-in-transcendence of man to give himself (to) himself as this transcendence, without having once more to re-transcend toward himself; and it is constitutive of man to be already in transcendence without having to transcend. It is affected (affects itself) ceaselessly and is exhausted at once without it having need of a decision to begin itself, of a plan or position to extend and realise itself. It is proper to man as One or individual that his human, non-philosophical transcendence should be an immediate and non-thetic lived-experience-(of)-self. But this non-thetic transcendence is but one mode of the real essence of man, and is determined in the last instance by the latter.

XIV

Dasein or Being-as-a-being is not only Being. Human-reality-as-One is not only *Dasein* or Being-as-a-being, it is not limited to having a relation of being to self, it is more radically non-thetic Transcendence-(of)-self. But Human-reality-as-One, moreover, is not limited to being this transcendence. Not only is it via the unary distinction or real essence, but it is also now the non-thetic vision of the mixed nature that it has in the World and as Being. *Dasein* or Being-as-a-being is the necessary signal or support of this human or non-thetic transcendence, a support now lived by the latter and perceived according to this experience of exteriority. All metaphysical ontology, and also all ontology-as-ontic, is now experienced by real man as a non-thetic event of exteriority – decision as absolutely undecidable, position as absolutely non-positional. It is constitutive of human Reality to experience without any delay, albeit in a non-thetic mode of exteriority, the auto-affectation of Being and its chiasm. It is proper to it that this auto-affectation should be given to it yet more originarily and radically than in its own mode of auto-affection (or of hetero-affection). Understanding of Being is not necessary to define the essence of man, but it is the determination in the last instance of the latter. The unary distinction of human Reality lies in the fact that it lives in a non-ontological mode, and thus also in the fact that ontology, for it, is experienced as a non-ontological affect.

XV

Human Reality is a One that is not limited to experiencing the affect of an ever-undecided exteriority; of a division forever undivided and given (to) itself as undivided; nor to experience thus all ontology, the mixture of *Dasein* or of Being-as-a-being, in that non-thetic mode and to be able to generate ontology in this mode. Rather it has the following unary distinction: it can also make and let float away from it, indifferently, the whole set of these objects, including transcendence, drawing from them a non-specular image or reflection that has still less reality, still more contingency than them. It is constitutive of this One that it can experience, not only as lived real, but as henceforth non-thetic knowledge of this lived, the auto-comprehension of Being, all the circles and chiasms of philosophy. Thus Being is not only disclosed to itself; this disclosure is not only the lived of a non-thetic object; it itself passes into the state of a non-thetic reflection of self, a reflection without chiasm, a knowledge that neither posits nor modifies and is content to reflect 'absolutely' and 'vacuously'. Being-as-a-being, but also the essence-of-Being-itself, all ontology, all deconstructions, are not only events of a non-thetic exteriority; they now become mere descriptive and non-constitutive representations of themselves. From now on they belong to a uni-versal and abyssal reflection that reflects in non-specular manner man or the One. And now they are even stripped of the non-thetic Transcendence under which they formerly appeared.

XVI

Two series of variations distribute Philosophical Decision and open it to 'non-philosophy'. On one hand we have variations on the circle, or the circle as variation: Being-as-a-being, Saying-as-said, Logos-as-Differe(/a)nce, Desire-as-lack, Actuality-as-subject, and even Difference-as-One. Logos, the ontologos, turns itself in sudden inversions and chiasms around beings, like a function (that is also a variable) around a variable (that is also a function). The ontic root subsists in it as the pivot of these inversions and recurrences, but the circles thus engendered are not limited to appearing within the circle of ontology, but have the ontic distinction of being modes of the latter, or chiasms. On the other hand, though, we have variations affecting the ontic itself, which is said as being, as Other, as lack, as substitution – finally as One. This last variation brings to bear ontological variations on the real, and ontic variations on the ontological – a real around which turn the logos and its satellites – on an in-variable real, the One. The One or man is thus, on one hand, the highest point of philosophical revolutions, the absolute limit of their successive torsions, beyond which it is no longer possible to spin the philosophical or to make implode the circle of circles; and on the other hand, the real which is never limited to appearing among Being and to serving as a pivot for its circles: Vision-in-One, which lets the philosophical cosmos float freely in infinite spaces. When finally man, through Vision-in-One, in whose mode he 'is', before all understanding of Being, sees the circle of circles passing by again, it is to perceive it outside the One and passing under the One, below it, and even 'upon' it, like clouds over the moon, or the sun of reason upon the unalterable opacity of man. Thus philosophy floats, indifferent, in the 'non-philosophical' element.

Leibniz Variations

(1988)

Translated by Robin Mackay

I

1.1. There exists something rather than nothing

1.2. There exists a statement rather than nothing at least a statement rather than no statement at all it says that beings exist rather than nothing or that the nothingness-of-beings or that the nothingness that being exists rather than nothing or that the nothingness-of-being or that beings that the One exists rather than nothing or that the nothingness-of-One or that Being it says that rather than negation (n')[17] – not beings not being not One – exists that which is determined by the function (n')

---

17   Laruelle plays throughout on an ambiguity between 'not' (as in *n'est* – is not) and a differential function *n'* – thus dramatising the function of the 'non' of non-philosophy.

1.3. There exists rather than nothing a philosophy that says that a philosophical exists at least a philosophy rather than nothing it says that the contrary of a statement is not a simple privation but that there exists – rather – in its way in so far as that statement that the nothingness of the statement is not a lack but that there exists – rather – in so far as the statement that says that there exists something rather than nothing than the absence of beings the not being exists just as positively as being that being as not being in so far as being that being as not One in so far as the One there exists rather than nothing a philosophy that says that the nothingness of philosophy exists – rather – in so far as a philosophy that nothing exists in so far as something rather than nothing

1.4. There exists rather than nothing a statement that says that a philosophy exists at least a philosophy rather than nothing it says that there exists rather than nothing a philosophy which inverts that which says that there exists a statement rather than nothing in that which says that nothing no statement at all exists rather than a statement or the existence of beings rather than of nothingness of beings in the existence of the nothingness of beings rather than of beings the existence of being rather than of the nothingness-of-being in the existence of the nothingness of being rather than of the being the existence of the One rather than of the nothingness-of-One in the existence of the nothingness-of-One rather than of the One the existence of something rather than nothing in the existence of nothing rather than of something

1.5. There exists rather than nothing a philosophy that says that rather than nothing a statement exists to say that a philosophy exists at least a philosophy rather than nothing it says that there exists a supplementary statement to that which says that something a statement exists rather than nothing exists rather than the statement and despite this statement that says that the nothingness of the statement exists rather than a statement that it exists of beings rather than of the nothingness of beings exists rather than the existence of the nothingness of beings rather than of beings and despite the nothingness of beings that there exists some of being rather than of not being exists rather than the existence of not being rather than of being and despite this not being that there exists some of the One rather than of no One exists rather than the existence of no One rather than of the One and despite this no One that there exists something rather than nothing exists rather than the existence of nothing rather than of something

1.6. Existence wills something rather than nothing and even nothing rather than not to will there exists rather than nothing a will of philosophy that wills rather than nothing a statement to say that a philosophy wills the nothing rather than not to will that it wills a statement of nothingness even the nothingness of the statement rather than not will than not will statement of All that it wills beings of nothingness even the nothingness of beings the being of nothingness even the nothingness of being the One of nothingness even the nothingness of the One rather than not will than not will at All

II

2.1. One exists rather than something than nothing than the existence of something rather than nothing One exists rather than nothing rather than All rather than nothing at All

2.2. One exists rather than a statement than the existence of a statement rather than nothing than no statement at All One rather than the statement that says the One or that says that that which is not truly *a* statement is also not truly a *statement* a statement rather than nothing One exists rather than the statement that does not exist except as One and that says that there is no *being* that is not *a* being and that beings are One rather than the nothingness-of-beings is not One that there is no *being* that is not *a* being and that being is One rather than the nothingness-of-being is not One that there is no One that is not *a* One and that the One is One rather than the nothingness-of-One is not One One exists rather than the statement that is One rather than what the statement says of the being of the being of the One rather than that which is determined by the function (n') One exists rather than the function (n') or (non-) One that exists thus as One rather that as nothing and rather than something than nothing than something rather than nothing

2.3. One exists rather than a philosophy than nothing than the existence of a philosophy rather than nothing or than no philosophy at All rather than the philosophy that says that what is not truly *a* philosophy is also not truly a *philosophy* a philosophy rather than nothing One exists rather than the philosophy-One that says that the contrary of a statement is not a privation but in its way exists just as much as this statement and exists as One that no statement at All is not a lack but is One just as much as the statement that says that a statement is One rather than the nothing is not One than the nothing of beings is just as positively One as beings as beings as nothingness of being is also One than being than being as nothingness of One is also One as One

2.4. One exists rather than a statement-One that says that there is no philosophy that is not One and that there exists rather than nothing a philosophy that inverts that which

says that a philosophy exists and exists as One rather than
the nothing does not exist as One in that which says that
nothing no philosophy at All exists and exists as One
rather than a philosophy that nothing-of beings is One
rather than beings is than the nothingness of being is One
rather than being is not than the nothingness of One is
One rather than the One is not One exists rather than a
philosophy that says that there is not such an inversion
that is not One

2.5. One exists rather than a philosophy-One that says
that One exists rather than a statement-One exists rather
than nothing One exists rather than a supplementary
statement-One that says that a statement that exists and
exists as One rather than the nothing does not exists as
One exists as One rather than and despite the statement
that says that the non-existence of a statement exists as
One rather than a statement exists as One than something
that is One rather than nothing is not exists as One rather
than and despite the One of nothing which is One rather
than something is not than being which is One rather than
the not being is not is One despite the One of not being
which is One rather than the being is not that the One
which is One rather than the One is not is One despite
the One of not One which is One rather than the One is
not One exists rather than a philosophy-One that exists
despite the nothingness-of-philosophy and rather than it

2.6. One exists rather than a will-One of philosophy that wills rather than nothing a statement-One to say that a philosophy-One wills the One of the statement and the statement of the One rather than nothing or than not willing that it wills as One the statement of nothing even the nothing of the statement as One the beings of nothingness even the nothingness of beings as One the being of nothingness even the nothingness of being as One the One of nothingness even the nothingness of the One rather than not willing to will nothing at All One exists rather than a philosophy-One that wills the One of willing the willing of the One rather than not willing One exists rather than not existing as One the willing nothing rather than the not willing nothing

III

3.1. (not-) One exists an *chôra*-One rather than something than nothing than something rather than nothing than a philosophy rather than nothing there exists or not indifferently indifferently rather than nothing indifferently in so far as rather than nothing a statement or a philosophy indifferently a *chôra* that says that there exist indifferently rather than nothing 'a statement' a 'nothing' an 'a statement rather than nothing' a 'nothing rather than a statement' a 'rather than' an 'in so far as' or an 'indifferently' or indifferently that there exists indifferently in so

far as nothing an 'a statement' a 'nothing' etc. an 'Etc.' or
indifferently an 'a statement' in so far as an 'there exists'
a 'nothing' in so far as a 'something' a 'being' in so far as
a 'One' a 'nothing' in so far as an 'Etc.' or statements that
say indifferently rather than indifferently that something
exists rather than nothing or indeed rather than rather-
than that nothing exists rather than something or that
rather-than that rather-that exists rather than something
or something or that nothing or again indifferently in
so far as indifferently that something exists in so far as
nothing or as rather that something exists in so far as
something or that rather than rather-than exists in so far as
something or that nothing or again indifferently because
indifferently that something exists rather than nothing or
rather than rather-than because nothing or rather exist
rather than something that nothing exists rather than
something or that rather because something or rather
exists rather than nothing that rather exists rather than
something or that nothing because something or nothing
exist rather than rather-than or again indifferently that
indifference wills the indifference of nothingness and of
something of rather and of the in so far as rather than
nothing or indifferently in so far as nothing that something wills the statement of nothingness or indifferently
the nothingness of the statement rather or in so far as to
will nothing at All that something wills the nothing of
nothingness or indifferently the nothingness of nothing

rather or in so far as to will nothing at All that is wills the rather-than of nothingness or the nothingness of rather-than rather or in so far as to will nothing at All that nothing wills the something of nothingness or the nothingness of something rather or in so far as to will nothing at All that it wills the rather-than of nothingness or the nothingness of rather-than rather or in so far as no rather of All that rather-than wills the something of nothingness or the nothingness of something rather or in so far as to will nothing at all that it wills the nothing of nothingness or the nothingness of nothing rather or in so far as to will nothing at All in so far as or rather indifferently a *chôra* ...

IV

4.1. Rather-One exists rather than something than something rather than nothing rather-One that is to say that that which is not truly *a* rather or rather-One is also not truly a *rather* One exists rather than rather-One and rather-One rather than rather-than

4.2. Rather than a statement that says that there exists a statement rather than nothing there exists as rather-One a statement that says that rather than a statement and that no statement at All there is no statement that is not One rather – a rather-One – than nothing and that does not say that rather is rather-One rather than something or that nothing that something or that nothing is not One that beings or not beings that beings or not beings is not One that being or not being that being or not being is not One that One or the not One that One or the not One is not One

4.3. Rather than a philosophy that says that there exists a statement rather than nothing there exists as rather-One a statement that says that rather exists as One that the equality of non-beings to beings exists as rather-One rather than its inequality is not rather-One that the equal-ity of non-being to being exists as rather-One rather than its inequality is not rather-One that the inequality of non-One to the One exists as rather-One rather than its inequality is not rather-One

4.4. Rather than a statement that says that there exists a philosophy rather than nothing there exists as rather-One a philosophy that says that rather exists as One that there exists a statement that inverts that which says that there exists a statement that is rather-One rather than a statement or that nothing that a statement or that nothing is not One in that which says that no statement is rather-One that not beings exist as One – Onenotbeings – or as rather-One rather than the being that the not One is One – OnenotOne – or rather-One rather than the One and that this inversion exists as rather-One that as rather-than or that as inversion

4.5. Rather than a statement that says that there exists a philosophy to say that a statement exists rather than nothing there exists as rather-One a statement that says that there exists a philosophy to say that a statement exists as rather-One rather than a nothingness of statement and despite this nothingness or that a statement that says that there exists a statement-One rather than nothing is itself One and rather-One rather than a statement and despite the statement that says that no statement is One that a something is One and rather-One rather than nothing is One this is One and rather-One despite the existence of nothing as One and rather One rather than of something that being should be One and rather-One rather than the not being is One this is One and rather-One despite the non-being being One and rather-One rather than being that One should be One and rather-One rather than the non-One is One this is One and rather-One despite the non-One being One and rather-One rather than the One

4.6. Rather than a will of philosophy that wills willing rather than nothing or than not willing there exists as rather-One a statement that says that a will of philosophy wills the rather-One rather than the rather-than or than not willing the rather-One rather than willing the statement of nothingness even the nothingness of the statement being of nothingness even the nothingness of being the One of nothingness even the nothingness of the One it wills the rather-One rather than willing nothingness rather than not willing at All it wills the rather-One of this willing rather than this willing that nothing that willing this willing rather than nothing

V

5.1. One exists rather than a something-One that is to say that this that that which is not truly *a* something is also not truly a *something* One and rather-One exist rather than something-One and rather-One and something-One rather than something than nothing than something rather than nothing

5.2. Something-One exists rather than a statement-One rather than nothing a statement-One that says that there is no statement that is not something-One and rather-One rather than something that there are no beings that are not beings-One and rather-One rather than beings than not beings than beings rather than anotbeing that there is no being that is not being-One and rather-One rather than a being thananotbeing than a being rather thanabeing that there is not a One that is not One-One and rather- One rather than a One thanaOne than a One rather thanaOne

5.3. Something-One exists rather than a philosophy-One rather than nothing a philosophy-One that says that the non-existence of a statement is not an absence nor an absence of something-One but that it is just as much something-One as a statement is that there is no equality of beings and of not beings of being and of not being of One and of not One that is not something-One equality-One just as much as an equality as an inequality as an equality rather than an inequality is One

5.4. Something-One exists rather than a statement-One rather than a statement rather than nothing a statement-One to say that there is not a philosophy that is not philosophy-One if it must invert that which says that a statement is One rather than nothing or that no statement is One in that which says that nothing no statement at All is One and statement-One rather than a statement is not or that anotbeing is One and being-One rather than a being is not that anotOne or thatnooneONE is One and One-One rather than a One is not it says that there is no such inversion that is not One and something-One rather than a non-inversion is not rather than an inversion that nothing that an inversion rather than nothing

5.5. Something-One exists rather than a philosophy-One rather than nothing a philosophy-One to say that a statement that says that there exists a statement rather than nothing is something-One rather than the statement that says that no statement-One exists rather than a statement that a statement that says that a statement-One exists and exists as rather-One rather than nothing exists as something-One and as rather-One rather than the existence of nothing rather than a statement that a being-One exists rather than a being this exists as being-One and as rather-One rather than the existence of notbeing existing rather than being than a One-One exists rather than a anonOne this exists as One-One and rather-One rather than the existence of anonOne existing rather than a One

5.6. Something-One a will-One of philosophy exists that wills rather than nothing a statement-One to say that a philosophy that wills something rather than nothing exists as will-One and rather-One rather than as will that something that nothing that will of something rather than nothing rather than nothing than a philosophy-One wills beings-Ones of nothingness even the nothingness-One of beings the being-One of nothingness even the nothingness-One of being the One-One of nothingness even the nothingness-One of the One rather than no One at all but that it wills also rather-One rather than rather-than or than willing nothing at All

VI

6.1. Rather than something than nothing than some something rather than nothing there exists the occasion for which there exist rather than nothing to signal the existence of something-One and of rather-One and to signal this signal itself as something-One and rather-One rather than as signal something nothing something rather than nothing beings and nothingness of beings being and nothingness of being One and nothingness of One exist rather to signal that something nothing something rather than nothing exist as something-One and rather-One rather than as something nothing something rather than nothing and as occasion that signals it

6.2. Rather than a statement that says that a statement exists rather than nothing statement that exists as rather-One and as something-One rather than as the statement of which it says that it exists rather than nothing there exists a statement that says that a statement exists rather than nothing or that no statement exists rather so as to signal that this statement-One exists and that it exists as something-One and as rather-One rather than no statement at All that a statement or even that no statement exists a statement says that this exists rather than as the occasion that signals that the statement exists that says that there exists something rather than nothing also that his signal as rather-One and as something-One

6.3. Rather than a philosophy that says that the nothing-ness of the statement exists just as positively as a statement philosophy that exists as rather-One and as something-One rather than as the statement of which it says that it does not exist any more than the lack of statement there exists a philosophy that says that the statement that says that the nothingness of the statement exists in so far as a statement or that the nothingness of beings exists in so far as the beings of nothingness in so far as being the nothingness-of One in so far as the One exists rather so as to signal itself and this occasion itself as existing as rather-One and something-One rather than a statement that an occasion that the occasion of a statement rather than nothing

6.4. Rather than a statement that says that a philosophy exists that inverts the statement that says that there exists a statement rather than nothing in that which says that no statement exists rather than a statement there exists a statement that says that this inversion and that the statement that says that the nothingness of beings exists rather than beings the nothingness of being rather than the being of nothingness of One rather than the One existing rather as occasion to think the statement that says that the nothingness of the statement exists rather than a statement and that this statement and this occasion itself as rather-One and as something-One rather than as a statement

6.5. Rather than a philosophy that says that the statement that says that a philosophy exists rather than nothing exists rather than the statement that says that the nothingness of philosophy exists rather than a philosophy there exists a philosophy that says that this statement serves rather as occasion to signal that itself and the occasion by which it exists exist as something-One and as rather-One rather than as this statement and this occasion that the statement that says that beings exist rather than the nothingness-of-beings exists rather than the nothingness of beings exists rather than beings or that being exists rather than the nothingness of being exists rather than the nothingness-of-being exists rather than being or that the One exists rather than the nothingness-of-One exists rather than the nothingness-of-One exists rather than the One exists only to signal that there exists it or that it says it and it as occasion as rather-One and as something-One rather than as this statement and this occasion

6.6. Rather than a will of philosophy that wills rather than nothing a statement to say that a philosophy wills a statement rather than nothing there exists a philosophy

that says that the will of the statement exists as occasion
to exist itself and the occasion that it is as rather-One
and something-One rather than as will than will beings
of nothingness and the nothingness of beings the being
of nothingness and the nothingness of beings the One
of nothingness and the nothingness of One rather than
will nothing is rather that which gives the occasion for
there to exist this will as rather-One and something-One
rather than as philosophy than as willing than as willing
a philosophy rather than nothing

VII

7.1. One exists rather than (non-) One and (non-) One
rather than rather-One and something-One (non-) One
exists rather than the statement that says that a statement that is not and does not say truly the One – One
rather than rather-One – can also not truly describe the
statement that says that rather-One or something-One
exist rather than the statement that says that there exists
something rather than nothing

7.2. (non-) One exists rather than a statement that exists
as rather-One and something-One rather than as statement that says that beings exist rather than non-beings
and exist as rather-One and something-One rather than
beings non-beings beings rather than non-beings that

being exists rather than non-being and exists as rather-One and something-One rather than as the being of non-being being rather than non-being than the One exists rather than the non-One and exists as rather-One and something-One rather than as One non-One One rather than non-One

7.3. (non-) One exists rather than a philosophy that says that a statement exists as rather-One and something-One rather than as the statement that says that a statement that does not truly say that the equality of beings and non-beings of being and non-being of One and non-One exists rather than their inequality and exists as (non-) One rather than rather-One and something-One can also not truly describe their equality as existing rather than their inequality

7.4. (non-) One exists rather than a statement that says that a philosophy exists as rather-One and something-One rather than as a statement that says that non-beings exist rather than beings and exist as rather-One and something-One rather than as non-beings beings non-beings rather than beings that non-being exists rather than being and exists as rather-One and something-One rather than as non-being being non-being rather than being that the non-One exists rather than the One and exists as rather-One and something-One rather than as non-One One non-One rather than non-One that a statement that does not truly say that the statement that inverts that which says that beings exist rather than non-beings or that being rather than non-being or the One rather than the non-One in that which says that non-beings exist rather than beings non-being rather than being the non-One rather than the One exists as (non-) One rather than as rather-One and something-One also cannot truly describe this inversion as existing rather than nothing

7.5. (non-) One exists rather than a philosophy that says that a statement exists as rather-One and something-One rather than as a philosophy that says that this the statement that says that there exists something rather than nothing exists rather than the statement that says that nothing exists rather than something or that the statement that says that being exists rather than non-being existing rather than being or that the One exists rather than the non-One existing rather that the One exists rather than the statement that says that non-being exists rather than being or that the One rather than the not-One or that the statement that says that the statement that says that something rather than nothing exists rather than the inverse exists as rather-One and something-One rather than as statement exists itself rather than this statement that this also cannot truly be described unless by a statement that is (non-) One rather than nothing that non-being non-One or nothingness-of-statement (non-) One exists rather than a statement that if it is not and does not truly describe the (non-) One rather than rather-One and something-One also cannot truly describe the statement that says that something exists rather than nothing or the statement that says that a statement-One exists as rather-One rather than as the statement that says that no statement exists as rather-One

7.6. (non-) One exists rather than a will of philosophy than a will of nothingness or of a nothingness of will (non-) One exists rather than to will nothingness rather than not willing at All (non-) One exists rather than the statement that says that (non-) One exists rather than this statement or that the statement that says that a statement cannot say that there exists a statement that wills the statement of nothing even the nothing of a statement as (non-) One rather than not will if it is also not truly (non-) One rather than nothingness of statement or that there exists a statement that wills beings of nothingness and even non-beings as (non-) One rather than not willing if it is also not truly (non-) One rather than nothingness of beings or that there exists a statement that wills the being of nothingness and even not-being as (non-) One rather than not willing if it is also not truly (non-) One rather than nothingness-of-being or that there exists a statement that wills the One of nothingness and even the notOne as

(non-) One rather than not willing if it is also not truly
(non-) One rather than nothingness-of-One

Letter to Deleuze

(1988)

Translated by Robin Mackay

What distinguishes the One from Spinoza's substance?
LETTER FROM DELEUZE TO THE AUTHOR

1.1. By *Philosophical Decision*, I understand that whose essence encompasses existence to the nearest nothing, or indeed to the nearest non-existence, or indeed to the nearest difference, or indeed to the nearest Other, or indeed to the nearest negation of negation, etc., to the nearest Etc. In other words, that whose nature can be conceived only as existing to the nearest 'to the nearest Etc.'.

1.2. By *real*, I describe that whose essence is indivisibly without the nearest nothing or difference or Etc., reality rather than existence or difference, Etc., in existence. In other words, the Identity whose nature can only be described as real rather than conceived as existent or as different, etc., in existence.

2.1. A thing is called *finite* in extrinsic manner when it can be limited by another thing of the same nature, however it may remain infinite in another aspect, or when its limitation encompasses its illimitation to the nearest nothing, difference, etc., the nearest Etc. For example, a philosophy is said to be finite because we can always conceive of another possible philosophy, just as a decision is limited by another decision. But on the contrary, a philosophy is not limited, as simple position, by another philosophy.

2.2. A thing is described as *finite* in intrinsic or immanent manner when it is limited in itself, when it is itself through this limitation and cannot be limited by another. The real is limited or finite in itself and not by virtue of the possible or by effective existence. For example, an individual is said to be finite because we conceive him as real and cannot conceive a merely possible or existent other that would limit the real one. But on the contrary an existing decision is limited by another possible or existent decision.

3.1. By *sufficiency*, *Principle of Sufficient Existence*, or *objective philosophical appearance*, I understand that which, existing in itself and being conceived by itself, claims to be real and concludes from its existence to its reality. In other words that whose existence claims to suffice to be real and not to have need of the real to be determined.

3.2. By *last instance*, I describe that which is real in itself, that is to say that which has no need of existence in order to be real. Or that of which the description as real in itself has no need of this description in order to be real in itself, and of which it must be constituted.

4.1. By *attribute*, I understand the dimension, at once finite, infinite and empirically determinate, that thought grasps of the objective philosophical Appearance or of Philosophical Decision.

4.2. By *real a priori* I describe the essence of existent things, an essence that thought describes as determined in the last instance by the real.

5.1. By *empirical givens*, I understand that which is posited by Philosophical Decision and its sufficiency to affect the latter, in other words that which is in Philosophical Decision by means of which it is also interpreted.

5.2. By *support* or *occasion*, I describe the empirical or ideal givens that are necessary as materials from which thought extracts the real a prioris, in other words that which, existing in Philosophical Decision, has its condition of reality in something else or in the real as last instance.

6.1. By *chaos*, *chôra* or (*non-*)*One*, I describe an absolutely infinite and indivisible receptacle, containing an infinity of philosophical decisions, each of which expresses an essence at once finite and infinite.

Explanation: I say *absolutely infinite*, and not a mixture of finite and infinite at the same time, for from that which is merely finite and infinite at the same time we can deny an infinity of philosophical decisions; on the contrary, the real or intrinsically finite essence of that which is *absolutely infinite* means that it contains all that is expressed by a decision at once finite and infinite.

6.2. By One, I describe an individual that is absolutely finite or stripped of attributes or of philosophical decisions, that derives its essence from its identity without which it would be necessary to express it in a universal attribute; that is to say a last instance that is not infinite and constituted by a universal collection of individuals, but which is immediately a multiplicity of individuals that know themselves to be multiple and solitary without ever forming a collection or a universality.

Explanation: I say *absolutely finite*, and not *finite in extrinsic manner*; for, from that which is merely finite in extrinsic manner, we can deny that it could also be a merely real, and not logico-real or universal, multiplicity of individuals; on the contrary the essence of the individual or of that which is absolutely finite implies that it must be multiple not despite its finitude but because of it.

7.1. A thing, a philosophy, will be called free when it exists as cause of itself or through the sole necessity of its nature, and when it is at once determinate and determinant itself. On the contrary, a thing will be called constrained or conditioned when it is determined by another to exist and to operate, according to the fixed and determined law of some philosophical decision.

7.2. A thing, the One or the individual, will be called determinant when it is real or sufficiently determined by its sole passivity toward itself which is its essence, and when it is incited to act only on the occasion of another, World or Philosophy, acting under condition of the (non-) One. On the contrary, a thing will be called determinate in the last instance when it is determined without reciprocity in its reality, rather than incited in its existence and its operation, by another: the One.

8.1. By *objective eternity* or *eternity of existence*, I understand the existence itself of philosophy in so far as it is conceived as resulting necessarily from its sole definition or its essence.

Explanation: For such an existence is conceived as an eternal truth, as well as the essence of the thing; thus the eternity of philosophy cannot be explained by way of duration or time or by the given multiplicity of historical philosophies, even if duration is conceived as having no beginning and no end.

8.2. By *subjective* or *real eternity*, I describe the reality itself of the individual in so far as it is identically, with no approximation, its essence and the joyful immanence of this essence.

Explanation: For such a reality of the individual is thought as an eternal truth, as well as the essence of the individual; thus it cannot be explained by way of duration or time or historicity, even if duration is conceived as having no beginning and no end, or by way of the objective eternity or eternity of existence of philosophy.

9.1. All that is, is either philosophy or interpretable by philosophy or, better still, is the difference of philosophy and the non-philosophical.

9.2. All that is, is either immanent and in-itself, or mixture and immanent-and-transcendent.

10.1. That which cannot be conceived by way of the non-philosophical must be conceived through the philosophical, or, better still, through their difference.

10.2. That which cannot be described as being of itself or as immanent-(to)-self, must be thought by way of transcendence, that is to say by way of the a priori amalgam of immanence and transcendence.

11.1. From a determinate philosophical decision results necessarily certain effects, and every philosophy draws at every instant all its consequences; and on the contrary, if apparently no philosophical decision or causality is given, it is impossible that an effect should follow from it; but a philosophical decision is always given and the philosophical explanation of a phenomenon is not only required, but always assured.

11.2. From a determinate cause in the last instance there does not necessarily follow any effect, for this supposes an occasion or an incitement in existence; but, on the contrary, if no cause in the last instance is given, it is impossible that a real effect should follow.

12.1. Knowledge of the philosophical cause and that of its effect mutually encompass one other.

12.2. Knowledge of the real effect depends on the knowledge of the cause in the last instance and encompasses it; but not reciprocally.

13.1. Things which, exceptionally, have nothing in common with one another, also cannot be understood one by means of the other; in other words, the philosophy of one does not encompass the philosophy of the other.

13.2. Things that have nothing in common with one another or which are in chaos, also cannot be understood reciprocally one by means of the other; in other words their description does not encompass the concept of Philosophical Decision and no longer has philosophical meaning.

14.1. A philosophy claims to accord with the real.

14.2. A true representation accords only in the last instance with the real that it describes.

15.1. Of all that can be conceived as non-philosophical, its essence and existence do not mutually encompass one another.

15.2. Of all that can be thought as non real or as effective, its essence is not identically reality, but only encompasses existence.

Universe Black in the Human Foundations of Colour

(1988)

Translated by Miguel Abreu and Robin Mackay

I

In the foundations of colour, vision sees the Universe; in the foundations of the Universe, it sees man; in the foundations of man, it sees vision.

The Earth, the World, the Universe have to do with man: the Earth a little, the World a lot, the Universe passionately. The Universe is the inner passion of the Distant.

Man works the Earth, inhabits the World, thinks according to the Universe.

The Earth is man's ground, the World his neighbour, the Universe his secret.

The Earth is the strait through which light from the

World finds its way; it is the tongue made of sand and water upon which, upright, man strides against the World.

The World is everything too vast and too narrow for the Earth, and again too narrow for the Universe.

Man gropes around the World and the World floats in the Universe unable to touch its borders.

Man brings into the World of narrow-minded thoughts the emotion of the Universe.

The Universe isn't the object of thought, a greater object than the World; it is thought's *how* or its *according to*.

The Universe is an opaque and solitary thought which has already leapt into the closed eyes of man like the space of a dreamless dream.

The Universe isn't reflected in another universe, and yet the Distant is accessible to us at all points.

The World is the infinite confusion of man and of the Universe; the Universe being treated as man's object.

The forgetting of the essence of the Universe is more inapparent than the forgetting of the World. The forgetting of man as One-(of)-the-Universe and that of the Universe as One-by-man is more inapparent than the forgetting of being-in-the-World.

II

In the beginning there is Black – man and the Universe, rather than a philosopher and the World.

Around the philosopher everything becomes World and light; Around man everything becomes Universe and opacity.

Man, who carries the Universe with him, is condemned, without knowing why, to the World and to the Earth; and neither the World nor the Earth can tell him why: The Universe alone responds to him, by being black and mute.

Black is neither in the object nor in the World, it is what man sees in man, and that in which man sees man.

Black isn't merely what man sees in man, it is the only 'colour' inseparable from the hyper-intelligible expanse of the Universe.

Solitude of the man-without-horizon who sees Black in Black.

The Universe is deaf and blind, we can do nothing other than love it and assist it. Man is the being who assists the Universe.

We can unfold the future only with closed eyes and can believe we enter it only with opened eyes.

Light strikes the Earth with repeated blows, divides the World infinitely; solicits in vain the invisible Universe.

The Universe was 'in' the World and the World didn't see it.

Black, before light, is the substance of the Universe, what escaped from the World before the World was born into the World.

Black is the unGround which stares at light in the Distant where man observes it. Here lies the mad and catatonic light of the World.

Man reaches the World only by way of transcendental darkness into which he never entered and from which he will never leave.

A phenomenal blackness entirely fills the essence of man. Because of it, the most ancient stars of the paleo-cosmos together with the most venerable stones of the arché-earth, show themselves to man as being outside the World, and the World itself shows itself as outside-World.

III

Universe Black is the opacity of the real or the 'colour' that renders it invisible.

No light has ever seen universe black.

Black is prior to the absence of light, whether this absence be the shadows where it is extinguished, whether it be its nothingness or its positive opposite. Universe black is not a negative light.

Black is the Radical of colours, what never was a colour nor the attribute of a colour, the emotion that seizes man when affected by a colour.

As opposed to the objectified black from the spectrum, Black has always already manifested itself before any process of manifestation. This is vision-in-Black.

Black is definitively interior to both itself and man.

Black is without opposite: even light, which tries to turn it into its opposite, fails to do so when confronted with the rigour of its secret. Only the secret can see into the secret, like Black in Black.

The essence of colours is not colourful: it is universe black.

Metaphysical white is a mere blanching, the prismatic or indifferent unity of colours. Phenomenal blackness is indifferent to colours, for it is their ultimate tenor in reality, that which prevents their final dissolution into the mélanges of light.

Philosophy, and at times painting, treat black and white as opposites, colours as contraries, colours as opposed; mixing them under the authority of light as the supreme mélange.

The human science of colours is founded on black known as 'universe'. It thinks together man, the Universe, and theories of colour – and their tone of Black which is their common reality (but in the last instance only).

A human science of colours makes universe black the real or immanent requisite of their physics. Black is the very stance of science and of its 'relationship' to colours.

IV

Science is a thought in black and white which studies the light of the Cosmos and the colours of the World. Black in its stance or its inherence to the real, white in its representation of the real. A thought in which white is no longer the opposite of black, but rather its positively faded reflection.

Science is the mode of thought in which black determines white in the last instance.

Universe black transforms colours without mixing them. It simplifies colour in order to bring out the whiteness of knowledge in its essence as *non-pictorial reflection*.

Our uchromia: to learn to think from the point of view of Black as that which determines colours in the last instance rather than that which limits them.

Philosophical technology was drawn mimetically from the World, to reflect and reproduce it. It is inadequate to thinking the Universe.

We are still postulating that reality is given to us through the paradigm of the World. We perpetuate the inhuman amphiboly that confuses World and Universe. We believe that reality is horizon and light, aperture and flash, whereas it resembles more the stance of an opaque non-relationship (to) light. At the very moment we explore the uni-versal dimension of the cosmic, we remain prisoners of cosmo-logical difference. Our philosophers are children who are afraid of the Dark.

Philosophy is thinking by way of a generalized 'black box'; it is the effort to encase black into light and to push it back to the back of the cave. But the cosmo-logical generalisation of black doesn't save it, quite the contrary, from still having the status of an attribute. Black alone is subject and may render manifest the philosophical encasement of concepts.

Don't start by thinking technology: rocket and launch-ing of the rocket. Instead look, as in the depths of a closed eye, into the opacity of the knowledge through which, becoming one with it without distance, the rocket crosses infinite distances. Think according to the knowledge that steers it as in a dream, heavier and more transparent than the boundless night it penetrates with its silent thunder. Start by thinking science.

Stop sending your vessels through the narrow cosmo-logical corridor. Stop making them climb the extreme walls of the world. 'Allow' them to leap over the cosmic barrier and enter the hyperspace of the Universe. Cease having them compete with light, for your rockets too can realise the more-than-psychic, postural mutation, and shift from light to universe black, which is no longer a colour; from cosmic colour to postural and subjective black. Allow your rockets to become subject of the Universe and to be present at every point of the Distant.

Simplify colours! See black, think white.

See black rather than believe 'unconscious'. And think white rather than believe 'conscious'.

See black! Not that all your suns have fallen – they have already returned, only slightly dimmer – but Black is the 'colour' that falls eternally from the Universe onto your Earth.

What the One Sees in the One

(1989)

Translated by Robin Mackay

PROSE FOR PHYSICS

The opaque foundations of
knowledge remain in man
There where the invisible Manifest did
name itself
More than Being-in-language
It called itself the vision
that is neither seen nor seeing
The one to whom, looking
in itself, is proved
the solitude of vision.

For it the World is described
without it having to go out of itself
For it all the things
of the World without going out of itself
nor becoming World.

For it the stars
more profound than history
without it having had to make itself
light of time.

All totalities without delirium
All the exteriorities
without hallucination
The proximities and
the coiled distancings
in the infinite and even
the interior and sensible body of the Distant
without making itself either horizon
or mass, neither force nor gravity.

The shock of simultaneities
and the ardour of instantaneities
without knotting itself in itself
like time
Like the wave of time
contracts itself to expel

the World
For it all the computers
that reflect the glory
of the universe and multiplying it
All the bodies that light
observes from the depths of matter
Without entering the eye
of reason.

The effusions of space and
the insensible slidings
of the Cosmos
The excessive universes
and the discretion that surrounds
the birth of World
Without entering into the ring
of Tradition

All the chaos and hubbub
babels and hurly-burly
all the zigzags and artefacts
And the tortuous ways of God
Without borrowing
the rectitude of God.

SOLITUDE OF PHRASES

The opaque foundations of
language remain in man
There where the phrase the Solitary
named itself
More than language-in-Being
it named itself the phrase that
is neither spoken nor speaking
That to which, looking
in itself, has proved to itself
the solitude of phrases.

What the One says when it looks
in the One:
that there is nothing in the World
or outside the World
to separate it from itself;
or unite it to itself;
that separation exists only
in things already
separated and unity
in things
already united.

What the Contrary says when it
looks in the Contrary:
that there is nothing
in philosophy
or outside of philosophy
to thwart it or to
continue it;
that contrariness exists only
in things already contrary
and continuity in things
already continued.

What the Opaque says when it
looks in the Opaque:
that there is nothing in light
or outside of light to
manifest it or obscure it;
that light exists only
in things
already illuminated
and obscurity in things
already obscured.

What the Eagle says
when it looks in the Eagle:
that there is nothing in the sky
or outside the sky to nail it down
to the peak of its flight or to cast it
into the hallucination of the fall;
that suspense exists only
on earth and the fall
for things that have already fallen.

What the Serpent says when it
looks in the Serpent:
that there is nothing on the ground
or outside the ground to knot
or unknot the ruse;
and that only
already broken rings
celebrate
the multiplication of rings.

What the Sea says
when it looks in the Sea:
that it is impossible to be
the enemy of the Sea, and
that there is nothing in the wave
or outside the wave
to quell it or

to swell it.

What the Phrase says when it
looks in the Phrase:
that there is nothing
in speech or outside
of speech
to render more solitary
the black diamond
of phrases.

LETTER FROM THE ONE TO THE MOST-DISTANT

We the Anteriors
Anteriors of the future
not of the past
Precessors
of the restraint of time
We remain in the Before
of every thing
We hold our life from the Before
that is in the Before,
More interior to ourselves
than the first
and the originals
are to time
Whence we institute
the Precession of rigour
And pay the oracle
of the in-place.

We the Insouciants
Insouciant of the contrary and
of its contrary
Indifferent to this and to that
We remain in the intimate
emotion of the One
More interior to ourselves

than the Dyad to the One
More shut up in the vision
of the World than
in the World itself
Whence we receive
the endless rolling of logos
And pay the oracle
of Suspense

We the Unhabitants
Unhabitants of the sky
and of the earth
Driven from the luminous soil
of the World
We remain
in the unsuspected
foundations of the fold
More interior to ourselves
than ourselves to space
Of all the lives
our life is
the most foundational
Whence we warn
the phrases
And pay the oracle
of the Distant

We the inapparents
Inapparent of the invisible
as of the visible
Unscathed by the occidental
fall
We remain in the Night
that is in the Night
Anterior to the creative fall
of suns
More interior to ourselves
than solitude is to solitude
Whence we drink at length
the vigilant Night
And pay the oracle
of Universe

WHAT THE ONE SEES IN THE ONE

SHORT TREATISE ON THE SOUL

Definitions and Axioms of the Soul

1.1.
I call Soul that which suffices to the soul

1.2.
The Soul is the multiple and solitary daughter of the Soul rather than the daughter of the World.

1.3.
The Soul is that which is seen in the Soul rather than in the Distant as in something-Other.

2.1.
I call Distant or something-Other that in the world which is seen in the Soul in the Soul's way.

2.2.
The Distant is that which, as something-Other, is seen in the Soul rather than in the Distant.

3.1.
I call World that which is seen in something-Other rather than directly in the Soul.

3.2.
The World is that which the Soul sees in itself rather than in it, at the same time as it sees it in the Distant.

4.1.
I call Time the Before that does not turn, the Infallible that has its essence in the Soul rather than in the World.

4.2.
Time flows from the Soul to the World.

4.3.
Time Infallible separates Time and the World.

5.1.
I call Philosophy what philosophy sees in philosophy without seeing it first of all in the Soul.

5.2.
Philosophy sees in philosophy the Soul as soul of the World or else as soul of the Other man.

6.1.
I call science of souls or non-psychology these definitions and axioms with the theorems that follow from them.

Theorems of the Soul

1.

In the freed Soul, freed from the Distant, the Soul sees the Soul before seeing the Other soul; the Other soul before seeing the soul of the Other man; the soul of the Other man before seeing the soul of the World, the soul of philosophers playing the soul's turn.

2.

In the freed Soul, freed from the Distant, the Soul sees the Soul before seeing the chaos of the World and the soul of the World, the chaos of equivalent philosophies before seeing the blackest soul of philosophy: 'the soul's turn!'.

3.

In the freed Soul, freed from the Distant, the Soul sees the Soul before seeing the Other soul as interior image of the World and of the soul of the World; its un-altered height, its imposed extent; it sees the interior image of the soul of the World before seeing the chaos of the soul; the chaos of the soul before seeing the soul of the philosopher making the World turn around the soul.

4.

In the freed Soul, freed from the Distant, the Soul sees the Soul before seeing the science of the World and of the soul of the World; their inert reflection, their sterile representation; it sees the science of the World and of the soul of the World before seeing the Other soul as their interior image; their interior image before seeing their chaos; their chaos before seeing the philosophers making the soul turn around the World.

5.
In the freed Soul, freed from the Distant, the Soul sees the Soul before seeing the Infallible of time; the Infallible of time before seeing what it locates in the Distant; the interior image of the soul outside the science of the soul; the chaos of the soul outside its interior image; the soul of the World and the turnings of the soul outside the chaos of the soul.

6.
In the freed Soul, freed from the Distant, the Soul sees the Soul rather than the turning of the soul, and the World in the Distant, far away from the Soul rather than around the soul.

APPENDIX II

Transvaluation
of the
Transcendental Method

Transvaluation of the
Transcendental Method
(1979)

Translated by Robin Mackay

Meeting of the Société française de Philosophie, 24 March 1979.

PROGRAMME

A transvaluation of the transcendental method is proposed, so as to relieve the latter of its epistemological,
logical, and moral hypotheses and to overcome the classic
objections to it (those of vicious circularity and sterility). This transvaluation thinks the method no longer
according to its objects, but according to its essence (or
the immanent rules of its becoming-transcendental). It
attempts to deliver the *eidos* of the transcendental from
its empiricist and formalist limitations by assigning it
'reality' as instance.

Systematic Exposition of the Rules of the Transcendental Method or its Transvaluation

(1) First rule: Constitute a 'factum' under already transcendental conditions; do away with the question *quid facti?* as question (the method is a continual process of reduction rather than a description) and in terms of the 'fact' sought (it is a transcendental and synthetic residue rather than a 'fact'); in turn, treat the residual factum as capable of being reduced (dissociate ideality and the a priori).

(2) Second rule: Proceed with the continuous given, by way of two cuts (ontic or realising, ontological or idealising); define the 'transcendental reduction' as 'unilateral' cut and synthesis, and its objects as 'residual transcendental objects' (destruction of the 'analytic').

(3) Third rule: Define an additional cut or reduction that extracts a supreme synthetic Principle or Essence responsible for unifying the diversity of 'residual objects'; assign to this factor a non-logical and non-ideal type of reality according to which the technique of cuts receives a 'transcendental' status.

(4) Fourth rule: Define a 'transcendental genesis', i.e. the particular modes of synthesis of residual objects or reality and ideality under the conditions of the immanence of Essence (destruction of the question *quid juris?*).

PRESENTATION

FRANÇOIS LARUELLE: In a word – an apparently simple word, but it is only a word – I seek a return, a return to Kant that would be an 'eternal return'. Is it now possible for such a repetition no longer to be what it was in a former era: the lot of unfortunate heirs, disinherited by the ruin of Hegelianism, and suddenly in want of epistemology? Nor that which it is on the way to becoming: the act of those who have been deprived of all hope by the fall of Marxism, and find themselves demoralised? Can a new return to Kant cease to be this reaction of defeat, this suspect vocation of modesty, to become finally what it ought to be – an inventive recurrence? Such, at least, is the cause – the wager, perhaps – for which the goodwill (and, I fear, the temerity) of the *Société Française de Philosophie* will allow me for an instant to don the colours of 'transcendental philosophy'.

If we are particularly in need of something, it is not objects (we have far too many); and it is not even theory; it is *method*. Since we are constrained to palliate the distress in which the political and theoretical evacuation of Dialectic and Structure has left us, is it possible to rediscover some kind of living force in the transcendental method, without re-enacting the neo-Kantianism of the nineteenth century, or palaeo-Kantianism, as some today attempt, out of spite (that is, out of morals)? Armed with new techniques, having undergone several non-Kantian and non-Husserlian mutations, can it become that 'new kind of order' that we all seek, capable of taking up anew modern tasks (political and revolutionary tasks, for example) that have fallen dormant, but also classical tasks: What is it to think? What is Being? What is it to speak? Is it, above all, capable of re-unifying the two, within a new project that would change the very style and the force of these questions?

The critique of the transcendental method oscillates between two contrary objections: On the one hand, it denounces this method's vicious and circular character, the raising of the empirical properties of the object into the sphere of the essence of experience: In Kant, the properties of the Newtonian scientific object, in Husserl the properties of the perceived and more generally of the empirical paradigm of seeing. Both come to be reflected in their proper essence, the conditioned reflected in the condition, giving rise to those *mixtures* that are transcendental epistemology or the critical theory of cognition, phenomenological psychology – or even Husserl's absolute transcendental philosophy, in so far as it still continues, despite itself, to secrete the properties of the perceived into the a priori structures of pure consciousness. If one admits – a postulate that is perhaps part and parcel of the method – that there is 'a transcendental truth' distinct from the truth proper to the sciences, then it becomes an urgent matter to overcome this objection and to exorcise, from within what moderns call the 'empirico-transcendental doublet', and Husserl the 'parallelism' of the psychic and the transcendental, all trace of this vicious 'reflection' of the founded in the foundation. The battle against empiricism is perhaps an infinite project, but imperative nonetheless; it merges with a true 'becoming-transcendental' of method, even if it is only a means for the latter.

On the other hand, the critique of the transcendental method denounces its sterility, formalism and will to purity: that which, since Hamann at least, has been known as the purism of pure reason.

Whether the transcendentals preside over experience, as in the scholastics (since Being, the *ens*, to which all relate, is itself the first of the transcendentals), or whether they relate to experience, they do so qua pure form and ideality, too universal for the singularity of experience and its contingency. The transcendental method proposes 'pure cuts', but the destiny of purity is either the sterility of formalism, or compromise with the empirical, or else that form of spiritual materialism which Jacobi denounced in Fichte.

It is appropriate not to respond in an external manner to these critiques, which denounce inherent traits of the classical method. On the contrary, a good strategy is to accept them, but to make their destruction, if not the constitutive problem and the principal aim of the transcendental method, at least one of the resources for its renewal. The whole strategy here consists in provisionally redefining the method according to new aims, and according to these aims alone. On one hand, against the first objection, it must be admitted that the method consists in determining the a priori structures – i.e. the being – of *any* being whatsoever, not including in this being in general, or in its a prioris, its determinate properties whatever they may be (scientific, logical, perceptual, aesthetic or moral). It is obviously this generality that is important. To decide thus between a being and its being is perhaps not immediately possible, but is the object of a rule that only defines a tendency or a becoming. But to distinguish being as such from its reputedly empirical properties, which are bracketed out, is at least the aim that must be fulfilled in order to free the method from its traditional subjection to regions of objects that are privileged for cultural reasons, reasons that must indeed be called political in the broad sense of the word. It is enough to interiorise this programme in the very definition of the method to render the latter capable of thinking the conditions of any object whatsoever. Its aim is no longer to found this or that science, or 'Science' as such – an ambitious task whose sterility no longer needs any demonstration – nor even to serve as organon for a science or a philosophical logic that would be one of those mixtures that we refuse.

The 'higher form' of the transcendental method lies in its becoming-immanent: in keeping it within the limits and the very power of thought qua power of evaluation and of critique of the 'any being whatsoever'. The higher interest of a simply thinking thought necessitates that it content itself with penetrating the interior life of this power, so as to think on the basis, as Kant says (albeit of reason) of its 'original germs'.

But, in order not to be vicious, it must court the risk of being sterile. We shall annul this risk by means of a second rule, apparently contradictory to the first, and which will complete the definition of the method according to its aims. This rule is as follows: although the empirical properties of the being are bracketed out, the being is still always determined and individuated, but under transcendental and internal conditions and perhaps, further, under empirical or *merely* empirical conditions. The method is thus transcendental and not transcendent: it does not preside over all experience, it determines only an object that is already determinate – but which is nonetheless 'any object whatsoever' from the point of view of its empirical properties in so far as it is thus transcendentally determined! It is the object indifferent (or which *becomes* indifferent) to its mundane properties, but whose indifference is one of the ingredients of difference or determination. The two preceding rules will no longer be contradictory if they are united in this one, which is characteristic of thinking in the transcendental mode: the a priori is distinct from the empirical, but reconstitutes a new a priori (and no longer empirical) unity with the empirical. Or again: Being is distinct from the being, but re-forms a new higher – transcendental – synthesis with it.

Everything will thus depend upon the extension we can give to the empirical and consequently to the a priori – upon the generality of their respective domains. In particular, ideal and formal properties, which define the object according to a logico-scientific point of view, must perhaps suffer the fate of everything empirical. There will be no transvaluation unless one begins by severing the alliance between the transcendental method and rationalism (not to mention logicism), and thereby detaching it from reason's self-interest. It will therefore not be enough to extend the field of the a priori by extending the field of reason, as Cassirer does. Because the question is not so much the one which drives all returns to Kant – With what new objects can we replenish the transcendental field? – as the following: What new, non-rationalist conception to make of the a priori itself and of the transcendental field? Kant himself (not to mention Husserl) proceeded with just such an extension, recognising that there existed an a priori in the judgement of taste and in the faculty of pleasure and displeasure. From this, we can imagine a tendency that would require us to seek an a priori of linguistic reason, etc… But such a prioris would still give

rise to a critique not only *of* reason, but *by* and *for* reason –
something that, for us, can no longer constitute either the
means or the end: if there is, for example, a 'linguistic' a
priori (and why not?), it need no longer be a rational one.
In order to be able to extend the transcendental to cultural
dimensions, we must firstly modify the concept that we
have of the a priori and of essence, or the transcendental
principle, so as to sever – not immediately, that would
be impossible, but as a tendency or an aim (at the 'limit',
really) – the 'Greco-occidental' alliance of the a priori
and ideality. More important than the new objects with
it is to be replenished, there is, on one hand, the style of
the cutting-out of the a priori field, and on the other, the
'objectively real' status of those techniques of cutting,
or the type of reality of the agent who assumes them.
On one hand, true transcendental cuts which determine
Being from beings; on the other hand, the very being of
these cuts themselves. Not only the difference between
Being and beings, but the being of this difference. Philosophy has always been an art of cut-outs, and transcendental
philosophy more than any other, because it is perhaps
the only philosophy to have been able to elevate cutting
to the power of the subject, to that of a substance even,
and its technique to the height of a *techné* that makes of
philosophy itself a *physis*, that is to say an autonomous
'nature', the object of a *jouissance* proper to it.

It could be that this programme contributes to rendering the transcendental to us – that is to say, rendering it to its essence. Kant and Husserl were only able to build on this essence such as it was delivered to them by the scholastic tradition, which made of the transcendentals the predicates or the passions of beings in general; to build on it by imposing upon it idealist-style epistemological and logical decisions that would function as so many founding limitations for its later history. Since we renounce any definition of the method (even a partial one, as in the classical thinkers) on the basis of its empirical regions of objects, i.e. of empiricist and formalist local restrictions which it has folded back onto, we are obliged to think it on the basis of its essence – the *eidos* or the *Wesen* of the transcendental – which alone is capable of restoring its generality and its power of genesis, its generativity.

Neither Kant nor Husserl really interrogate themselves about the historicity and the 'status' of the transcendental motif. By 'really', I mean *beyond* the more or less common idea they have of the 'reason' within whose limits they take it to be enclosed. For is the 'reason' of philosophers really anything other than a mixture of the transcendental as tendency and an historical, all-too-historical idea of science? The transcendental motif – they describe it, they exploit it, they limit it, they invest it with various tasks and aims of diverse origin, but they never really critique it … in the name of the transcendental itself.

Because ultimately, if this method determines the status of objective reality, what is going to determine the status of these procedures of evaluation? The response is as follows, once we admit that it is no longer 'reason' as seat of the a priori: Only the transcendental method is authorised to critique and to reproduce itself – in short, to transform itself. It is enough to conceive of it in such a way to see that (at least at the level of its internal conditions or its essence, because as to this metamorphosis itself, it is perhaps an infinite process) it belongs, in turn – this is indeed the least we can require – to 'transcendental truth'.

If there is a critique and an extension of this method, they must be immanent to the very process of the transcendental operation. Now rather than submitting to this rule of immanence that is perhaps the secret, the last word, of the transcendental method, something like its *telos*, Husserl, for example, proposes that dubious compromise that consists in separating the description of the fact of the transcendental from its critique.

On the contrary, I call *transvaluation* – it is the aim and it is already the means – the set of immanent rules that describe the method according to its essence alone, and which make of this essence the unity of the genesis and the critique of its classical procedures. The essence is the set of rules that precede and govern (a priori, then) the historical and systematic possibility of empirical limitations and rationalist decisions about method, at the same time that they precede and govern (still a priori) the overflowing of these limitations, the 'generalisation' of the method beyond its restrictions. This essence is thus none other than what there is, within the heart of the classical transcendental method (but restrained, bridled) of the force of destruction of its historical forms. The rules to be put forward below will describe the broad outlines of the classical usage, but always in formulating at the same time the conditions of its transformation in view of a new usage.

It is only in giving the detail of these rules that one can, here and there, and obviously with a certain reference to the Nietzschean project, perceive in what sense, and within what limits, this term 'transvaluation' is historically justified.

But in all probability, in this 'transvaluation', we need not expect to hear of some unprecedented, extraordinary operation; it consists in a precise inventory of gestures – in the form of determinate rules, indeed. No, trans-valuation is the transcendental method itself – up to a transformation that remains to be determined, and which cannot but be its essence. It is thus the true sense of that enigmatic formulation that can be taken up again in order to try and give it a minimally articulable content: the 'transcendental of the transcendental' – and it is not I who advances this 'abstraction'. Transvaluation is not a super-method or a meta-method, it merges with the transcendental itself, or rather, with its will to auto-suppression or decline. It is the *telos*, at once internal and external, of the method – implying a correction of what I said about aims: a *telos* that programmes its own destruction, a destruction that will come to it, however, from the outside – that is one of the definitions of 'Nietzschean' transvaluation; and this is, in any case, what I understand by the 'essence' of the transcendental method. We must define a transcendental concept of the 'limit' that would be simultaneously a limit of (the production and destruction of) the field of transcendental philosophy.

But as unity of these classical limitations at the opening of this border, the *eidos* that we envision can no longer be a pure logical signification. To determine the *eidos* of the transcendental, the transcendental conception of *eidos*, and ultimately the *eidos* as last procedure of the transcendental analytic (the essence of experience) – here are a few operations that we must undertake simultaneously and circularly, every characterisation of one serving to problematise the others. Not only is the transcendental, qua gesture immanent to the real movement of thought, not exhausted in the external architectonic or the semantics of a philosophy; but it would be like some kind of alchemical transmutation to expect this transvaluation to emerge from a body frozen by rules, like a dove appearing before your eyes from the hat of pure reason. For reasons that will become evident below, a concept of transcendental status cannot be a pure and closed signification – it is a limit or an a-signifying cut on a signifying and semantic chain. But a limit that is at the same time illimiting for thought, or which induces new signifying and semantic continuity. In which case it is impossible to posit the essence in the mode of logical representation. I sample the concepts of the transcendental, cutting them from the texts of Kant, Husserl, Heidegger, the Scholastics; but these cuts will in turn define becomings or tendencies. Everything is under condition and in progress. We *are* not transcendental philosophers; we have to *become* them, which is an infinite task. This is why the transvaluation of the transcendental is both a twofold and a unique operation: on one hand, it involves gathering its invariant historical traits into an essence; on the other (but this may well be the same gesture) in bringing this *eidos* to a limit-state, on the basis of which can be determined a recommencement of thinking, a new usage, new forces of the transcendental.

There is no reason to be surprised by this word 'transvaluation'. Because Nietzsche is perhaps the thinker who gathers the essence of all the forms and powers of transcending, and who assigns to this power an unprecedented force. The nineteenth century is for Nietzsche the 'era of methods'. As it is for Hermann Cohen, who taught us that the transcendental is method and nothing but method? No doubt – and it is true that Nietzsche is one of those who, at the end of the nineteenth century, made a return to Kant – but the one, precisely, who made of the transcendental the method of thinking thought co-extensive with the encyclopedia of culture, and not the mere thinking of science. For he was not content to say, banally, that method overrides object; he spoke of a triumph, of a victory of method over science itself. Which is also to say: science is only one method among others. It is this victory of method – its universal reign, method becoming a thinking thought and thought becoming a nature – that we must think as its entering into the law of its essence.

Perhaps you are waiting for an example to shed some light on this transvaluation. I only have time for an example that may suggest to you the aim of this operation, but will not exemplify the steps of its method. I shall be rather caricatural and schematic on this point. If I were to reprise just one thing from Kant, it would be the famous example of the mercury sulphide, which philosophers still call vulgarly (i.e. in the Greek fashion) 'cinnabar'. In the name of its 'conditions of possibility', the classical method set out the inventory of a priori elements which are all, or nearly all, ideal, but at the same time are sampled from the real faculties (intuition, understanding, etc…). Now, these a priori elements are perhaps only mere duplications, doublings or redoublings of the *given* identity of the object or of the unity of experience; so the latter is not at all explained by them. As Nietzsche said of Kant and the idealism that followed him, one contents oneself with repeating the object of the question in the response: for every sort of synthetic a priori judgement discovered, one invents a 'faculty'. It is more appropriate instead to return to the simplicity of the hypothesis – that is, of any object whatsoever – and to its a priori conditions, with the same conditions being valid for every region of objects. Thus the rarity and univocity of the transcendental method. For it is rather those forms and those idealities that require explanation. Rather than going from the empirical manifold of the cinnabar toward its objectivity, one goes from the latter toward an entirely other, a priori, even transcendental, manifold that will now furnish a true explanation. The dispersion of sensible qualities that Kant threatens us with, in order to make us accept the rules of the imagination and all the factors of order, is but a parody of an entirely other, pre-phenomenal – that is to say, noumenal – dispersion, where these qualities pull so indiscriminately in all sorts of divergent directions at once, that the understanding would indeed be hard-put to recognise in them its categories, the imagination its rules of reproduction, the phenomenology of perception its horizons. We must re-immerse the object cinnabar in this veritable transcendental *background noise* for which the Greeks invented the word *chaos*, and which forms the element of the internal constitution of things.

The aim of a transvaluation is thus very simple: it is a matter of understanding why mercury sulphide is not merely mercury sulphide, but an ideality whose a priori constituents are not only scientific laws. 'The' cinnabar is part and parcel with its circle of determinations that inscribe it into the web of culture, and first of all into the Greco-occidental field; with its poetry, with its force of imposing itself on us as a myth, and as a joke; of imposing itself on Kant also as an ideal object, an example of an example – without which imposition, perhaps, Kant (as obsessed by chemistry and perception as he was) would have seen that it was also cinnabar that Roman ladies used as lipstick; or that 'the alchemical sign for cinnabar is a circle with a central point ... [or that] the same symbol was later used, toward the end of the middle ages, for the philosophical egg, for the sun, and for gold'. 'Whence [so the encyclopedia I have just cited concludes sagely, more Kantian than Kant himself] various confusions, against which one must be vigilant.' Even more so, Kant could have known that cinnabar is also that red paint known as 'minium' with which any Sunday philosopher, returning to his country home as to his island of truth, would begin by painting the shutters of his understanding, before clothing them in the discrete colours of morality. Did Kant know this? In any case, the *Critique*, which demonstrates so many things, does not demonstrate the true reasons that make of cinnabar an ideality, and of that ideality an encyclopedia – that encyclopedia of knowledge for which Nietzsche quite rightly re-invented the rigorous name 'eternal return', and which is still not quite the same thing as that dictionary-knowledge by which you are not fooled. This is to say that a transvaluation proposes to furnish (but it would be the most naive insolence to believe that it could furnish them *all*) the reasons why Kant did not have more reasons to write the *Critique of Pure Reason* – or, since he had to write it, to demonstrate why it was precisely this positive absence of reasons that served as the reason for him to write a critique. It is the meaning of this abyss – whence the 'Critique', and indeed the cinnabar itself, derive reasons to render themselves necessary and to impose themselves upon us, with their self-evidence and their force – that we must now recognise.

> First rule: *Against empiricism, which subordinates cuttings-out to the articulations of the given, engender the* a priori *factum on the basis of transcendental-style cuttings; against rationalism, dissociate the a priori from ideality.*

To determine an a priori 'fact', to cut out a field from the a priori that might serve as primary matter for further cuts – such is the object of this rule, which we shall call the rule of factualisation, and which institutes the struggle against all empiricism.

The philosopher finds before him *continua* that will only later appear as illusions, but which make themselves evident to him as common sense. Continuity of perception and of science in the equivocal notion of the object; continuity of empirical properties of the being and of Being itself in the equivocal word 'being'; continuity of the perceived and of perception in the belief in a perceived-in-itself; continuity of pure will and desire in the immediate experience of the will; continuity of given forms of power and the a priori of power in the ambiguous concept of the institution, etc...

The first rule necessitates that we divide up these mixtures, cutting out an a priori field such that although it sets out, doubtless, from experience (from those continuities within which it is immersed) it does not derive from it. Deducted from these continuities by means of a cut that is not just any cut, a cut we shall determine as transcendental – a reduction – it cannot be an object 'in itself': we must here make of the noumenon and of the limit a weapon against every attempt to conserve, this side of the empirical, a fact or a given (albeit a priori) for a description (albeit pure or eidetic). Even the pure sciences that Kant places in the factum suppose a first reduction which bears upon the judgement of perception, and which is all too often forgotten. Husserl recognises the necessity of this preliminary suspension that isolates pure, albeit mundane, psychism. So that, even if there is something originary, it is perhaps not, despite Kant, the a priori as 'fact', but the operation of reduction that produces the fact. One cannot abstract the a priori from the totality of conditions of its obtaining: the factum exists only through cutting and suspension. We must speak of *factualisation* rather than of a factum, and subordinate all description to the work of cuts. Produced under these conditions, the factum is always itself a transcendental residue, the remainder of an operation of bracketing out that can be generalised as continuous and incomplete. Formulated in view of its transvaluation, this rule will say that there is no fact of reason in the sense that reason itself would be, in its own way, a fact. 'Reason' is no more than the set of cuts that engender the 'given', which should not be confused with the divisions of the given, and which it remains, moreover, to determine, under non-rationalist conditions of practice. The method is constitutive from its very first gesture, or, if not, must renounce all autonomy – it cannot allow itself to be guided by specific and generic distinctions between things, it indifferentiates them and renders them contingent in favour of its own cuts, which it imposes upon nature. It abhors so-called 'given' nature, that is to say (if you will allow me the expression – in which I include myself) stupidity, and not just illusion. But this is a transcendental abhorrence – for it remains, in any case, forever immersed in this real.

The question *quid facti?* is no longer, in Kant, anything but a rationalist, and indissolubly empiricist, interpretation and fixing of reduction; a halting of the continuous process of cutting at one of its provisional stages. Such are the conditions of what I will call the transcendental destruction of the question *quid facti*. Destruction, that is not to say negation (here, negation is an effect, not the essence), but critique and displacement (we shall see how); another cutting-out according to a gap governed without negativity as principle, an other economy of this question, whcih must be displaced into the margins of the terrain where Kant and Husserl placed it during their joint, fascinated struggle against Hume. Although it has its own concept of what is empirical and susceptible to being destroyed, the *principal* objective of the transcendental method is not the struggle against empiricism in the historical sense; this combat is the aim and the affair of rationalism. It need not rely on Kant and Husserl's aims and means of combat in favour of the 'fact' of science. Its affair is elsewhere; it retires from a game where there are more accomplices than real rivals, let us say more complementary than 'supplementary' positions; it proposes as its aim the genesis and the critique of culture, and also of history, where the subject is 'interested'.

To integrate the question *quid facti?* into a continuous process of reduction is only the first step, however. Because what really needs to be changed to give the struggle its full extension, this time against rationalism and idealism themselves, is the content of the reduced side and the residual side – and even more than their content, these classical concepts themselves, that is to say the *rationalist* concept of the a priori and the *rationalist and empirical* concept of the empirical; and to proceed with a simultaneous overthrowing and displacement of the rationalist hierarchy. On the empirical side, reduced or suspended, we shall place (not all at once, that would be impossible, but via repeated reductions) *all* given forms of continuity, of synthesis and thus of ideality. Even the Kantian formal a priori, even the Husserlian material a priori (which are not yet a priori enough for us, for they remain too empirical, too given) will fall within the sphere of the reduced. Ideality and formality are thus suspended, but not negated; they become, in turn, objects that demand a transcendental genesis. To know now what we shall place in the a priori as residue, we begin by dissociating the other alliance, the other chain of Kantianism and phenomenology – that of the manifold and the empirical. We shall make a certain manifold – but obviously not the so-called sensible manifold of space and time, empirical or even pure, for that manifold is always presented as such in a synopsis which is already an ideality – we shall make a certain manifold pass over to the side of the a priori and into its functions.

It is indeed a reversal of Kant and Husserl's idealising positions, but also their displacement; because the content of the terms has changed, and has not merely been inverted. On one hand we now see as empirical every form of ideality or synthesis, identity, formality or presence; but more generally everything that can be given – even to pure intuition. Givenness, evident or not, is no longer the criterion of the transcendental residue (as it is for phenomenology). On the contrary, it is now the criterion of the empirical. On the other hand, the manifold that now constitutes the residue in the new sense of the word can no longer be, by definition, a given manifold as is that of synopsis, simple presence but presence all the same. *It is a manifold that precedes* a priori *synopsis or intuition itself.* And it is no longer given, but merges with its own production, since it merges with the cut itself. The manifold is subordinated to the immanent divisibility of the residue. It is less a manifold than a continuous division. If givenness is the criterion of the empirical, (re)flexivity or splitting will be the immanent criteria of transcendental residues. Heidegger evokes a certain 'transcendental dispersion' which suggests that we speak of a *dispers* rather than a manifold [*divers*]. It is essential to remark: (1) that these residual objects that merge together with the cut of reduction (or at least tend to do so) are by definition anterior to (that is to say are a priori conditions of) all species of synthesis, continuities or totalities, whose derivative status consigns them from now on to assuring only the reproduction of this manifold; (2) that at this level of the a priori, which is not the truly transcendental level, the two sides are still mixtures, and contain at once both forms of this manifold and forms of this ideality, mixed together but in the process of separation. Here it is a question of the concept of a residual object as a priori, and no longer of its (essential and purified) concept as transcendental (Essence). All that matters is the movement of reduction and the tendency.

A transcendental manifold that precedes the unity of experience and renders it possible – this is the only 'factum' that the transcendental method can 'give itself', i.e. produce immanently, if it would free itself from the start from its logicising limitations. It then has at its disposal the means (in the long term) to cease reflecting viciously the syntheses found in experience, in the form of those transcendental idealities that are the forms of intuition, the pure concepts and the 'I think'. It will treat them, on the contrary, as objects to be engendered, and will make of transcendental genesis a theory of idealisation, of the production of idealities – a theory that will be its very own concept of the critique of ideology.

Generally speaking, synthesis as given is something to evaluate, the object of a transcendental genesis, or one whose degree of objective status is to be sought; it is not a means of explanation. To be freed not only from psychologism, from the confusion of the a priori and the innate (as Husserl, just as much as Cohen, aimed to be), one must also free oneself from the confusion of the a priori and form, and assign to the a priori, as its transcendental essence (as we shall see below) only the flexivity, the irreflective self-division, that should be written *division-(of)-self*, and of which the residual objects are the correlate. The struggle of neo-Kantianism and of Husserl against psychologism in favour of the transcendental must be relayed and completed – from now on, against both of them – by the struggle against formalism and rationalism. Experience might then be extracted from its (still naive) logical possibility, to be brought into its real possibility.

> Second rule: *Rediscover the true transcendental cuts*, as *opposed to empirical, quantitative and qualitative, generic and specific differences.*

The essential point of the second rule is already contained in the first, which defines residual objects, or cuts out the singular being according to its a priori, i.e. its individuating being. The second and third, in a certain way, break down the content of the first. The second bears more especially upon the articulation, the syntax, or (as Kant says) on the 'manner' and the 'mode' of the a priori; the third on the status or the transcendental reality of that a priori residual object.

Once the factum or fact is established, transcendental philosophers, in general, conjugate two types of cut: on one hand, a cut between *real* factors (for example Kant's distinction between the faculties, intuition, understanding, reason, imagination; or Husserl's between the spatio-temporal world and pure psychism). We shall call this one, if not 'real distinction' like the Scholastics, at least a realising or ontic cut (reserving 'factualising' for the initial cut). And on the other hand, a cut that distinguishes the real from ideality, and which we shall call an idealising or ontological cut. One is the cut of fact, the other of sense; between them, they decompose the factum, which is synthetic from the point of view of its content, always real and ideal at once (the Kantian factum of the sciences contains the real affect and the ideality of the a priori; the Heideggerian factum of the being in general or of the being's being-in-the-midst-of-being, contains the real being, but grasped in its ideal and non-empirical generality, etc...).

In general a cut can be called transcendental on the following condition, which we draw from the rule that serves us as organon, or again from the factum: the residue deducted by the cut, or that which is called the a priori, is identical to the cut itself; the reduction is transcendental if it is the fact of the residue in person. Transcendental means to say immanent, and the transcendental method is not at all the act of a philosopher *ex machina*. The cut being solely the work of the residual side, it can be said to be unilateral. Since the residue, in cutting into the empirical continuities, in fact cuts itself, it can be understood how the a priori is always that which *precedes* experience and conditions it: after the withdrawal of the cut, the donation of condition and genesis. There is thus, if not a synthesis, at least an immanence – properly residual or transcendental, specific – of the manifold of self-cuts, and which is the work of the a priori, in such a way that we shall say: the side that divides or residualises is at the same time the whole of the two sides; in short, the cut that defines the residual object or the transcendental limit includes an illimitation. As to the reduced, cut, or empirical side, it is this side that contains the synthetic factors and ideal givens, and which unites, in its own way and by virtue of them, with the residual side. A unilateral synthesis also, ideal and no longer residual immanence, and to be regarded from this point on as empirical and no longer transcendental – that which Kant has in mind when he says that understanding begins *with* experience. The meaning of the Transcendental Analytic will consist, as we have already seen, in passing from the empirical synthesis that defines the mixtures of representation and illusion, to the affirmation of real transcendental immanence, to 'transcendental truth'. Synthesis does indeed remain the horizon of the Analytic, but in the same way that, in Husserl, the object remains a transcendental guide – changing in status, it derives from the a priori as from a manifold upon which, however, it folds back.

The classical thinkers obviously understood the cut as a synthesis: it is always, to some degree or other, the residue of the a priori, and then the supreme transcendental condition, that operates differences or cuts. But this is the point at which it is possible to reverse Kant and Husserl's transcendental logic: because, for them, *only* the idealising cut is really transcendental.

Certainly Kant is constrained (lapsus of transcendental logic) to double and to reinforce his a priori forms and categories, Husserl his transcendental ego, through reference to real agents qua 'powers' (the power of reception, the power of concepts, the power of rules); not to mention imagination as time, which resumes all there is of the real, i.e. of the repressed, in Kantianism; or indeed by reference to immanent psychism. But the real cut is often simply traced from psychology – it is accessory, or serves at best as a support to that which detaches form and in general ideality as sole content of the a priori. The real factors, in any case, play a secondary role and are idealised, sublimated, raised up as 'forms'. This is surely to identify the immanence of the a priori, which is or which must be *real*, with all the forms of *ideal* synthesis or unity, which obviously do exist, but which are only derivative, and which only intervene later in transcendental genesis. Transcendental idealism is condemned to conflate the immanent production of the a priori manifold with its ideal forms of *reproduction*.

To transvaluate the method would be to subordinate the idealising cut to the real (but not empirical) cut, the ontological to the ontic. If Kant seeks the conditions of possible experience and not of real experience, then let us reprise and radicalise, perhaps against Kant, and against Husserl also, a Scholastic tendency: not only are the transcendentals, and all ideal elements in general – *not just the categories* – relative to the real; but the primacy is that of the ontic over the ontological, it is the being (but which being? here lies the whole question) that cuts and transcends. The transcendental method begins neither with God, nor with things, nor with man; it begins with nothing, that is to say with a cut – but this cut is perhaps identical to the real itself. Whoever said that the real comprises nothing more than God, things, and man?

Which brings us to the third rule.

Third rule: *Define a transcendental cut* par excellence *that isolates an Essence as supreme synthetic principle or unity of reality and ideality; define this unity as that of a hierarchy, of a primacy of the real over ideality.*

All the techniques, all the objects of the analytic, are brought together into a last problem, that of the principle that unifies them and governs their economy so as to produce the unity of experience. This principle, this Essence that all operations of cutting-out come down to, contains all of the preceding cuts and the whole of their reality. But it is an additional *reduction*. It brings together the preceding cuts, and presupposes them, for it cannot relate itself directly to the empirical instance, but acts solely through a priori residual objects, which it raises, moreover, to the power of transcendental conditions. The preceding cuts do not deserve the name 'transcendental' unless they postulate their unity, which is only posited confusedly in the factum. On the contrary, it is this Essence, itself coming out of the movement of the Analytic, but which completes or closes it in opening up the possibility of a transcendental genesis, that merits *par excellence* the appellation 'transcendental'.

On one hand, it is the unity of the preceding cuts, of what one might call the manner, the trope, the how or even the syntax of the a priori factors, whether or not they are those of the understanding; on the other hand, it is the essence of this a priori and of these cuts, the agent that evaluates and measures immanently the degree of their objective reality. It thus contains the *how* and the *that* of the unity of experience. But it unifies the two contraries – on one hand the syntax of the a priori, on the other the power of the a priori – without itself reconstituting a third term. As essence, it is one of the contraries and simultaneously the unity of contraries; and thus, from the point of view of its own syntax, it responds to the definition we have given of reduction – in other words, it is, in turn, a *residual* object.

There is thus a *parallelity* [*parallélité*] (to take up Husserl's word) between the residual objects corresponding to anterior cuts, postulated as transcendental, and the residual object of the Essence in which they are differentiated and which is, itself, the truly transcendental. Which arouses our suspicions: What prevents this parallelity from falling into parallelism [*parallélisme*], and the whole mechanism from giving rise to a vicious reflection of the empirical into the Essence? For if this reduction resumes, reprises and extends those that preceded it, it only bases itself upon the latter, which are turned toward the object, because it distinguishes itself from them in so far as it is non-synthetic self-cut and thus, as transcendental, is the subject itself, the only subject possible. This subject is no longer a real instance in the sense of being constituted and claiming to be constitutive; it is no longer a representation or a generality drawn from the empirical (I think, Ego) and the transcendent real, then endowed afterwards with a power of idealisation and infinite reproduction. In point of fact, it is only the cut, but the cut *in itself* and outside all ideal relation with an other, pure dispersion, which is here identified, *entirely*, with the residual object of which it is the (re)flexive or subjective (albeit 'irreflexive') face.

In a sense it is not distinguished from a priori objects except in so far as there is, immanent to them, the principle which at the same time gives an objective status or an empirical field to this manifold. It is that in them which cuts or reduces, that which synthesises or unifies, but also that which is cut and synthesised. It is the a priori and it is the empirical, but in relations that, from this point on, conform to transcendental truth. Co-extensive with residual objects, it is a transcendental principle, i.e. a principle of non-synthetic or real immanence. But here, already, is the second side of Essence, according to which it is an evaluating agent of the transcendental, i.e., objective status of the a priori. There is a power proper to the a priori, but the question is now that of the possibility of this power, that is to say of the power of power, since Essence implies a redoubling of power.

But what type of reality to put under the name of this second power? Essence is not only that which relates to the real of the a priori, which determines, on its side, beings or what there is of the ideal in beings. Essence itself determines the a priori in its relation to beings. The whole anti-idealist thesis, the thesis that is the last step in the transvaluation, consists in affirming that it is the real itself that is essence, that it is the being itself, but obviously only in so far as it is no longer grasped through its ideal determinations as object, in its *objectivity*. Essence is, from this point of view, noumenon – it is the being or the real in itself. But noumenon in so far as (*contra* Kant) the latter receives a positive (albeit non-empirical) content; noumenon grasped from the side of the transcendental and as constituent of the *a priori* manifold, and no longer from the side of the empirical of the spatio-temporal manifold of affection. In short (*too* short), noumenon is the a priori manifold in so far as it is self-subject or self-affection.

Let us consider three points, in order to explicate this thesis:

(1) Essence is indeed that which renders possible, but that which renders possible should not be confused with possibility as a pure logical form to which is raised a real of the type 'I think' or 'Ego', and which remains secondary qua real; even if it permits the passage from logic to the transcendental. The ascent of ideality into Essence is the basis of transcendental logic, and of neo-Kantianism in particular, but it conflates the *possibilitas* as *Wesen* – as active and productive essence, as real condition – with a simply possible possibility, doubling itself in an ideal and invariant form that is afterwards endowed with a transcendental function. The transcendental method might find a future in the thesis that essence is the being itself (not the 'objective' being), and in positing a primacy of

the ontic, of the real, over the ontological. But, of course, just as the *Critique of Pure Reason*, according to Kant's celebrated phrase, teaches us to take the word 'object' in two senses (as phenomenon and as thing-in-itself), we must also learn to consider the word 'being' in two senses: as empirical being and as being-essence or as noumenon. It is true that we take noumenon also in two senses: in the negative, Kantian sense, which marks the primacy of its limitative function at the expense of its potential function in a genesis or a production of experience; and then in a positive sense – positive but obviously not empirical, for this would see us fall prey once again to the Kantian critique. Residual objects, and above all Essence, are a noumenon whose function is no longer merely limitative, but which is instead subordinated to a genetic and productive function. Noumenon is auto-limitation of experience because it is first of all production-(of)-self (rather than 'auto'-production).

(2) What, from the point of view of its reality and not only that of its syntax, distinguishes Essence from residual objects, if, in its turn, it is one? From now on we shall assign one instance, and one only (real, or ideality), to each of these functions: It is the real that is preeminently the power of cutting, and it is the ideal that is the power of synthesis. So that, in order to reduce the two types of cut to one only, we shall hierarchise them. We shall oppose real cutting, which does not proceed by following the

generic and specific articulations of things, to cutting by and for ideality, which in general distinguishes one ideal generality from another, and is consequently carried out under the auspices of representation – a cut impregnated with negativity and giving rise to oppositions, or even contradictions. Real dispersion or transcendental division is a priori in relation to ideality; it forms an absolutely singularising cut, and, since it is not mediated by the whole that precedes it, it is without negativity. The hierarchy of the real and the ideal thus signifies that even in the idealising cut itself, nothing but the real or the being can cut, and can thus be the power that unifies, even in the activity of the unification of syntheses. But from now on the real or the cut is entirely on one side, ideal synthesis entirely on the other. This is what distinguishes the transcendental concept of the residual object from the a priori concept of the residual object.

In short, beings have power or sovereignty over Being because we are no longer talking about the empirical being in its ideality, but the noumenal being as immanent power of self-cutting. It is perhaps not Being that must be barred – that is a project still marked by the old transcendental idealism. Being is barred only because it receives from the being, itself barred, the bar of the transcendental cut. What is more, the being is not only barred qua ideal, i.e. empirical in the new sense of the word; qua Essence, being is nothing but the bar itself in its sovereignty over Being.

The bar is (re)flexive and dispersive, but it is the true transcendental subject. As to the Ego and the 'I think', here we must salute Sartre: they are transcendent entities, our own 'beings of reason' which would have us readily think that reason itself is but a being of reason. They are mixtures, empirico-transcendental doublets – they are necessary to transcendental logic, but not to the transcendental method considered in its essence, i.e. considered with regard to its future.

(3) What now to put under the name of Essence or of real, what to put in this power-to-differ which Heidegger tells us is the power to hold jointly and severally together Being and beings, the ideal and the real? The bar or the cross is indeed the Essence of Being; but this cross is the one from which Antichrists are made. Here an abyss opens up, an abyss where Transcendental Idealism, and many other good things (like Marxism) complete their course. If there absolutely must be a name to occult it, a name which itself has abyssal consequences, why not (this is a question open to debate, not a solution) that of 'will-to-power', which perhaps is not only this Essence of Being and of beings, but the being itself, that assigns its Being to the cut? The 'will to power' is a new way of replenishing the supreme synthetic principle of experience, the way in which Nietzsche pays homage to Kant even as he buries him. It designates the very abyss of the real as transcendental cut, a real but not empirical matter

upon which, here, I can say nothing. In any case 'will to power' is necessarily a *quid pro quo* and the name of a snare that can mislead only we, those who are astray. In evoking the will to power as the world of the multiple, did Nietzsche wish to designate anything other than an a priori dispersion which, beyond the pure forms of intuition and the categories themselves, beyond pure time (always hybridised with space), resonates precisely like that immense *transcendental background noise* that is the true subject of the universe? When Heidegger says of the Essence of Being that it is desire and power, he takes a Nietzschean step – however hobbled by idealist reminiscences – along the road of the transvaluation of the transcendental method. This conception of Essence gives us the unique chance, the rather serious opportunity, of a transcendental materialism which we all know is the 'dead dog' of the idealism that goes by the same name. I have been so bold as to think it would be possible to fish it out of the same Heraclitean river twice. I would add that this real condition of experience should not be confused in any way with an originary temporalisation or a productive imagination, except in considering that this dispersion without negativity or this positive division is that of an intensive temporality, *hyle* or transcendental matter, as is perhaps the 'will to power' – but I leave this question in suspense, because it is not even certain that the notion of *hyle* is here sufficient to satisfy this concept of real immanence.

> Fourth rule: *Define a 'transcendental genesis'*, i.e. *the particular modes of synthesis of residual objects, or of the real and of ideality, under the conditions of immanence of Essence* (*destruction of the question* quid juris?).

The three first rules have allowed us to take stock of the a priori materials at our disposal. But it is not as 'pure reason', nor upon it, that we have made this survey. The transcendental method is 'residual' rather than 'elementary'; its model is surgical just as much as (and perhaps more than) it is chemical. As its elements, it knows only the techniques of cutting, procedures of evaluation, rules that in any case define only becomings, tendencies, limits. The task is now to rebuild the temple, to reconstruct the edifice on bases of 'transcendental truth' infinitely more unsteady than that 'complaint of experience' evoked by Kant. It is time to place ourselves in the conditions of the re-unification of residual objects in view of the unity of experience – in short, to proceed toward a new distribution of these materials.

This economy serves at once as 'transcendental deduction' and 'transcendental genesis'. Essence is the highest result of the Analytic, but it is the means of genesis itself; the production of residual objects or of manifolds is immediately their reproduction. As Being, it has still to become what it is, through that which it is capable of producing – namely, the forms of unity of this manifold, forms we do not yet know.

On one hand, since an Essence of this type is unifying and immanent, by virtue of its very dispersion (otherwise, it would not be transcendental), it is a principle of legitimation or evaluation of the objective reality of residual objects in so far as they are always invested in experience. The evaluation of their objective status, that is to say their capacity to relate to a transcendental object = X, which they precede a priori and produce, and which meanwhile always accompanies them and makes them converge in it. It is a true transcendental deduction, because they are constrained not only to unite, but to abandon forthwith their empirical and transcendent forms, which are critiqued and delimited, so as to re-enter, with the object = X itself, into the heart of Essence, that is to say to form really (but this can only be a tendency) nothing but a transcendental dispersion. For Essence makes them become what it is, that is to say, this dispersion. It is animated by a tendency or an intention, a becoming-really-residual that is the same thing as a becoming-immanent. It achieves this by laying down in itself the obligation for the two sides of every residual object (the real a priori and the ideal empirical, the ontic and the ontological) to unify or rather to re-unify on new bases, bases that will no longer be empirical, after having been separated by the transcendental reductions. That Being, for example, must be the Being of a being, we have always known this – it is a knowledge inscribed in our language; but we will now be equipped to think – that is, to transform – this relation of synthesis according to transcendental truth or the Essence of Being – *Wesen des Seins*.

On the other hand, as an Essence of this type is the real condition of experience, it is at the same time the principle of a genesis. One can only destroy the idealist interpretation of the question *quid juris?* by re-inscribing the latter within a real, and no longer ideal, genesis. It is Essence as real and no longer as ideal that determines the objective 'status' of residual objects, even if, to this end, it also has recourse to synthetic (that is, ideal) procedures. We no longer have any reason to separate, as Kant and transcendental idealism were obliged to do, the ideal condition of experience (the 'I think') and its real condition (the imagination); nor, as Husserl was often tempted to do, transcendental description, critique, and genesis.

We cannot detail the content of this rule here. On one hand, what is essential in transvaluation is established as a passage to Essence as real transcendental dispersion. With it, we thus acquire the principle of every genesis (an equivalent of the Objective Deduction) – a *productive acquisition*, we must say, to parody Kant who speaks of an 'originary acquisition' of the a priori. On the other hand, it is the least inventive part of the method, the most dry and mechanical. Once we possess the concept of residual objects, it is enough to seek (we do not have time here) the two or three modes of their synthesis, the *how* of their articulation that permits them to form aggregates or objects – this object as any-object-whatsoever – according to the form of objectivity = X. To analyse the three ways in which the a priori or residual manifold relates to the form of objectivity (an equivalent of the Subjective Deduction) one can take as one's model (albeit a little misleading, a little empirical) the three Kantian syntheses. Thus thought penetrates into the internal life of power, the internal life of the real or, ultimately, of matter; and the subject, which is thus within the secret of matter since this matter is the subject itself, recognises itself to be of the same stuff as cinnabar, at least in so far as it ceases to be mercury sulphite and becomes that object inhabited by a background noise, an evil genius, fugitive and surreal, that seems to trouble Kant so.

DISCUSSION

ANTOINETTE VIRIEUX-REYMOND: I have listened with much interest to M. Laruelle. I must say that I was very troubled, because, in seeking the method, he cannot destroy the question *quid juris?*, since a method implies something that must be followed. Thus, there is a reference to right. I do not think one can evacuate (if this is the meaning of the word destruction) the question *quid juris?* Even if you were to reconstruct the fact as something that is not given, that is in part constructed, after all, fact and right are opposed, and I don't believe that you can eliminate the question of right.

What's more, I was a little perturbed when you spoke of a cut on the basis of nothing, if I understood you correctly; because it seems to me that a cut always exists *between* things situated on two sides of the cut; and, on the other hand, it seems that, if one brings in the nothing at the origin, it would take a divine power to create something from nothing – creation *ex nihilo* has always been considered to be the preserve of the divine. Those are the questions to which I would like to hear your response.

FRANÇOIS LARUELLE: On the first question, I am entirely in agreement with you. 'Destruction' of the question *quid juris?* does not mean negation – I did not repeat this a second time, having already said so for the question *quid facti*. We cannot simply shake off, as if by magic, what Kant wrote, and in particular this question, which is consubstantial with the transcendental method. Even in Nietzsche – in fact, above all in Nietzsche – there is always a problem of right for any affirmation or 'value'. I know no greater philosopher of right, besides Fichte and Hegel, than Nietzsche. 'Destruction' means displacement

according to a controlled distance – according to a cut, precisely, which is the whole object of the question and which
has effects of negation, but which is not essentially negative.
With regard to what I call residual objects – that is to say, a
prioris that are not (or not just) ideal a prioris – the problem is always posed of their validity, i.e. the degree of their
objective reality, of measuring their capacity to enter into the
empirico-ideal constitution of an object. Because it is not a
question of suppressing, in the transvaluation of the transcendental method, the problem of the objectivity of objects
or of their constitution. It is precisely their unity, their identity, that we must account for, and which is thus suspended
by the method. This is exactly what I wanted to suggest
when I spoke about the 'cinnabar' as I did. The cinnabar is
indeed something other than mercury sulphite. The ideality
of cinnabar, Cinnabar capital C, is an identity that is a circle
of reproduction; it supposes the passage, the composition or
the synthesis of a multiplicity of determinations. There are
also various jokes that could be made about the cinnabar.
Cinnabar is an encyclopedia. The problem always arises,
therefore, of a legitimation of residual objects. The transcendental method must, whatever happens, remain critique – a
critique of illusions that arise with respect to experience.

As to your second question about the cut and the nothing, if I said that the transcendental method begins from
nothing, it was as a provocation, for I immediately added:
through a cut, and the cut is the real in the non-empirical,

noumenal sense of the term. Thus, it does not begin with a *nihil*, but with the fullness of Being. But this fullness of Being is not substance, it is Essence, it is the fullness of a manifold, it is immanent. This is how the transcendental method begins, its concrete beginning, the 'site' where it always already is, the non-region it has always already trodden. Incidentally, I did not go into *the very complex relations internal to this manifold of cuts*, I just produced it without analysing it. Difference is not 'between' two things, it *is* one of those two 'things'...

JACQUES MERLEAU-PONTY: It seems as if you have destroyed chemistry. You yourself said 'mercury sulphite'. What does that mean? Are there not questions to ask about mercury sulphite, about what the empirical is and what the rational is, what the formal is, what content is, perhaps what experience and the transcendental are? All these questions can be asked of cinnabar, because there are electrons, wave functions, experiments, etc. in there, but you did not pose them. Lipstick, very well, but ...

FL: And why not! There are verses in La Fontaine where he speaks of cinnabar in relation to the complexion of young girls.

JM-P: There are also treatises on chemistry that speak of it.

FL: Chemistry enters partially into 'culture'. Precisely the object of the transcendental method is to take culture as its object and to 'destroy' it.

JM-P: So chemistry must be destroyed in the process.

FL: Not entirely. The problem you raise is either one of chemistry, in which case it has nothing to do with the philosopher; or one of epistemology or the theory of science. As to the latter, I said just now, in responding to another question, that the philosopher intervenes therein only to 'destroy' the strictly philosophical part that enters into that 'mélange' that is epistemology.

JM-P: Cinnabar is a 'being'. If you preserve cinnabar's property of being a lipstick, this proves that you have not stripped the being of all its properties. So why not keep the others, too?

FL: I seek the determination or the proper internal difference of cinnabar; which is indifferent to its properties, but precisely makes it not only mercury sulphite, since it accumulates the latter simultaneously with various other, non-scientific, determinations. Cinnabar is a point of condensation of *all of* culture, and not *only* an object of science.

JM-P: Yes, but don't neglect the fact that there is culture in wave functions, in atoms, etc.

FL: I entirely agree: in science, too. The difficulty, then, is to determine that specifically philosophical element that enters into the constitution of science. Not only aims, values and ideologies; not only the philosophemes and theories that may play the role of 'relations of production' in the process of production of science; but something that is perhaps even more profound, and which affects the idea that scientific producers have of 'objectivity'. The latter may well be a hybrid theme, referring at once to internal criteria or precise procedures of verification, and to a philosophical (*too* philosophical?) idea of objectivity as 'auto-position' of reality. To be brief, I would say that scientific work needs a concept – a philosophical category – of 'position' or existence, but that it does not need that of the 'auto-position' of empirical reality, which belongs to common sense and thus still to a certain philosophy, from which I suggest the transcendental method must demarcate itself – if need be, against Kant.

GILBERT KAHN: I do not really understand on what basis you make a distinction between 'beings'. Do you wish to begin from the ontic and not from the ontological, and from a 'being' that would not be empirical?

FL: Just as Kant asks us to take the object in two senses (a cut that is the effect of the transcendental method), i.e. the object as phenomenon and the object as thing-in-itself, so a transformed transcendental method will always imply a cut (but now displaced) between a transcendental and an empirical concept of the 'being', a concept that is still transcendental in its way.

GK: But on what basis?

FL: It is the very definition of the transcendental method to impose this cut between empirical and transcendental. The latter is nothing other than its own proper difference (cut) with the empirical. But this is an invariant trait of any form of the transcendental method, whereas what characterises its transvaluation is the new economy that this cut brings about, the new distribution of the real and ideality. I define as empirical, beings such as they are given in their spatio-temporal form. Even ideality and scientific 'laws' are said to be empirical, through an additional extension of what is 'empirical' outside the limits fixed by rationalism, thus overthrowing-displacing Kantian idealism. One is then obliged to distinguish, from this empiricist concept of the real (which is nothing other than 'reality', the ontological ideality of the real) the transcendental and 'true' concept of the real, that is to say 'essence'. This real still merits the name of 'being' (whence the Scholastic communication between the *ens* as the first of the transcendentals and *essence*), but it is a being *indifferent* to its ideal determinations of identity, a noumenon in the state of an a priori and even transcendental manifold – and this is no longer the manifold of 'formal intuition' ... If this being, a manifold-being rather than a being, were determined empirically, we would obviously fall prey to Kantian critique. It seems to me – this is a very important point for the organisation of the philosophical field after Heidegger, and I will come back to it soon – that the primacy habitually attributed, upon a reading (in my opinion an overhasty reading) of Heidegger, to Being over 'beings', must always be corrected: In Heidegger, one must never neglect 'beings', and even less the essence that is (the) being upon which Being depends. As soon as Heidegger poses the problem of the essence of Being, he establishes in fact the problem of the power-to-differ Being from being, and this power-to-differ is noumenon. But the content of noumenon is 'transcendental dispersion', for noumenon can perhaps receive a positive concept.

BALDINE SAINT-GIRONS: Are we saying – to parody a well-known phrase – that 'a being is that which represents a subject for another being?'

FL: A being, at least qua residual object, is effectively that which the subject, or a subject, represents for another being; and Lacan's formula (or Peirce's, as Pierre Kaufman reminds me) is wholly suitable in this context. However, the true subject is the residual object, and above all it is subject not relative to another residual object, but in so far as another residual object is relative to it. A formula that I doubt would be acceptable to structuralism: On one hand because structuralism distinguishes the differential object from its correlate, the subject, and subjects the latter to the former. On the contrary one of the theses of the transvaluation of the transcendental method is that the residues, the manifold of cuts, are the subject itself, the *self* of the dividing [*se-deviser*] (no longer, perhaps, the 'complete' or even 'whole' subject, but the matrix of the subject). And on the other hand because structuralism knows the residual object only as the signifiant or differential relation of two phenomena *relative to each other*.

A relation is necessarily an ideality: structure is therefore entirely relative to itself, a relation of relations. Which is to say that it is vain and empty, a pure ideality that sinks into relativity, a relative autonomy that has not succeeded in founding itself in any 'instance' endowed with an absolute autonomy. On the contrary, the essential thesis of 'transcendental materialism' is that residual objects are not, in themselves or qua essence, relations. They are *non?-relations*, they are *contiguous* or *positively dispersed*. This anti-idealist, and consequently anti-structuralist thesis 'supposes' an absolute, endowed with an absolute autonomy – the subject as positive dispersion or transcendental abyss (the refusal to make a relation of it does not lead back to substance, but constrains us to *differ* the classical opposition of Relation and Substance, of substantial relative and absolute). A 'transcendental materialism' supposes a rupture with the idealist ontological postulates that made possible structuralism and its avatars – psychoanalytical, Marxist, and even 'Nietzschean', for there was a structuralist version of Nietzsche's thought... Thus, by residual object, we do not understand, like Lacan, something like the signifier. The content of the residual object, the content of the cut, will not be the signifier.

BS-G: Isn't there the problem of the ultimate indestructibility of the signifier?

FL: It's true, it is an extremely difficult problem. It's the problem of the indestructibility or (perhaps one could formulate it otherwise) of *the final invariance in the last instance* of residual objects. This poses the problem of the unconscious, if that which is indestructible is the unconscious. I think that, in this context, there is an unlimited destruction of invariants. Residual objects are not formal indivisible objects, as would be the signifier or even the 'distinctive trait' that rests on the same unthought ontological postulates.

Residual objects are not susceptible to a finite inventory. There are no invariant residual objects; or, more exactly, their invariance is 'at the end' of their internal variance in principle, it is the objective appearance of their internal multiplicity.

ANDRÉ JACOB: In the context of this recusing of rationalism, what is the least worst qualification?

FL: Above all not irrationalism. Irrationalism is the affair of rationalism, not that of the transcendental method such as I see it at work partially in Nietzsche. Why give it a name? 'Surrationalism', that would be a possible formula. I would add, all the same, that all this is only a sketch, an attempt and a temptation...

AJ: That term has already been used by Bachelard.

FL: I believe Bachelard used it in a text where he speaks of Nietzsche...

PHILIPPE ENCRENAS: In assigning the instance of *reality* to a *positivity* or *transcendental matter*, you effectively render obsolete the traditionally empirical determinations, at least in philosophy, of the concept of matter... If you had to give, even in brief, some criteria for the description or determination of this transcendental matter, what would they be?

FL: I cannot give you any more than I have already given – that is, the rules... Your question could not be more pertinent, and yet it is beyond my capabilities.

PE: I am not speaking here of the cutting-out to be operated, the articulations to be effectuated, but of the very being of that which is cut and articulated... You even spoke of the Being of the cut... Of what order is it? Of what order is the transcendental matter of the residual object?

FL: You allude to the problem of intensive magnitudes, of the will to power as fluctuation of intensity. I said that I would not say anything on this question, I would like to reserve this... It is an immense problem, a largely unknown territory. On the other hand, the problem of intensity is also an historical problem that has its origins in scholasticism.

To begin treating it with materials, one must put into relation the usage of the transcendental method in the scholastics with their concept of intensity, i.e. of quantitative variations of qualities (charity, for example); and one must refer to the work of the Parisian physicists of the fourteenth century. Not to mention the obligatory passage via thermodynamics... I will content myself for now with doing what all transcendental philosophers have always done: with putting in place the notions of the real, ideality, and objective reality – which is, after all, the beginning of a response to your question. It is certainly the case that, up to and including Cohen, the classical transcendental method and the problem of intensity maintained very close ties.

PIERRE KAUFMANN: I was struck by the fact that the allusion you made to an anticipation of the positive critique of Kantianism was drawn from the sphere of communication, since this allusion related to the third *Critique*. I would ask whether it is not within this sphere of communication that the problem is posed of that positivity of the non-empirical; or, if you go by way of Husserl, it would be in the fifth *Cartesian Meditation* that we would have to seek an anchor point. But doesn't the pure appresented precisely have something to do, as to its status, with what you envision, and in liaison with it – I refer to the question that was posed earlier about the *de jure*, the *quid juris*. I thought that I spotted something there about guilt. Isn't the question of guilt at issue here (and this would be my third question) concerning Heidegger? Is it not this theme of guilt, along with the problem that you have posed, that allows the clarification of the enigma that remains attached, in Heidegger, to the coexistence of the metaphysician and the Rector of 1933, whose initiatives and activities might appear as a sort of reprojected guilt or sur-guilt? And this touches on the very ground of our problem. For I believe that in this regard Heidegger is the most interesting of philosophers, for he presents the unique case of a philosopher who was writing staggering texts in the period around 1933. We have other great philosophers. But it is a matter of a unique case of residues. Finally, it is as if there were residues above and residues below: Jean Wahl's 'transcendence and trande-scendence'. Can the method be called the constitution of criteria? What criteria, in the event?

FL: It is difficult for me to respond to the problem of appresentation, unless I say that appresentation is the relation to the alter (ego), as these 'objects' by definition are, and that this relation conditions the constitution of the form of ideal objectivity, as is still the case here. As these residues are the matrix of subjectivity, they imply that subjectivity is multi-or pluri-subjectivity (rather than 'intersubjectivity'). In Husserl's own work, however, appresentation is but a *mode* of absolute presence to self of the living Present; and it is only outside Husserl, with another method, another 'reading' of his text, that one can suggest that, ultimately, in his work, appresentation conditions the constitution of a field of presence to self.

As to the problem of political guilt that may be at the origin of a political engagement by a philosopher, personally I would not pose the problem only in terms of 'guilt' and of 'sur-guilt', in order to explain Heidegger's deviation (if indeed it is a deviation). I wonder whether we must not first proceed from the very interior of Heidegger's thought. A thought whose aim is to overcome or displace (to 'differ') all the contradictions, all the oppositions handed down to us by the Greeks, will necessarily – owing to the very fact that it assumes one of the 'contrary' positions that itself assumes the power-to-differ and no longer the power-to-contradict – find itself in the position of a contrary in relation to another contrary. Politically, I believe that on the basis of Heidegger's thought, and more clearly Nietzsche's, it is impossible to content oneself with thinking the relations of power in terms of contradiction. They are relations of difference, of proximity and of contiguity, and also of continuity, and proximity is a risk to run that must always give rise to compromise and treason. I believe that in a thinking such as Heidegger's, and such as Nietzsche's, treason is a possibility that belongs to that mode of thinking. One must run this risk. It has become decidedly too easy to reject the adversary, in this case fascism, as a simple contrary, outside oneself. A thinking in the transcendental mode feels itself responsible for that which dialectic is made to wash its hands of. Irreducibly compromised by fascism, nevertheless irreducibly resistant, such is the paradox of the politics of residual objects...

PK: I don't believe there was any 'treason' on Heidegger's part. You used Heidegger in your discussion of the cut. I believe, on the contrary, that there was on his part a fidelity to a very particular sensibility to guilt, and that it is on the basis of the theme of guilt that one can address the theme of reprojected guilt. For me, I am infinitely grateful to Heidegger for having given to philosophers the unique example of having written and said what he wrote and said, and of having had the political investments he did. I believe that one cannot find within the whole history of philosophy anything approaching this. His bust ought to be present in all Societies of Philosophy. It is a unique case, in some sense a mystery that must be explored. We never speak of these things any more, and yet we touch there on the problem of the cut. But we had better not continue too long on Heidegger.

FL: Just a brief word. I entirely agree with all that – and I come now to the problem of guilt – but beginning from other bases, to say that much guilt remains with Heidegger, but I say this in opposition to Nietzsche. Everything that differentiates Heidegger from Nietzsche seems to me to have been accounted for by a remainder of guilt – of which he, in turn, accuses Nietzsche, of course... All the same, have we any criteria by which to assign guilt or innocence? A prejudicial question. These criteria cannot be transcendental, that is to say immanent. Innocence is *index sui et mali*, and if it is part and parcel of the innocence of the dispersion of cuts, it cannot be assigned to a subject 'in person' – no more to Nietzsche than to Heidegger. And neither can guilt. Unless we admit that the innocence or guilt of a thinker – or any individual whatsoever – pervades the *whole* of his existence and his acts, is as one with his *proper name* or *person* – which, also, condenses all of culture...

PK: This was just a commentary on the question of the person who preceded me, on the *de jure*.

Anne-Françoise Schmid (read from a letter): Your programme proposes a *trans*valuation of the *trans*cendental method. If we are to take seriously this double usage of the 'trans-', the transcendental no longer belongs so much to a typology as to a topology: a continuous passage, as you say elsewhere, an errance perhaps, a line of flight (the object (r) of your *Au-dèla du Principe de pouvoir*).[1] So that your method is not thought according to its objects. Which suggests to me two reflections:

---

1 [*Beyond the Power Principle*]; Paris: Payot, 1978.

How do you think the passage of this method to the 'disciplines' and 'objects' of which you speak elsewhere – power, language, linguistics (a passage that would be, apparently, the simple inverse of the approach that you have presented today)? How do you evaluate these 'objects' – if one can still treat them as such? Is it through the notion of the 'residual' that you think this passage? Is it equivalent to that of the 'fractionnel' in *Au-dèla du Principe de pouvoir*? This is the question of the 'applica-tion' of your method (although the term is inadequate). This transcendental thought at once relativises (through auto-affection) and revalorises 'theory' in philosophy, by operating a displacement characterised in particular, it seems to me, by the passage from 'external' referents to a referential internal to thought; this is the limit you 'impose' upon 'relativism' in philosophy. Do you think that it would be possible today to 'surpass' this 'limit' – that is to say, also, for you to do without the notion of the object (in general) and its (positive) critique? This is the question of the 'absolute' and the 'relative' in philosophy. These two reflections are also suggested to me by your reticence to use examples ('if such a thing exists', you say somewhere...)

FL: The pertinence of these questions comes from the fact that they touch on the thing itself. But the thing, as you have seen, is not just the object; the thing is the gesture, the continuous movement of a displacement. In this movement, I try to reconcile the trans-cendental and trans-valuation as being the same apart from one disparity, which is that of the displacement itself, the 'trans-' itself; which is, in short, no doubt, the 'transcendental of the transcendental', the term that I have reprised and which, as you have been able to see, contains two gestures that belong together, a gesture of overthrowing and a gesture of displacement in relation to the positions of Transcendental Idealism.

Consequently, the reference of this mode of thinking to what it is convenient to call 'object' becomes problematic – which is not to say inexistent, but simply open to question. In so far as, under the name of 'method' – of a method become subject and substance, production and nature – I understand thought as nothing but thinking or *simply* thinking, it becomes easy to imagine that, in clearing its head of the intoxicant of objects, it becomes drunk on itself and becomes even more sterile than its classical forms. For what a risk it would be, apparently, if philosophers allowed themselves a little to enjoy philosophy itself – to enjoy, that is to say to live and die of thought alone; if they suddenly asserted a will to sterility, to non-production and uselessness. What risk, and above all what wastefulness! If I may be permitted to place under the patronage (or the 'matronage ...') of Socrates (childbirth) and Nietzsche (pregnancy) this obstetric figure of the transcendental method: It is a woman who remains united with her child, in an infinite parturition. An uncomfortable situation that cannot be tolerated by one who is eager to have a son or to recognise a father, or simply to get on with attending to worldly matters. Or just to end the suffering...

And the relation to objects, to experience, to facts? And the examples that you have not given, or only so as to mock them? I thank you for posing these questions in a spirit that is not philistine. The method would not be transcendental if did not relate to real experience, and not only to experience 'in general' – it would be transcendent... The a prioris, even qua residual, are always and by definition invested in empirical instances, through which they pass, with which they begin, without ever deriving from them. But the thesis that seems to me consubstantial with all transvaluation is that of the univocity of method – it is the 'same', it enjoys a continuous validity for all regions of the object, it produces from itself, *with no separation*, its own field of 'application'. Hence, no typology (at least in the classical sense of the word), but a transcendental topology that is, if not the whole *manner* of thinking, at least half of the method (the other half being the dispersion of cuts...) Not even the self, or the *Ego*, can any longer benefit from what Heidegger calls ontico-ontological primacy. Not even Science – for example, mathematical physics, as in Kant. Not even 'discourse' and 'works', as for contemporary hermeneutics.

The indistinct object is not the indeterminate object. However empirically determined, this empirical determination is suspended, reduced: the empirical instance becomes indistinct from the transcendental, which does not supress it, but suspends it. And what is isolated by these reductions or these cuts, are the cuts themselves and their syntheses qua transcendental determination of the object. The object thus 'residualised' is transcendentally individuated. It is already a residual object, even if a whole (*perhaps* interminable) chain of reductions or cuts is necessary to draw out its a priori. If 'for example' (but the theoretical conditions of possibility of the 'example' are destroyed here) I were to try and draw out a linguistic a priori (to make a transcendental, rather than Cartesian, linguistics) I would seek to elaborate a residual object of language. Let's call it the *phonese*. I would distinguish it from the phoneme, which is a 'Kantian' concept, i.e. a hybrid entity of empirical speech and ideality. It is the *phonese* that is, beyond the phoneme but also in the phoneme, the true *real* power-of-differing. And also the true *ideal* power-of-differing? Doubtless, but such that the two sides, real and ideal, of the *phonese* are no longer held in a relation mediatised by a totality – that is, by what linguists call the 'system'. For a phoneme does not relate *immediately* to another, as one might wish. Its ontological constitution as ideal indivisible entity proves that it exists only surreptitiously, through the mediation of a whole or a system – in short, an empirico-ideal entity. And then one will have to isolate the diverse concrete and historical forms of *linguistic* a prioris, i.e. the different manners in which determined languages have found to link, close, suture, code the abyss of the *phonese* or of the power-to-differ, *thus rendering possible the reproduction of language.* For, needless to say, language conserves and reproduces itself, but structural linguistics only exploits this reproduction, without being able to explain how it happens – I mean to say, its internal transcendental production. In particular, the phoneme will be interpreted as one of the fundamental means found by languages (and abusively generalised by linguists) to suture and 'overcode' the *phonese*: one 'techno-linguistic' procedure amongst others.

Obviously the same *schema* (i.e., these three or four rules) is valid for every other region of objects. The transcendental method is a sort of universal or singular writing (a residual writing...) sufficiently plastic to be adapted to *every* object and to transform itself with that object: because it produces problems, and only produces solutions as an extension, without any rupture, of problems.

Let it not be said that it is incapable of explaining such and such a determinate object, its properties, etc. That is the work of the sciences, not of philosophy. But what about the properties of that special object that is called science or knowledge, and which, as we know, was Kant's object? The response must be that epistemology, which concerns itself with this object, takes the considerable risk, whether it wants to or not, of presenting itself as a science, or of falling under the criteria of a science (history, for example). It takes the risk of no longer being philosophy, or of playing on two tables at once... *Perhaps* a science? That is its own affair, or rather that of the sciences, which are the judges of epistemology... As to the transcendental method, it is not responsible for deciding what is science or non-science, it is incapable of doing so. Only science is judge of itself and *index sui* (which is not to say that it has no need of 'philosophical' concepts to establish itself... but so-called 'philosophical' concepts and the internal essence of philosophy, its transcendental aims and style, are two very different things...)

To come now to the notion of the object, *the residual object* is the non-idealist concept of the a priori; it does not at all designate an empirico-ideal object. I now prefer to speak of residual rather than *fractional*. For 'residual' has the advantage of attaching this enterprise to a tradition (that of Husserl) and to its terminology enough so that the gap thus imprinted on the notion of residue comes to perturb the conceptual field of transcendental phenomenology (a problem of strategy and palaeonymy...) Because, consequently, 'residual' allows one to avoid the confusion with the partial object of psychoanalysis and the (potential) misfortune of a Nietzschean usage of the 'partial object' in an analytical usage. And finally because the term 'residual' cuts short, hopefully at least, any positivist attempt to make the manifold of cuts, the dispersion of essence fold back onto *micro*-physics or *micro*-something.

The transcendental sense of the residual object, or of its cut (but the transcendental, here, has but few traits in common with the classical transcendental), it seems to me, prohibits us from folding the residual back onto the two extreme poles of representation, the Large and the Small, since it precedes a priori every form of representation. This is important for the cutting-out of a political or techno-political a priori, of an a priori of power. If I insist, as I did today, on the transcendental function of the concept of 'residual', it is so as to struggle against the positivist and empiricist insipidity of a certain usage of Nietzsche. And also, on a second front (but one that has much in common with the first), to struggle at the same time against the Heideggerian interpretation. What a great thing this Heideggerian interpretation of Nietzsche was. But on one hand it has become a breviary that even journalists can now recite, and which prohibits any re-evaluation of Nietzsche's importance, his step beyond 'metaphysics'. On the other hand, the insistence on Being at the expense of beings is an idealist archaism, at least in the interpretation that the 'young' Heidegger gives of it, for it is true that he increasingly 'reduced' it in insisting (but only on his own account) on the *Essence* (*of Being*). Heidegger showed us little by little that it is the meditation on Essence rather than Being that is the non?-philosophical object of thinking thought. Unfortunately, as far as Nietzsche is concerned (who he read regularly and at the closest level – 'Being' is but the 'closest level' of the Greco-occidental text), he proved less generous: Not only does he enclose him in the nihilist circle he traces (but which Nietzsche himself had also traced) of occidental metaphysics, a circle that he can only trace in already overstepping it; he can only allow himself *this denial*, *this incarceration of Nietzsche*, because his own insistence on Being at the expense of the being still belongs to what I have called the primacy of idealising cuts over real cuts. They make him conflate the Nietzschean thinking of the *essence* (of Being) with a 'brute' philosophy of empirical beings. His own concept of difference (the power-to-differ) – this is my hypothesis – is still a mélange (an *Aufhebung*) of the real cut and the idealising cut ... But that's not the most serious thing. The most serious thing is the conjuncture – that is, the 'sociological' effects of repetition, of automatism and of a training by rote that this reading had on contemporaries – the now famous vulgate of Nietzsche, last metaphysician of the West, that is to say of Being! And the incapacity one finds oneself in of reading Nietzsche outside of this reductive framework. This Nietzsche is already a part of our philosophical common sense, a Nietzsche who would inspire the disgust of a thousand Zarathustras!

JM-P: When linguists talk about a system, this concept is proposed as an operatory concept, which allows the understanding of everything you have explained. The concept of system must prove whether it is or is not operatory for the knowledge of languages, whereas your *phonese*, it exhausts itself in itself, it cuts and reforms itself, it is not comparable.

FL: You're right, it is not comparable. Phoneme and system are operatory concepts, 'phonese' is a philosophical and transcendental concept. But, on one hand, what is the 'operatory'? Doesn't it suppose philosophical conditions of possibility, isn't it a notion that, like that of cinnabar, is a selective sample taken from a whole encyclopedia? And, on the other hand, 'phonese' is not a transcendent or abstract concept, but transcendental: it has no use except in linguistic experience taken in the totality of its aspects and not only in the closed corpus of complete statements that the structuralists extract from it in order to be able to make their concept of phoneme function. In these conditions, moreover, the 'operatory' is certainly a good criterion – a good criterion for a philosopher, that is.

As to the introduction of the notion of 'phonese', it responds to exigencies which, in spite of not being 'operatory', are nonetheless precise. It is a question (to sum up some work done elsewhere) of re-introducing into linguistics: (1) against structuralist anti-humanism, the speaking subject, but as producer and agent of the *unity of the chiasm* of *langue* and *parole*. A unity that is no longer this side of their Saussurian distinction, but *beyond*: the two series of phonematic phenomena and phenomena of *parole* extending each other continually and *at the same time* cutting each other each time perpendicularly, a 'torsion' that only the phonese immanent to the two series can support; (2) against the psycho-physiological subject whose remainders or avatars haunt almost all of linguistics, the radical subjectivity of linguistic existence conceived as that of a power-to-speak. Phonese is thus an 'active' and 'productive' concept of a *real* power-to-differ pendant to, or rather, supplementary to, the abstract and ideal concept of the phoneme. The phonese does not exclude the phoneme (which is necessary to assure the social reproduction of *parole*); it permits the description of a generativity at the level of the phoneme rather than that of the phrase.

It comprises, like any residual object, a double face: on one hand, a differenciating power that is the *genetic a priori* of the phoneme itself, too abstract and general, too idealised to take account of *all* the real 'facts of language' of the speaker; on the other hand, a power of continuity, of continuation and of synthesis which, without being a *form* opposed to a *substance*, animates the ideal form of the phoneme and explains the possibility of forming a quasi-infinity of words and phrases, but this time in respecting strictly the immanence of language and without suspending the spoken in relation to extra-linguistic 'innate' essences. (3) Finally, it permits an 'affirmative' critique of the dissociationist and abstract postulate of *langue* as instrument of *parole* (albeit in the form of an element of pure negative, and without-existence relations that come to animate a *parole* that sinks into this 'defile'); of the corpus as a spoken that is supposed terminated and dead; of the primacy of receiver and hearer over producer, an old-hermeneutic primacy that still animated structuralism.

The notion of *phonese* corresponds to the introduction of a materialist *and* transcendental point of view into linguistics, and to the simultaneous critique of structuralism and generative grammar. It does not reintroduce the 'phonetic' point of view against that of phonology, it is an entirely other problematic. If we remember the inspiration that Jakobson and phonology drew from the Husserlian theory of 'wholes' and 'parts', why not try to animate (from afar...) the linguistic field with a theory of residual objects that is a form of anti-idealist radicalisation of the Husserlian theory? An overthrowing-and-displacement of structuralist idealism...

JM-P: It is you who spoke of the critique of the indistinct object, but if it is indistinct, then what is the object of critique?

FL: Precisely the 'indistinct': it is determined transcendentally as empirically indeterminate. What makes the object of critique is the confusion of the empirical determination of the object with its transcendental determination.

JM-P: What is its transcendental determination?

FL: The set of syntheses of cuts that are programmed by the fourth rule. But this is all too brief, it's true...

PATRICK HENRIOT (read from a letter): I would have liked to have posed the question of the status of time in the perspective of the transvaluation you evoked. Wouldn't it be one of those 'hypothecations' of which the transcendental method must be disencumbered? What I wonder, personally, is whether the theory of the transcendental ideality of time furnishes the means to found the historicity of history (the time of nature opposed to properly historical time). For example: doesn't the double immortality, of humanity in fact (species) and of each man as reasoning person, call into question the ontological status of time? How, for example, to link phenomenal time and the ideal of a noumenal 'progress'?

It may seem as though these questions remain external to your problematic. But I wonder whether there is not the occasion for an interrogation of the notion of 'destruction'.

FL: These questions, not being solely internal to Kant's problematic (does such an interiority exist other than as a semantic illusion, other that as an artefact linked to the history of philosophy?) are also not entirely external to those of transvaluation. They form instead the common border of the two perspectives, extending one into the other. Effectively, the question of time is not a 'hypothecation' in the sense of a simple obstacle of which thought can disencumber itself without any risk. But it is, if one understands it *as a right* of the tradition over thought – one that we might believe thought would seek to absolve itself of, as one pays off a debt. Whether it is a matter of time or whatever other 'concept' ('form', 'condition', 'a priori', 'transcendental', etc.). For I consider that the univocity of the transvaluated transcendental method (its equal validity for all regions of objects) demands that one begins, precisely through an observance of 'method', by according no particular privilege even to time; and by 'streamlining' all concepts, i.e. by proceeding upon them, considered as indistinct objects, with cuts that isolate their (residual) a prioris. Time, also, is first of all a given. Even as ideal continuity, it remains 'empirical', up to the point where successive reductions 'purify' it of its spatial elements (here the spatiality of extensive-being stands as an index of given-being, and thus of that which, from my point of view, still needs to be reduced).

This is to admit that one does not disencumber oneself all at once of the 'hypothecations' (even epistemological, even moral – above all moral – ones, etc...) that form the continuous fabric of a tradition that closes itself up *behind* and *upon* each cut, and that the transvaluated 'transcendental' character can only define a limit, at once a tendency and a mutation in the becoming of a concept. This limit is still 'transcendental', but in a sense new, precisely transvaluated – or on the way... 'Destruction' is a process, not a magic spell.

One is thus constrained by the tradition, simultaneously and strategically, to recognise a certain privilege or primacy of time, even if this primacy recedes and sees its domain and its meaning change. From this point of view, one can say – this is an entirely possible strategic, but at the same time contingent, thesis, from which it suffices to draw and limit certain effects – that 'will-to-power' is a Nietzschean concept of temporalisation as production of time, it is intensive and intemporal time which is immanent to empirical time and even to Kant's ideal time, as their genetic a priori. On this point, it appears to me that every theory of the ideality of time ends up privileging its consistency and reproduction. We see this in Kant, where time manifests a veritable lack of being and a petitioning of space – as good a way as any of giving reality to ideal time by giving it objectivity – at the expense of its production on the basis of cuts-sources, or of its 'real' transcendental history.

The transcendental manifold of residual objects, which merge with their production by immanent division without negativity – here is true temporalisation, it is the radical, finally de-spatialised concept of 'originary' temporality, and it is a condition – a real (in the non-empirical sense) and non-ideal condition – of history.

The transcendental ideality and empirical reality of time? Allow me to reverse and displace this duplicity: the ideality of time is empirical, its reality is transcendental – but this thesis does not just give rise to a 'transcendental realism'. For the residual manifold is time as noumenal self-producer, and no longer as phenomenon. All the same, given the univocity I spoke of earlier, I would prefer to say that the residual and real manifold is noumenon in relation to time itself. As to the distinction natural time/ historical time, it is transcendent and must be reduced; it is not 'external', but, from my point of view, transcendent and not transcendental. It is fitting to seek the residual object – the a priori that relates one to the other, at the same time as it divides them, natural time and historical time.

Of course, all these concepts no longer have *quite* their Kantian sense, otherwise no transvaluation would be possible. I can only distribute otherwise and 'displace' your questions themselves: all the rest, all my responses, result from that recutting, or only continue it by further determining it.